Women and the labour market

Teresa Rees

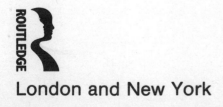

London and New York

First published in 1992 by
Routledge
11 New Fetter Lane, London EC4P 4EE

Simultaneously published in the USA and Canada by
Routledge
a division of Routledge, Chapman and Hall Inc.
29 West 35th Street, New York, NY 10001

© 1992 Teresa Rees

Typeset by Witwell Ltd, Southport

Printed and bound in Great Britain by
Mackays of Chatham PLC, Chatham, Kent

British Library Cataloguing in Publication Data

A catalogue record for this book is available from the British Library.

Library of Congress Cataloging in Publication Data

Rees, Teresa L.
    Women and the labour market/Teresa Rees.
        p.   cm.
    Includes bibliographical references (p.   ) and indexes.
    1. Women – Employment – United States. 2. Sex discrimination in
employment – United States. 3. Sex role in the work environment –
United States. 4. Labor policy – United States. I. Title.
HD6095.R44   1992
331.4′12′0973–dc20   92-10512
                                                                            CIP

ISBN 0–415–03801–4
        0–415–03802–2 (pbk)

The ... In
par... sitive
acti... nder
seg... e of
inte... t of
curr...

B... and
Aus... and
trai... size
of la... ving
how... the
excl... pon
wor... r of
patr... ket
also... me
effe...

A... ard
prac... uit-
men... ide
reac... ies,
soci... ent
and... ers,
Tra...

Ter... in
Soc...

Also available from ROUTLEDGE:

Professions and Patriarchy
Anne Witz

Women, Work and Protest:
A Century of US Women's Labor History
Edited by Ruth Milkman

Young, Female and Black
Heidi Safia Mirza

Training at Work:
A Critical Analysis of Workplace Training and Development
Jeff Hyman

For Ieuan and Dyfrig,

without whom this book would have been written much more quickly, but without whose forbearance, it would never have been written at all. Diolch yn fawr i'r ddau o chwi.

Contents

Tables and figures

Preface and acknowledgements

Over the years, with colleagues in the Social Research Unit of University of Wales College of Cardiff (UWCC) I have conducted a large number of empirical, policy-related research projects on aspects of the labour market. These have been undertaken for a range of bodies such as the European Commission, government departments and agencies, the Economic and Social Research Council, and trade unions. The studies explored employment, unemployment and training; evaluated policy initiatives; documented international comparisons; and investigated barriers facing women at work. While the work has been written up for the sponsors concerned in the format that they required, the results have not yet systematically found their way to academic and policy audiences more generally. In this book I have synthesised the findings of sixteen of these projects into a number of themes, and sought to integrate them with current theoretical and policy debates.

There is a distinguished feminist scholarship emerging which seeks to explain gender segregation in the labour market: this book draws heavily on that work but puts an emphasis on what I think is the neglected role of training as a factor in the equation. It also focuses on three key areas currently undergoing considerable change: education and training, labour supply and the labour market itself.

The book includes work from projects in many European countries and Australia, although the majority are based in the United Kingdom, and there is a special emphasis on data from Wales. I hope the latter will, to an extent at least, offset the Anglocentricity of many purportedly British studies, which Lyn Jamieson, David Raffe *inter alios* in Scotland and Celia Davies, Bob Cormack and others in Northern Ireland have done so much to seek to balance. I have tried, moreover, to offer a flavour of the lives of the women who have taken part in the various studies. This ranges from describing the future which schoolgirls from the industrial towns and villages of the valleys of South Wales see in front of them, to feeling the material of the silk dresses of the femocrats of Perth (Australia), and conveying the fear with which Turkish women in Berlin face the introduction of new technology in the factories where they work. The book is, in a sense, then, a collection of structured observations of women's position in the labour force, and an exploration of potential for change offered principally through training, from different sectors and various countries of the global village we now inhabit.

Whatever the academic merits or policy insights the book may or may not offer, I was fascinated by the people I met in the course of the research work upon which it is based. I also thoroughly enjoyed the adventures which field work so often affords and which I suspect provide the essential nicotine to the addicted researcher. I have tried to present the ideas and observations in this book in an accessible form, and to share some of those adventures.

As a complete addict of award-giving ceremonies (Oscars, Sports 'Personalities', BAFTA Lighting Technician of the Year, it matters not what), I particularly enjoy recipients' speeches, and the long list of thanks that are given to sundry people who made it all possible. John Cleese excelled, to my mind, by acknowledging both God and the laundry maid. Indeed, I agreed to become a judge in the Welsh Arts Council Literature Book Prize, thereby committing myself to reading over sixty works of high culture in one year, solely for the prospect of at long last attending such a ceremony. Alas, the winners were sent a cheque by post.

So, albeit in altogether more modest circumstances, I should like to take the opportunity to record my own thanks to my collaborators, funders and all those who encouraged and supported me in writing this book. I clearly owe a big debt of gratitude to them and to the thousands of people whom I interviewed, surveyed or observed.

A large number of people worked on the projects with me in various capacities; I have identified them at appropriate junctures in the notes to each chapter. I should especially like to record my thanks to those with whom I have worked collaboratively for a good many years; they are Sara Delamont, Kevin Doogan, Sarah Fielder, Martin Read, Gareth Rees and Howard Williamson, all of UWCC. Sara Delamont and Caroline Joll kindly read the whole manuscript and didn't spare my blushes with their comments: the mark of true friendship. Paul Atkinson enquired after its progress with a kind but unremitting tenacity which ensured that there had to be progress to report. Andrew Metcalf, of the University of New South Wales, persuaded me that the difficulties of combining work, children and writing a book could be overcome with a little more determination. Numerous friends and colleagues have read chapters, expressed interest and generally been supportive, in particular Gill Boden, John Craig, Val Feld, Freda MacNamara, Anne Murcott, Jane Pilcher, Anna Pollert, Juli Southall and Chris Weedon. Students on the M.Sc. Econ. Women's Studies option 'Women and Paid Work' (run by Caroline Joll and myself), and those on my undergraduate course 'Gender, Work and Employment' provided useful stimulation and feedback on ideas. I am very grateful to them all.

I should especially like to acknowledge Gareth Rees, many of whose ideas are reflected in joint projects we have worked upon that are drawn on in the book, and who falls into the 20 per cent of men who – according to Arlie Hochschild (1990) – seriously do the business at home. Finally, I'd like to thank Vera Geddes-Ruffle, for setting me an example.

Abbreviations

ALP	Australian Labor Party
APACE	Appropriate Technology Development Group Incorporated
BIBB	Bundesinstitut für Berufsbildung
BIFU	Banking Insurance and Finance Union
CAD	Computer Aided Design
CBI	Confederation of British Industry
CEDEFOP	European Commission's Centre for the Development of Vocational Training, Berlin
COHSE	Confederation of Health Service Employees
CWTR	Cardiff Women's Training Roadshow
DES	Department of Education and Science
EC	European Commission
EEPTU	Electrical, Electronic, Telecommunications and Plumbing Union
EITB	Engineering Industrial Training Board
EPOS	Electronic Point of Sale
ESF	European Social Fund
ESRC	Economic and Social Research Council
ET	Employment Training
FRG	Federal Republic of Germany
GAOC	Girls and Occupational Choice
GATE	Girls and Technical Education
GIST	Girls into Science and Technology
GMB	General, Municipal, Boilermakers and Allied Trades Union
HTNT	Higher Technology National Training
IMS	Institute of Manpower Studies
IT	Information Technology
LEC	Local Enterprise Councils
LFS	Labour Force Survey
MESP	Mini Enterprise in Schools Project
MSC	Manpower Services Commission
NALGO	National and Local Government Officers' Association

NEDO	National Economic Development Office
NOW	New Opportunities for Women
NUCPS	National Union of Civil and Public Servants
NUPE	National Union of Public Employees
NUT	National Union of Teachers
OECD	Organisation for Economic Co-operation and Development
OMCS	Office of the Minister for the Civil Service
OPCS	Office of Population Censuses and Surveys
SGWW	South Glamorgan Women's Workshop
TA	Training Agency
TEC	Training and Enterprise Councils
TGWU	Transport and General Workers' Union
TUC	Trades Union Congress
TVEI	Technical and Vocational Training Initiative
UCATT	Union of Construction, Allied Trades and Technicians
USDAW	Union of Shop, Distributive and Allied Workers
VDU	Visual Display Units
WISE	Women into Science and Engineering
WOW	Wider Opportunities for Women
WP	Word Processors (*sic*)
YTS	Youth Training Scheme

Chapter 1

Women and training in a changing labour market

Every generation perceives the speed of societal change, the sophistication of the development of new technologies and the shift in the roles of men and women to be unprecedented: this age is no exception.

Industry and employers more generally certainly face a daunting package of changes towards the turn of the century. The facilities offered by telecommunications and telematics coupled with international developments simultaneously make the world smaller and increase the opportunity to expand into new markets. The growth in significance of the Pacific Basin, the emergence of a single-market Europe, the developments of links with Eastern European countries all indicate a need for more global approaches to product and service development and marketing. The use made of human resources increasingly provides the competitive edge between companies, as technological standards harmonise. Moreover, changes in technology and the development of new materials provide their own impetus for rethinking the use made of 'manpower'. They imply an overall decrease in the number of unskilled workers required in the workforce and the introduction of new training systems to update skills constantly. The number of jobs in the labour force will grow, in particular in the private services sector. The greening of the consciousness of both the state and the consumer provides an imperative for employers to undertake a substantial rethink on production processes, packaging, waste disposal and marketing. And then of course, there is the demographic time bomb, the projected slow-down in the rate of growth of the labour force, just as the demand for labour is expanding.

Such shifts and rethinks, it could be argued, will surely affect the significance of gender as a variable in determining the way the labour force is organised. An employee's gender, it might be rational to hazard, will become a less powerful predictor of occupational life chances than is the case at present. And yet these projected changes are perhaps no more dramatic than those which have characterised the post-war period so far. There have been paradigm shifts in the organisation of the labour process which have had significant effects on patterns of employment. Industrial restructuring has led to the decline of the once monolithic industries of coal, steel and shipbuilding with their powerful trade unions. They have been replaced by light manufacturing and service-sector industries: in the words of Max Boyce, the Welsh singer, the old pithead bath is a supermarket now. Part-time work has expanded enormously; its growth represents the biggest single change in labour-force patterns this century. Working from home, and more specifically teleworking, has become a way of life for many. There has been an increase in the numbers of self-employed and small businesses, heralded by the Conservative administration as evidence of the success of the 'enterprise culture' fostered in the 1980s. But despite these significant changes, and despite the fact that the number of women (particularly married women) in the labour force has increased substantially as a result of them, gender remains the single most important determinant of options chosen at school, industry worked in, occupation entered, amount of pay received, training opportunities received and taken up, promotion prospects, size of pension and so on.

For this reason, the subject of women and the labour market has received considerable attention in the last decade, from academics, particularly feminists, but also more recently from others directly concerned with the policy implications of a 'gendered' labour force. These comprise both those concerned with the labour market from a social justice perspective, such as the Equal Opportunities Commission, and those responsible for assisting in the efficient running of the economy; for example, central government departments and agencies, economic development departments of local authorities, Training and Enterprise Councils (TECs) in England and Wales, and the Local Enterprise Councils (LECs) in Scotland.

This book is aimed at both academic and policy-related audiences. It seeks to engage with academic debates about the reproduction of gender inequalities in the labour market, and to address policy issues about how to reduce the impact of gender as an organising principle in recruitment, training and work organisation. It has a particular focus on training, and sets out to demonstrate how the same sets of structures and impediments which restrict women's access to labour-market opportunities constrain and limit their access to training opportunities as well. Those opportunities could be transformative; that is, they have the potential to improve individuals' occupational life chances quite radically. Moreover, to respond to the global changes in the economy, training and the efficient use of human resources are increasingly important. Training for women therefore should be high on the agenda.

In all the chapters, the emphasis is on those policies and practices which can improve women's life chances, from those disadvantaged by, say, lack of qualifications or the impoverished opportunities in their local labour market, through to women seeking to break through the 'glass ceiling', which women in middle management perceive as an invisible barrier preventing their rise to the top. Racial discrimination of course cuts across sex discrimination and renders its own, differentiated patterns of circum-scribed 'choices': while all women share some experiences, there are also huge differences between them determined by race, class, country, region and indeed locality. I try to illustrate some of those differences in the case studies while also emphasising the commonalities.

Each empirical chapter (Chapters 3-8) begins with a review of the 'problem', and then moves on to provide a critique of policy responses and consider empirically based 'solutions'. Chapter 2 sets the scene by giving an outline of the position of women in the labour market and the theoretical framework for the book; it is principally designed for students and academic audiences. It argues that much of women's contribution to the national economy is rendered invisible through the social construction of statistics; nevertheless, those labour-force statistics among other sources are then used to chart the extraordinary impact that gender has on patterns of participa-tion and occupational and industrial distribution. It goes on to develop the theoretical underpinnings of the book, reviewing various economic, sociological and feminist approaches to understanding gender segregation very broadly, and presenting that perspective which has most influenced the writing of the book, the dual systems approach, whereby patriarchy and capitalism are thought to interact to produce the particular blend of recruitment, training and work-organisation structures constraining women in the labour market.

The chapters of the book are organised around three major areas of radical change, and have three recurring themes running through them. The three *areas* are education and training policy; changes in labour supply; and changes in the nature and size of labour demand. All the changes are likely to impact significantly upon women's experiences of paid work. The *themes* which weave their way through the chapters are among a number to have emerged from studies of women and the labour market over the last two decades; they are the ideology of the family, the limitations of material realities, and exclusionary mechanisms operated by men. These changes and the themes are foreshadowed here and developed in the concluding chapter.

POLICIES FOR CHANGE AND CHANGING POLICIES

Education and training

Major changes in education and training in Britain have been ushered in by the Conservative administration during the 1980s and early 1990s. The 1988 Education Reform Act moves much of the responsibility for governance and financial management of schools to parents – described by Brown (1990) as 'parentocracy'. Although the curriculum to which young people are exposed is harmonised across schools, the quality of education and access to resources is likely to become further polarised, given the increased involvement of parents and local businesses with different resource levels, despite the outward manifestations of fairness rendered by the formula funding system which is used to calculate the budgets for the local management of schools.

The school as the site of reproduction of the ideology of the family has received much attention (David 1983) with its implications for girls' attitudes towards jobs qualifications and careers. A series of special initiatives has been designed to attract girls into a wider range of jobs, particularly engineering, but they have not been matched elsewhere by initiatives to tackle the issue of the domestic division of labour which underpins much of the gender segregation at work. Chapter 3 focuses on the aspirations and choices of 500 South Wales schoolgirls in exploring some of these issues. It charts the impact of the ideology of the family and the material reality of their projected lives on those 'choices'. Those decisions in themselves contribute to the reproduction of existing patterns of gender segregation, and offer scope for 'blaming the victim'.

Education is undergoing major change, not least through facilities for schools to 'opt out' of local authority control. However, responsibility for training has shifted in a much more thoroughgoing way. Employers in the United Kingdom traditionally have been coy about their role in training, in particular the small business sector. The state assumed responsibility for training the unemployed at least, especially during the 1970s and early 1980s when unemployment levels, particularly among young people, were unacceptably high. What will be the impact of the TECs and LECs on training?

Their introduction combines two policy strands: the training function is in effect being both privatised and locally determined, and it will be difficult to disaggregate the impact of one from the other. Training needs are to be identified by boards overwhelmingly made up of the chief executives (who are almost exclusively male) of 'local' industry, although in practice this means the larger corporations, where they exist. Boards are advised by various committees, and it is clear already that the interpretation of local training needs will vary considerably. As local employers are expected to provide training for their employees, and to 'top up' training budgets allocated on a formula system, it follows that the local economy will determine the overall investment into the skills stock from which local employers and inward investors can then recruit. Despite the fact that the calculations for formula funding budgets take account of levels of registered unemployment, the existing economic base is likely to determine the future skills provided. Regional and indeed local disparities may therefore further polarise. Hence, individuals' access to training will increasingly depend upon where they live. Although training opportunities may improve because of local employers' needs in Swindon or the Thames Valley, the South

Wales Valleys, dominated by very small employers in low-skilled work, are unlikely to find that there will be training provided which will enable companies or individuals to transform their opportunities. The focus on existing employers' needs may impede 'training for stock' which would be of interest to potential inward investors.

It is too early to assess the impact of TECs and LECs, but the importance of training for breaking down patterns of gender segregation in the labour market is stressed throughout the chapters.

Changes in labour supply

The much-heralded demographic time bomb is largely misunderstood as a net decline in the workforce: in reality, the danger comes from a mismatch between skill needs and those available in what will become an ageing workforce. School-leavers should be a more valued commodity than has been the case since the early 1970s, and women wanting to return to the labour force after a period of child-bearing and -rearing are likely to experience solicitation about flexible hours and child-care responsibilities from employers which they have not enjoyed since the Second World War. Moreover, women in middle management or relatively unskilled jobs in traditionally female work may be looked at anew, rather than overlooked, in the context of labour shortage.

Training for women returners, and the mismatch between their needs and provision, is the subject of Chapter 4. The 'malestreamism' (or male orientation) of training provision has rendered women returners a 'problem' rather than a legitimate consumer group so far. The chapter examines their training needs compared with what is available, and draws on the experiences of a women's workshop to suggest what a package of training measures which could transform their life chances might look like. The increased interest in women returners as a client group as a result of the relative decline in school-leavers is already producing some changes to be introduced by training providers in order to accommodate their needs.

The changes in the workforce, and the increase in the numbers of women working, have of course been reflected in the gender make-up of the trade unions. Unions, it is frequently claimed, are becoming increasingly 'feminised' as a result of patterns of industrial restructuring and the growth of the proportion of members who are women. Does this mean that unions will increasingly take on board issues of prime concern to women, such as the persistence of pay inequalities and the relatively poor terms and conditions offered to part-time workers? Chapter 5 draws on two major studies of large unions (NALGO and USDAW) to illustrate that the same difficulties which impede women's progress in their careers at work inhibit their access to and ability to rise within the union. This in turn restricts their ability to influence agenda-setting within the union.

Positive action measures of all kinds have been prompted by labour shortages, and the need to make better use of human resources; they are the subject of Chapter 6. They have been given a boost by Business in the Community's 'Opportunity 2000' initiative, whereby major companies pledged to have more women at the top by the end of the century. Such measures fall broadly into two categories: those which seek to assist women in their dual responsibilities of home and work, and those which aim to maximise the use made of women as a resource. Measures which seek to make employers 'family-friendly' through accommodating parenthood include child-care and career break schemes, which seek to retain women through the child-bearing years or encourage them to return to work. The chapter also examines the glass ceiling and the experiences of the Civil Service in running women-only training courses designed to foster women in middle management and groom them for promotion. This is one route through which women can develop their own networks as well as providing role models and mentors. Senior women can also potentially legitimise flexible forms of working from the top.

Changes in the labour market

The labour market is changing dramatically; some of the ingredients of change have been described already. The final two chapters focus on two of these, the introduction and expanded use of new technologies (Chapter 7), and the growth of the 'enterprise culture' (Chapter 8).

New technologies can render existing jobs deskilled or be used to enhance jobs and allow individuals to invest more of their intelligence in the work that they do. Drawing on research conducted in the newly re-united Federal Republic of Germany (FRG), Chapter 7 suggests that the old barriers between manual and non-manual jobs, and technological, communication, management and business skills are breaking down. These trends clearly impinge upon the extent to which 'flexibility' is likely to become a reality. The increased fluidity in the organisation of work may well impact upon gendered patterns of work in the future. Moreover, training for the new technologies will become a lifelong process.

The final empirical chapter looks at the potential for women to opt out, to an extent at least, of discriminatory work structures by setting up their own businesses. State intervention in the labour market in the 1980s did little to break down remarkably rigid patterns of occupational segregation either by gender or by race. Some authors have argued, indeed, that training measures aimed at young people (Cockburn 1987) and at ethnic minorities (Cross and Edmonds 1983) reproduced patterns of inequality to a more marked degree than already pertained in the open labour market. But does state intervention aimed at fostering the 'enterprise culture' hold more potential for breaking down these rigidities? Is it the case that support for self-employment and small business proprietorship facilitates, or could facilitate, people traditionally disadvantaged in the labour market in opting out and bypassing discriminatory practices by starting up their own enterprises? Setting up their own businesses has been a traditional solution for members of some ethnic minorities in the face of discrimination in the labour market, but women have not historically taken this route. Nevertheless, the 1980s saw an increase in the number of women proprietors. Will the existence of more women 'entrepreneurs' loosen the grip of patterns of gender relations in the labour market and even potentially in the home?

In 1987, the State of Victoria in Australia produced a strategy document which identified social justice and economic development as its twin goals. Some would argue that these goals are incompatible, suggesting that gender-specific oppression (patriarchy) is necessary for capitalism, and indeed that class-specific social division and struggle are necessary for the sustaining of patriarchy. As Magarey (1984) asks, is social justice for women even possible under capitalism? There is clearly no reason to suppose that patriarchal relations are any less powerful in the small business economy than among larger employers. The gatekeepers of access to finance and support for small businesses may be motivated to maximise profit, but they are also informed by the same sets of assumptions and stereotypes that shape employers' decisions about granting individuals with particular ascribed characteristics access to opportunities in the labour market. But, although women may experience gender-specific barriers to setting up, is gender a less significant determinant of success once this has been achieved? Or are women in danger of merely exchanging exploitation for self-exploitation?

Chapter 8 explores these issues. It offers a critique of the concept of enterprise as it has developed in policy terms in the United Kingdom, and draws upon experiences of other countries, in particular Australia, to suggest how women can derive empowerment from setting up their own businesses.

RECURRENT THEMES

The first of the three themes to cut across the chapters is the ideology of the family and its impact in determining attitudes and practices of employers in recruitment, training and promotion mechanisms and forms of work organisation. The second is the notion of the impact of material realities facing women's 'choices' about their participation in the labour force. The third recurring theme is the raft of exclusionary mechanisms operated by men, both overtly and more subtly and subconsciously, which define, shape and constrain women's use of their talents in the labour market.

Ideology of the family

The family is universally presented as an ideal, and it is one to which we aspire despite our own learned experiences and despite divorce statistics, domestic violence and other evidence of casualties and failure. As a lived ideal, it is almost as elusive as the Holy Grail. Nevertheless, it is sanctioned and endorsed in every arena. Weedon (1987:103) draws attention to the centrality of the ideal[1] of family life, in the twice-weekly screened episodes of the highly popular BBC soap opera, *EastEnders*:

> Family relations, in particular the relations between women and men, are central to each episode. The two relatively stable marriages in the serial at the time of writing contrast with a whole range of broken relationships and with relationships in the process of breaking down or being established. Where marriages are stable other family problems with the young or old are paramount. Where relationships are in the process of change their effects on individuals are shown. These are devastating in the case of breakdown or a source of sanctuary from loneliness and unhappiness where new relationships are formed. In each case the assumption is that a stable heterosexual relationship is necessary to a happy or contented life.

Despite the manifest difficulties of living the ideal of family life, the *ideology* of the family, which in its present form evolved as a by-product of the industrial revolution, is all-pervasive. Whereas previous theoretical approaches focused exclusively upon the relationship between the family as an institution and other systems, taking the 'natural' roles of men and women within it as unproblematic, feminists have looked closely at the position of women within the family, and questioned the benefit of the influence of the ideology of the family on women's lives (for example, Barrett and McIntosh 1982; Beechey 1986; Smart 1984). They have documented, for example, women's unequal access to resources in the family (Pahl 1989), and their experiences of domestic violence within it (Dobash and Dobash 1980, 1992).

The ideology of the family is supported by the state (Wilson 1977) in a series of welfare and other provisions which are predicated upon a model of a family form (bread-winner husband, wife at home, two school-age children) which does not apply to a growing proportion of the population. Single-person households, co-habitation, reconstituted and single-parent families are all on the increase (see Central Statistical Office 1991: Table 2.3). The family is nevertheless seen as the location of 'community' care and the locus of sets of obligations for the care of the elderly and infirm, which in effect, women have to provide (Finch 1989; Finch and Groves 1980, 1983; Glendinning and Millar 1987; Parker 1988).

There have been criticisms of some of the work on the ideology of the family for focusing exclusively on white family life or taking white family life as the norm (Brittan and Maynard 1984). For many Asian and black women, family life is not experienced in the same way, and of course there are variations within groups of different ethnic origin, including whites. For Asian women, the extended family, while on the whole patriarchal and authoritarian, is often regarded as a refuge from racism and source of strength in combating it. The developed sense of family obligations can be protective. Afro-Caribbean families are often, by contrast, described as matriarchal: the influence of men is said not to be as strong within them (Carby 1982). Many Afro-Caribbean women are in any case single parents (Central Statistical Office 1990: Table 1.12) living outside the stereotyped white concept of a nuclear family.

The ideology of the family is highly influential in shaping both the supply of and the demand for labour: it structures individuals' choices, and employers' recruitment and human resource strategies. It legitimates the concept of the family wage and its corollary 'pin money' (Barrett and McIntosh 1980; Hartmann 1979a; Land 1980), even though, as Walby (1990) argues, the value of the family wage in sustaining an entire family is something of a myth. It is clear that women's part-time wages are essential to keep many families above the poverty line, and women are not, on the whole, at home looking after the children full-time. Nevertheless, the concept of the family wage has been crucial in suppressing women's wages.

The strength of the ideology of the family in justifying recruitment decisions is demonstrated by Collinson et al. (1990): whereas male 'bread-winners' are deemed suitable for jobs with good prospects, female 'home-makers' are recruited for temporary work. These stereotypes, and the ideology of the family, are found to influence attitudes and actions which sustain a gendered workforce, throughout the studies reported upon in this book, but most especially in the chapters on schoolgirls, returners, positive action measures and the enterprise culture.

Material realities

The second major theme is concerned with the restriction on choices which women can make in the labour market, affected as they are by the material realities of everyday life, a theme probably most associated with the writings of Cynthia Cockburn (1981). Women's location within the process of capital accumulation and within the family unit constrains choice because of the asymmetry of power relations. This is not to deny the power of agency to individuals, but rather to emphasise that material realities shape and inform those choices to a marked degree.

The organisation of work is the first major arena of constraint. Segmented tiers, with separate recruitment structures and little mobility between the tiers, means that the reality of work for many women is a ghettoised, low-paid job, deemed unskilled or semi-skilled women's work.

The 'factory studies', which graphically describe everyday life on the factory floor drawing upon interviews and ethnographic field work, identify for us the lived reality of patriarchal relations in the workplace (Cavendish 1982; Glucksman 1990; Pollert 1981; Westwood 1984). The highly segregated workforce, the control of technology by men, and incidents of sexual harassment are experienced by women as reminders of the hierarchy of the gender system. Westwood in particular shows how the work is organised in such a way that the skill component for women's jobs is minimal and the wages reflect this: the women read off from this the low esteem in which they are held, and internalise that sense of lack of value. The jobs have been designed so that workers need to be able to survive monotonous tedium. It is little wonder that for the young, single women, romance and the role of wife and mother is seen not simply as a more glamorous option, but as the only means of economic survival. The fiction of choice is a recurring motif.

Domestic commitments are the other major constraint. It is not simply the lack of state provision and workplace nurseries, but the cost of private provision which, coupled with women's relatively low wages, means that for many it does not make economic sense to go out to work once they have paid out for child care and travel costs. Lack of available, affordable child care not only prevents some women from participating altogether, but also reduces the hours of some who do. Unequal domestic loads further restrain women. The state, through its 'Care in the Community' policies, is putting more responsibilities on women: the Institute of Manpower Studies has calculated that 222,000 women may be prevented from participating in the labour market because they are caring for the elderly or infirm, and that 146,000 women may have their hours and occupations constrained by caring for dependent relatives (Metcalf and Leighton 1989:4).

The material reality of women's lives and the pragmatism of the decisions which they take are featured in particular in Chapter 3 on schoolgirls' option and career choices. The enterprise of women seeking to circumnavigate those constraints is illustrated in Chapter 8.

Exclusionary mechanisms

Many writers have examined the material of male power which transcends capitalist relations, but takes on particular forms under capitalism. Cockburn (1981) used a materialist analysis to look at the way in which the introduction of new technology in the newspaper industry was handled by employers and unions to the detriment of women workers. Walby (1986) provides case studies of various industries and occupations which chart the systematic exclusion of women from access to specific jobs and the labour force more generally.

The lack of women in top positions in the public and private sector is well documented (for example, Hansard Society Commission on Women at the

Top 1990). Some of the exclusionary mechanisms which restrict women's access to the top are explored in Chapter 6, such as the 'old boy' network, the gendered discourse of managerial potential, and the insistence upon unbroken work records for promotion. The effective exclusion of women from trade-union decision making is outlined in Chapter 5; and their difficulty in gaining access to male business networks, together with the control by men of women's access to loans to start up their own businesses, are described in Chapter 8 on women and enterprise.

CONCLUSION

This book is not simply concerned with underlining, if such a task were necessary, the power of patriarchy in shaping the labour force. It is also concerned with the development of policy measures which might have some effect on breaking down gender segregation. Many authors have argued cogently the need to beware what appear to be advances in equality which 'allow' more women into what were previously no-go areas, such as the Stock Exchange or the board room: in fact, patriarchy simply shifts and reshapes, like so much play dough, to reformulate the rules of territorial access *within* the organisation. Such arguments have been powerfully expressed and illustrated (for example, Walby 1986, 1990). Nevertheless, there is a danger in such an approach of invoking either passivity or full-scale separatism as the only responses. The studies reported upon here will, I hope, feed into academic debates but also offer some potential for adjusting the system at key points of recruitment, training and work organisation, all of which are sites of reproduction of gender segregation in the workplace.

Chapter 2

The reproduction of gender segregation

The subject of women and the labour market has received considerable attention in the last three decades. In the 1960s and early 1970s, much of the contribution came from feminists offering a critique of the androcentricity of empirical studies conducted by sociologists and economists which purported to describe the employment experience of all, while in fact they only addressed the experiences of men. Feminists developed theories of the labour market which sought to redress, in particular, the omission of women from Marxist analysis, and to develop theoretical approaches which took on board women's and men's position in both the class structure and in patriarchal relations – that is, the system by which men dominate and oppress women. Different theoretical perspectives lay varying emphasis on the impact of class and patriarchy, and although some see them as separate systems, others see them as inevitably linked, to a greater or lesser degree (Beechey 1987a; Brown 1976).

The 1970s to the 1990s have seen the mushrooming of empirical studies of women's work experiences. These have sought both to document and understand the everyday lived reality of working lives, and to feed observations into the important emergent theoretical developments. These insights were assisted considerably by the first major large-scale study of women's working lives, a survey conducted by the Department of Employment and the Office for Population Censuses and Surveys (OPCS) of over 5,000 women's lives (Martin and Roberts 1984). A rich seam of secondary analysis of this survey has greatly facilitated both our empirical knowledge and theoretical understanding of the gendering of the labour force (for example, Dex 1987, 1988; Hunt 1988).

The key question to emerge from writers of all theoretical hues is why patterns of gender segregation in the workplace evolve and persist, despite sex discrimination legislation, a growing liberal and social justice based concern with 'equality', and advances in some exotic arenas, noteworthy because of their rarity value. There are related questions which are interlinked. Why do women continue to earn on average less than three-quarters of men's wages? Why do they still shoulder the major responsibility for the domestic division of labour even when both partners are working? And why do employers systematically overlook women when searching for senior management potential, but seek them out for part-time, temporary work? In Cynthia Cockburn's (1987) phrase, why are jobs 'gendered'?

A theoretical pluralism has emerged over the decades, with emphasis being laid on different explanations for different facets of gender segregation in the workplace (see Crompton and Sanderson 1990). This book draws upon a range of theoretical insights in seeking to explain aspects of the findings presented, but is principally informed by approaches which lay emphasis upon the effects of the inter-relationship between systems of patriarchy and capitalism in given contexts.

The chapter begins by examining the social construction of labour force statistics and outlining the major shifts in women's employment patterns in the post-war period. It then provides a brief account of some of the major theoretical issues which both underlie the empirical chapters of the book and are elaborated upon within them.

WOMEN IN THE WORKFORCE IN THE POST-WAR PERIOD

Measuring women's work

Official statistics clearly do not simply measure a 'true' rate of a phenomenon: they are the result of whole sets of decisions about, in the first instance, what to measure and what not (see Slattery 1986). Moreover, the records of those activities which are to be measured are themselves the outcomes of sets of decisions about how to conceptualise and categorise certain activities. Bureaucrats then have to make judgements about the allocation of cases to those categories. Official statistics have built into them value loading about what should 'count' at a number of levels: they are socially constructed (see Hindess 1973; Kitsuse and Cicourel 1963).

Labour-force statistics privilege a particular concept of work and pattern of working in what they measure. More value is placed, in effect, on how men work. Such 'malestreamism' in the statistics percolates through to inform our understanding of the labour market and dominates debates about the economy and the practice of employment. It has a legacy in the way in which different occupations are organised, valued and rewarded.

One of the major contributions of feminist writing has been to correct our understanding of the role of women in the economy. Feminist historians have carefully filled in the gaps of a history which is androcentric at worst and gender-blind at best, and offered instead a woman-centred interpretation of the past. Rowbotham (1980), for example, provided an account of the women's movement which had not been systematically recorded. Some feminist writers reclaimed the contribution of women to the economy in the nineteenth and twentieth centuries (for example, John 1986; Lewis 1984;

Matthaei, 1982), or provided detailed accounts of their work in specific industries (Bradley 1989; John 1984). Some provided channels through which women's accounts of, for example, their war-time work experiences can be heard (Braybon 1981; Glucksman 1990; Summerfield 1989). Attention has been drawn too, to the fact that the social construction of statistics means not simply that women's work is under-recorded, but it is under-valued too (Allin and Hunt 1982; Beechey 1983; Beneria 1988; Oakley and Oakley 1979).

When the first British Census was held in 1801, literacy levels were clearly much lower than now; as a consequence Census enumerators' notebooks are a key documentary source. These are protected by legislation which safeguards privacy for 100 years; but as we approach the end of the twentieth century, access to records for almost the whole of the previous century is now available. Painstaking secondary analysis of them has revealed a systematic under-recording of women's economic activity, both in full- and part-time work (Alexander 1976; Hakim 1985; Higgs 1983; Roberts 1988). The Census began as a head-count, prompted by concerns that the population was falling. Information was collected about what people *did*; this included paid and unpaid work. As the industrial revolution progressed and the separation of home and work became more marked, so there was a shift of emphasis to gathering information about the labour force: information was collected about what people *were*, rather than what they did. Married women were often defined as just that: any involvement in paid work, either inside or outside the home was not necessarily recorded. Hence patterns of expansion and contraction of domestic service are now thought to be obscured in census returns, as many enumerators used the terms 'housewife' and 'housekeeper' interchangeably (Higgs 1983). The implication here is that work only takes place away from the home: even where that home is that of the employer.

These early sets of assumptions about what work should 'count' laid the basis for the under-recording of part-time employment, and irregular, seasonal and home-based work which remains a feature of labour-force statistics today. Moreover, this under-recording and undervaluing has led to what Hakim (1985) terms a 'twentieth-century myth' about women's patterns of participation. She describes how, through re-analysing nineteenth-century census enumerators' notebooks, the economic activity rate for women is revealed as being as high in 1861 as it was in 1961 (at 43 per cent). Indeed, the rate for married women was as high in 1851 as in 1951. The recent 'rise' in women's propensity to engage in paid employment is thus a fiction:

women were typically involved in work in the mid-nineteenth century (either in collaboration with their husband's or family's business or in their own independent occupation); they were then excluded from the labour force and confined to domestic activity in the home in the early part of this century; they have now resumed their role in the labour force in the second half of the twentieth century. This places women's current work activities in a new light. It suggests that we should be asking how and why it was that women were excluded from gainful work in the early part of this century instead of seeking to explain the recent rise in women's work rates.

(Hakim 1985:43)

But the representation of women's work in the twentieth century is scarcely more revealing. Joshi and Owen (1987) have argued that a 'head-count' approach to measuring labour supply remains problematic when looking at female activity rates. Major government sources systematically focus on certain kinds of employment: those predominantly undertaken by men on a full-time basis. The employer-based Census of Employment excludes small employers, domestic employment and the self-employed; the Department of Employment's *New Earnings Survey* leaves out non-PAYE employees (who are likely to be low-paid and/or part-time, and therefore women) and the Census of Production covers manufacturing industries only: most women are employed in the service sector (Beechey 1983). Women's contribution to the 'black' or informal economy is, of course (like that of men), also invisible (Pahl 1984), and home-working is grossly under-recorded (Allen and Wolkowitz 1987; Hakim 1988; Pennington and Westover 1989).

Women's unemployment is particularly difficult to measure. The unemployment 'count' comprises those people registered as unemployed and eligible for benefit. However, in the United Kingdom, the benefit system is arranged in such a way that married women who opted to pay the reduced National Insurance stamp before 1978 are not eligible for unemployment benefit: they are unrecorded in the statistics and do not 'count' as unemployed, even if they are seeking work and would take a job if offered. Changes to the system in 1978 mean that there are diminishing numbers of women in this category. Women only available for part-time work are not eligible to receive benefit. Many women without jobs do not qualify because they do not satisfy the conditions for eligibility: they may, for example, have been earning low wages or working insufficient hours to have made enough contributions to qualify.

The Labour Force Survey (LFS) is conducted on an annual basis in all member states of the European Community, and allows some international comparisons of unemployment rates. While the criteria for being registered as unemployed vary markedly across the states, the LFS uses the International Labour Office definition of unemployment which is in terms of availability for work and job-seeking behaviour. This is particularly helpful when trying to establish unemployment among women in Britain, given that so many are ineligible for benefit. Even so, many women will not actively seek employment unless they believe suitable work is available: the tremendous number of applicants for jobs every time a hypermarket opens in an area without substantial registered female unemployment bears witness to this.

The LFS has also been useful in widening the concept of work so that women who regard themselves as a housewife first and foremost can also record their part-time employment. It also facilitates international comparisons as definitions are standardised. But pitfalls remain in the use of labour-force statistics, particularly for comparative purposes (see Dale and Glover 1989).

The Department of Employment's *Women and Employment Survey: a Lifetime Perspective* (Martin and Roberts 1984) was a landmark in revealing patterns of women's activity over the lifetime and the complex relationship between economic activity and stage in the life cycle. By interviewing 5,588 women of all ages about what they did rather than what they were, a detailed picture was revealed which challenged some of the assumptions about women's relationship with the labour market. Attachment to the labour force was demonstrated to be high, contrary to prevailing myths. Women's conceptions of unemployment and their difficulty in identifying themselves as unemployed, even if they were seeking work and would take a job if offered, were brought to light (see Cragg and Dawson 1984). The classification of many jobs normally undertaken by women was found to be woefully inadequate (see below).

The survey also measured domestic and unpaid caring work. Such data are not collected in the Census because questions are decided upon according to the demand for them by government departments (the 'users' or 'customers' in the new business discourse, which is as much a growing feature of OPCS as it is in all other parts of the public sector). There is no 'need to know' about domestic work. This contribution of women is therefore completely invisible.

Valuing women's work

The concept of skill is also socially constructed. The power and status of the job incumbent is a determining factor in the assessment of its skill level: industrial muscle and, of course, gender are therefore crucial signifiers. In a highly gendered workforce, gender assumes vital importance in determining the skill component deemed to be attached to a specific job. That perceived skill level is then reflected in the level of pay which rewards it (Gallie 1988). Phillips and Taylor (1980), among others (Gaskell 1986; Horrell *et al.* 1990; Jenson 1989), have drawn attention to the relationship between the gender of those who do a particular job, the value put upon the skills involved, and the level of pay with which those skills are rewarded.

The social construction of skill depends not just upon which gender performs the task involved but also on how those skills were obtained. Skills acquired through education, training or experience are valued and rewarded more than 'talent' thought to be innate or skills learned on the job. Characteristics commonly supposed to be innate are different for the two genders. The physical strength of the labourer may not be particularly well remunerated unless supplemented with time-served, learned building skills. But by the same token, the 'talents' of women, such as the capacity for and skills involved in caring, are not rewarded either. However, the origin of those characteristics associated with women is more questionable: cleaning, cooking and caring are all low-paid occupations, but any difference in men's and women's ability to do those jobs is learned rather than in-born.

Time-served apprentices, however outmoded their skills, are respected and given the highest status in skilled work. Women tend to acquire their skills by other means, such as sitting by Nellie or in-house training (Training Agency 1989a). Such training is rarely credentialised or valued. When the learning takes place in the home, the perceived skill component is even further diminished (Elson and Pearson 1981). Employers sometimes use qualifications as a screening device, a short-hand exclusionary mechanism, rather than identifying them as a requirement for a job in any related sense: young unemployed people during the 1970s and 1980s found that the level of qualifications required for essentially unskilled jobs crept up while the state of the labour market allowed employers to pick and choose.

Feminisation of a particular occupation or profession is seen to have the effect of deskilling it. Where certain professions which previously excluded women altogether, such as law (Spencer and Podmore 1986) and medicine (Allen 1988; Lawrence 1987; Lorber 1984), have admitted women, new patterns of gender segregation emerge between specialisms within that profession: women do not necessarily enjoy the status and pay and conditions that previously accrued only to men.

Women represented by trade unions enjoy better pay and conditions on the whole than those who are not (Martin and Roberts 1984). Moreover, where trade unions are weak or non-existent, women's work is more likely to be defined as unskilled or semi-skilled (Mitter 1986). But unions of course, are largely male-dominated institutions (even where the majority of members are women). As Cockburn (1983) demonstrated all too clearly, they can be instrumental in defending the status of skilled work attached to men's jobs that have actually become deskilled. Industrial bargaining can be highly effective in maintaining differentials, despite changes in job content which undermine their rationale.

Job evaluation schemes have had the effect of recognising the skill content of many jobs deemed unskilled or semi-skilled because it has been exclusively women who perform them. Classification systems (such as the Registrar General's Classification of Occupations – CODOT, and more recently the Standard Occupational Classification – SOC) used to describe occupations are skewed in favour of jobs performed by men: the degree of gradation calculated in skill level, and the detail in differentiation between, for example, welders of different materials is almost loving in its meticulousness. The *Women and Employment Survey* (Martin and Roberts 1984) revealed by contrast that secretarial and clerical jobs, from company executives' personal assistants through to copy typists and data entry clerks, are afforded hardly any skill distance between them. This situation is common elsewhere. In Australia, for example:

> the Metal Trades Act lists hundreds of classifications, many describing highly differentiated and often obscure tasks. The majority of women covered by this award fall into just two categories – process worker and machine operator. These classifications describe vastly different jobs which share the common characteristic of being performed often by women who have lacked industrial strength, whose demands have been constrained by the interests of more highly paid male workers to maintain pay and status relativities and who have no trade or technical qualifications.
>
> (Windsor 1990:144)

The value placed on work is receiving increasing attention because of the shift in equal pay legislation to assessing jobs of 'equal value' (O'Donovan and Szyszczak 1988); because of the changes in skills required in the labour market as a result of new technologies, and because of the alleged growth in multi-skilling. As different skills evolve – for example, when Information Technology (IT) is introduced – so new, gendered patterns of ranking jobs in relation to one another and paying some workers more than others emerge. The inter-relationship between skill level and pay is muddied by the gender of the job occupants and their access to industrial muscle. This theme is developed in the chapter on new technologies (Chapter 7).

Recent studies of women's economic activity and the value put on women's work have demonstrated, then, how concepts related to work, such as part-time work (Beechey 1987c), unemployment (Marsh 1988) and skill (Phillips and Taylor 1980), are all predicated upon and take as their yardstick male experiences of work. Women's experiences of work have as a consequence been read in the light of that model, rather than in their own right.

Patterns of participation

The *Women and Employment Survey* (Martin and Roberts 1984) and a whole shelf-ful of excellent secondary analyses have illuminated the complexity of women's movement in and out of full- and part-time employment over the life cycle and the major shifts in the post-war period (Cragg and Dawson 1984, Dex 1987; 1988; Hunt 1988). More recent trends are observable from the annual LFS (Department of Employment 1990); from digests such as Reid and Stratta (1989) and from various smaller-scale studies (for example, Allat *et al*. 1987). Given that this is a well-trodden field, I propose here just to summarise the main patterns.

Martin and Roberts (1984) show that in each decade since the end of the war, the length of period taken by women out of the labour force for the purpose of child-bearing and child-rearing diminished. In the 1940s and early 1950s, it was common for women to leave work upon marriage; indeed, in some occupations a marriage bar made this compulsory. In later decades, women would be more likely to stay in employment until the birth of the first child, and then to return when the last child began school. This produced the 'bi-modal split', where the female labour force largely comprised two groups: young, child-free women, and older women who were mothers of growing children. In recent years, the pattern has shifted again, so that women are now quite likely to return to work between the births of their children. Increasingly, the initial return to work has been on a part-time basis; indeed, the United Kingdom has the second highest proportion of women working part-time in the European Community (Eurostat 1990).

Of course, these patterns are global; there are distinct variations between groups of women according to their occupation, qualifications, ethnic origin, region and, indeed, locality. Those women likely to take the shortest period out of paid work are highly qualified women in the professions, who enjoy employment protection in the form of maternity leave and whose salaries can better afford paid child care. At the other end of the continuum, unqualified women are likely to return to work soon after having each child as their families need the income: for them child care is more likely to be a complex system of family care. This link between level of education and time out of the labour force has been established too in a major study in the United States (Moen *et al*. 1990). For women in between these two extremes, such as those in clerical work or the retail industry, who comprise the majority, a longer break is the norm.

Afro-Caribbean women are unlikely to be out of the labour force for long irrespective of their occupation: their participation rates are higher than for any other ethnic group, including whites. They are also more likely to work full-time. This may in part be a factor of economic necessity; the rate of single parenthood is high relative to other groups, and disadvantage and discrimination in the labour market bring low wages which necessitate long hours of work. An economic activity rate is the ratio of women in the labour force – that is, either employed, registered unemployed or temporarily off work sick – to all women of working age. Women of Asian origin have relatively low economic activity rates, but for some this may to an extent be a function of the under-recording of their contribution to family businesses. Different birth-rates can also contribute to the variety of participation patterns among various ethnic minority groupings: women of Pakistani and

Bangladeshi origin in particular have high fertility rates and low economic activity rates (Central Statistical Office 1991: Tables 1.12, 4.7).

Men tend to remain in the labour force from leaving full-time education until retirement age (irrespective of whether they are in employment throughout that period). The *Women and Employment Survey* revealed that women have a rich variety of patterns of participation in the labour force, over their lifetimes. At one extreme, relatively few followed the male norm of being economically active for the whole of their adult lives of working age: at the other, a few stopped altogether on the birth of the first child. No one pattern of participation described the majority of women. Hunt (1988) illustrates the kaleidoscope of patterns of movements in and out of work, and in and out of full-time and part-time employment. As Main shows (1988:28), contrary to many dominant images and myths, women demonstrate a clear commitment to labour-market participation: 85 per cent of respondents in the survey had either never left the workforce or have returned to it at least once after a period of withdrawal.

It is clear from a variety of sources (for example, Bird and West 1987), including the *Women and Employment Survey*, however, that a break is bad for your career. This is particularly the case where women return to work on a part-time basis. The structure of work organisation is highly segregated; very few employers offer career-track posts to those on part-time hours. There are some moves in this direction on the part of certain employers loath to lose the services of highly trained and skilled women workers altogether; indeed, retention schemes are a more popular employer response to the demographic down-turn than recruiting from a wider net (see Chapter 6 on Positive Action). However, overwhelmingly, part-time work is highly limited in the rewards and opportunities for promotion that it offers.

Dex's (1987) detailed secondary analysis of life and work history data from the *Women and Employment Survey* shows that women both with and without children experienced downward occupational mobility over their working lives. She concluded that childbirth is undoubtedly the biggest single cause of downward mobility, the key factor being not so much having a baby, but the indirect effect of moving into part-time work afterwards. In essence, women have to choose between 'working full-time to keep their occupational status, or accepting a loss of status in order to get a part-time job' (Dex 1987:86). Dex (1989) has argued effectively that the relative abundance of opportunities for part-time work in the United Kingdom acts as a buffer against unemployment, explaining in part at least why, contrary to almost every other country in the European Community, the female unemployment rate is lower than that of males.[1] The effect of part-time employment is to lower women's wage rates when they return to work, even after they eventually move back to full-time employment (Main 1988:49).

The divisions between full- and part-time work can be seen as in themselves forming new patterns of segregation in the labour force, where gender is used as the organising principle. Beechey and Perkins (1987) have demonstrated the impact of gender on work organisation in the bread- and cake-making industries, for example, in their study in Coventry. Production activities were organised on completely different lines. Contrasting rates of pay, and terms and conditions of employment accrued to workers involved in the preparation of the two products. What differentiated the two labour forces essentially was not the nature of the work but the gender of those who did it: bread-baking was undertaken by men on a full-time basis, while cakes were produced by women on part-time shifts.

However, while resuming work on a part-time basis evidently implies downward mobility, even returning on a full-time basis is deleterious to those on career tracks, because of the privilege afforded to seniority over other considerations in the promotion process. Seniority is certainly easier to measure than ability to do the job, and skills that may have been learned during a period of child-rearing tend to be overlooked: it is as if the women concerned have been 'on ice' during those years. Moreover, where new technologies have been introduced, which applies to an increasing number of occupations in all sectors, the value of occupation-specific pre-break skills may indeed have eroded. The effect of the career break on women's working lives is discussed in the chapter on returners (Chapter 4).

Patterns of gender segregation

Analysis of occupational segregation patterns by Hakim (1979) and in *The Women and Employment Survey* (Martin and Roberts 1984) revealed to an extent not previously appreciated how an overwhelming proportion of women work exclusively, or almost exclusively, with other women. This segregation is both horizontal and vertical: men and women work in different industries and at different levels of the hierarchy in those industries. Women workers are heavily concentrated in a narrow range of occupations, particularly those which rely on part-time workers. Women constitute about 42 per cent of the workforce overall, but of the eighteen occupational groupings, account for over 20 per cent of the workers in only eight (Equal Opportunities Commission 1987). Three-quarters of the workers in the totally inadequately categorised 'catering, cleaning, hairdressing and other services' classification are women, the majority of whom work part-time. Men are much more evenly distributed throughout the occupations.

Patterns of horizontal and vertical segregation are immensely rigid and have attracted a considerable amount of attention from feminists seeking to explain their endurance (Crompton and Sanderson 1990; Walby 1988). There have been a number of empirical studies of women in specific professions such as teaching (Acker 1989), where, despite being successful in securing access, they have had difficulties in penetrating the upper echelons. There has also been a series of studies of women in 'male' professions (Allen 1988; Atkinson and Delamont 1990; Coyle and Skinner 1988; Delamont 1989; Fogarty *et al.* 1981; Hansard Society Commission on Women at the Top 1990; Silverstone and Ward 1980; Spencer and Podmore 1987). Such women develop coping strategies: those employed by some women in engineering and women senior civil servants in Australia are referred to elsewhere in this book. Breakwell (1985) explores the psychological strategies adopted by women in male-dominated occupations, such as fire-fighting, printing and motor-vehicle repair. Cockburn's study of the Youth Training Scheme (1987) found the barriers to acceptance encountered by both young women and young men who had attempted to enter a job traditionally the preserve of the other gender so insurmountable that the majority eventually gave up and conformed. By contrast, there is a growing genre of books of interviews with 'tall poppies' (Mitchell 1984) – that is, women who have succeeded in a 'man's world' in, for example, Scotland (Gerver and Hart 1991) and Australia (Mitchell 1984; Watson 1989).

Gender segregation has been described as 'the most important cause of the wages gap between men and women in Western economies' (Walby 1988:1). In the United Kingdom, patterns of gender segregation ensured that the 1975 Equal Pay legislation was decidedly muted in its effect on women's wages. In order to claim equal pay with a man, a woman employee needed to find a 'comparator', a colleague at the same plant of the opposite sex being paid more for the same or broadly similar work, with whose wages she wished hers to be compared. Given that women tend to work exclusively with other women, such male comparators were hard to find. Indeed, there is some evidence that in preparation for the legislation, employers divided their workforce even more rigidly by gender, precisely to avoid such cases being brought. In any event, the legislation had only a one-off improvement effect by increasing women's average pay as a proportion of men's from two-thirds to about three-quarters. Since then it has slipped back to around 72 per cent (calculated from Department of Employment 1991; Table 5.6). It is too early to assess the effect of the revisions to the legislation allowing equal pay for work of equal value; there will have to be a number of successful cases worked through the lengthy, costly and emotionally draining tribunal system (Chambers and Horton 1990; Gough 1979; Leonard 1987) before a judgement can be made. What is clear is that men and women do different jobs in different sectors, and that those done by men are more highly valued and better rewarded.

THEORETICAL APPROACHES

While specific patterns of gender segregation and pay differentials may vary over time and space, nevertheless, the impact of gender remains an overwhelmingly significant feature of labour-force organisation. Sociological and economic theoretical approaches to work largely ignored women until relatively recently: most of the contribution to understanding the gendering of the labour force and women's persistently lower rates of pay have come from feminists. There are already some excellent reviews of these theoretical developments (see, for example, Crompton and Sanderson 1990; Dex 1985; Walby 1990). My purpose here is to sketch very briefly the main thrust of the various perspectives, and to establish the theoretical framework within which the material in this book is couched; that is, the *dual system approach*, which argues that the position of women in the labour force is a consequence of the inter-relationship between capital and patriarchy.

Functionalism and human capital theory

Economic theories focus on aspects of labour supply and demand. Labour supply-side approaches have been heavily influenced by sociological and economic explanations rooted in Parsonian functionalist interpretations of the family and gender roles within it. Parsons (Parsons and Bales 1956) considered the family to be an organic unit essential to the survival of society, as it provided a secure environment for the procreation and rearing of the young of the species. Within the family, women were regarded as being best suited to carrying out 'expressive' roles such as caring, while men focused on 'instrumental' roles, such as bread-winning. This division of labour was considered functional for both the family and society more generally.

However, this division of labour clearly has ramifications for men's and women's relative marketability: as men accrue more experience in the workplace, they develop a competitive edge. As women concentrate on nurturing, and therefore have time out of the labour force, they inevitably amass fewer marketable skills than men. The relatively less skilled jobs they can then acquire are comparatively poorly paid. Economic human capital theory is informed by this notion when it argues that taking the household as the basic economic unit, it then makes sense for men to invest in their 'human capital' through the acquisition of skills, qualifications and experience: women by contrast would not be so motivated, since they are the ones to focus on care of the children and home, and fit employment around their domestic responsibilities.

The argument is clearly tautological, and moreover flawed in both empirical and theoretical terms (see Walby 1990). Owen (1987), indeed, has argued that the demands of economic efficiency at the level of the household no longer require household members to specialise in domestic or market tasks. She claims that, contrary to the 'new home economics', which suggests that productivity improves as more time is devoted to an activity, it is experience of, rather than the scale of involvement in, an activity which is crucial. As elements of housework become less complex due to changing technology, so it no longer makes economic sense for one partner to 'specialise'. Despite these and other criticisms, the notion of 'natural roles' within the family determining a gendered division of labour within and outside the home has been extremely influential, not only in theoretical terms but in the everyday actions of men and women, as both employees and employers (see Collinson *et al.* 1990).

The ideology of the family, and men's and women's ideas about their role within it, underpin many of the attitudes which inform the 'choices'. Those choices, in turn, lead to the acquisition of differentiated levels of human capital. Anticipation of a career break or return to work part-time is taken as given in many girls' decisions about options and careers (see Chapter 3 on girls' occupational choices). It can diminish their aspirations to invest in their own human capital. While the *level* of academic achievement among boys and girls at school is similar, the courses followed are remarkably gender-specific and the boys' choices are directed towards the higher paid occupations and professions; that is, those normally undertaken by men (see Cockburn 1987; Department of Education and Science 1991; Equal Opportunities Commission 1987). Boys are more likely to go on to higher education (Department of Education and Science 1991) and to jobs where employers provide training (see Chapter 7). Girls' option choices and career choices at school in effect shut off a whole range of education and training opportunities which in turn restrict their access to various occupations and industries. They are then less likely to earn a living wage, and will therefore be more likely to be financially dependent upon a partner or the state. As a consequence, sex-role stereotyping about appropriate roles in the home and in work can create self-fulfilling prophecies.

But to what extent is it actually true to say that women are clustered in a narrow range of industries and at the bottom of the hierarchies in those industries because they have inferior human capital in terms of educational qualifications and skill levels? The gap between women's and men's education levels and labour-market experience has been narrowing in the post-war period, but, as Walby (1988) points out, the gap in wage rates has not reflected this. She reports on research from the United States (Treiman and Hartmann 1981) which demonstrates that occupational differences in human capital explain less than half the gap between men's and women's wage rates. It is the arrangement of work into gender-segregated sectors which is crucial here: a major feature of such segregation in the United Kingdom is the limitation of opportunities for part-time employment to relatively low-level and/or poorly valued work.

Functionalist and human capital theories have been influential despite their acknowledged shortcomings. Feminist perspectives have emerged in the last twenty years as a reaction to the lack of satisfactory explanations for the impact of gender on occupational life chances.

Feminist perspectives

Feminist perspectives are differentiated from traditional economic and sociological theories in three significant ways. In the first instance, gender is clearly given a much higher priority as the focus of concern: indeed, the gender dimension was largely absent from much traditional social science until relatively recently. Secondly, feminists have looked not simply at the family as a unit or system in terms of its relationship with other systems, but they have also examined relationships within the family and in particular power relations between men and women. Finally, feminists have been concerned with practical action as well as theoretical explanation. Campaigns have regularly taken place alongside theoretical developments.

Liberal feminism

Liberal feminism has its roots in Mary Wollstonecraft's writings in the eighteenth century ([1792] reprinted in 1967) and her concern with equality for women through extending citizenship rights to them (see Chapter 3 on schoolgirls). Liberal feminist approaches to work have essentially focused on explaining inequality through the identification of barriers to women's full access to opportunities in the labour market. Campaigns have centred on legislation; for example, equal pay and the removal of more obvious forms of sex discrimination in education and employment. Liberal feminism offers no fundamental challenge to the status quo; rather, it seeks to secure equal access for women to the existing system.

Some of the studies described in this book were commissioned by organisations concerned to identify and remove barriers impeding women's progress. Employers and unions tend to be motivated more by the imperative of an efficient running organisation rather than inspired by social justice or liberal feminist concerns about equality. 'Positive action' measures more generally are on the whole predicated upon the belief that if women cannot gain access to the organisation, or its upper reaches, then there must be specific barriers which inhibit their progress: these are often construed as being located in women's own attributes, or lack of them, rather than in the structure of the organisation itself. Appropriate training, or the accommodation of domestic commitments through rearranging hours, are perceived as potential solutions. They leave the issue of power relations between men and women in the organisation and in the home, and the matter of the domestic division of labour, untouched.

Liberal feminism does not challenge the edifice of gender power relations and the organisational structures which support them by privileging men; rather, it seeks permission for women to join in.

Marxist feminism

Marx had little to say about women specifically when he developed his theories of the relationship between capital and labour, and the exploitation of those who sell their labour (the proletariat) by those who own the means of production (the bourgeoisie) in the process of extracting profit. Engels ([1884] 1972) did address the issue of the position of women, and argued that they would need to engage fully in the labour market in order to escape domination by men at home. Moreover, he asserted that the abolition of the family was necessary for achieving equality of the sexes. Although these ideas have never been fully implemented anywhere, various writers have examined Engels' ideas in the context of societies which have not actively fostered the ideology of the family and have moved towards the full involvement of women in production, such as the Soviet Union and Czechoslovakia (Heitlinger 1979). Contemporary feminists have continued to find Engels' ideas compelling, even if they disagree with them (Delmar 1976; Sayers *et al.* 1987).

Marxists, Marxist feminists and socialist feminists have struggled to insert women into Marx's account of class relations (Barrett 1987, 1988; Barrett and McIntosh 1980, 1982; Beechey 1987a; Vogel 1983). Marxist feminists see patriarchy, the oppression of women by men, as closely linked to, or indeed a by-product of the capitalist mode of production (Seccombe 1974; Zaretsky 1976). As a consequence, much of Marxist-feminist writing has focused on women as a distinct category of paid labour (in the sphere of production), and as playing an important role in capital accumulation through the bearing and rearing of the next labour force (the sphere of reproduction) and servicing the needs of existing male workers. Marxist feminists have also developed a materialist analysis of gender as well as class relations, which is empirically based and explores the reproduction of ideology and culture (for example, Kuhn and Wolpe 1978; Pollert 1981).

There is a wealth of writing in this field, but I propose to describe briefly just two areas germane to later discussion, the reserve army of labour thesis, and deskilling and the labour process.

(1) *Reserve army of labour.* Marx ([1867] 1954) described the reserve army of labour as a device to suppress wages through the availability of a surplus pool of workers. As such, it was essential to capital accumulation. Capital would both discard workers into the reserve, and recruit them again as and when the need arose. The very existence of a reserve army ensures that workers are unable successfully to press for higher wages in times of high labour demand. It comprises three main groups: the floating reserve – that is, the recently employed unemployed; the latent reserve – those whose

skills are redundant due to industrial restructuring; and the stagnant – that is, the underemployed and seasonal or intermittent workers.

Power (1983), drawing on US data, asserted that women could be seen as part of the latent reserve. Beechey (1977,1978), on the basis of British data, claimed that married women in particular can be seen as a flexible reserve army of labour, brought into the workforce when labour supply is short and then shed again when the demand for them dries up. She wanted to widen Marx's categorisation of the reserve army to include married women as a specific group. Certainly, the recruitment of women in large numbers during the two world wars in the United Kingdom and the United States, and their subsequent exclusion afterwards to vacate jobs fit for heroes, is often cited as a classic example of women operating as a reserve army. However, women's experiences of such war-time work did not liberate them from expectations that they would simultaneously continue to bear responsibility for domestic work, and job-gendering remained a feature of such work even though opportunities for moving into male-dominated areas were clearly, temporarily, greater (Braybon 1981; Milkman 1987; Summerfield 1989).

Breugel's (1979) search for empirical evidence of the reserve army thesis for the period 1974–78 found only limited support for it. The key element is the concept of disposability, but Breugel found that in the service sector, women are not necessarily the first to be laid off in a recession. Nor do women necessarily replace men as cheaper labour. In essence, gender segregation is a major stumbling block to the conceptualisation of women as a reserve army. The expansion of the service sector and its heavy reliance on women (particularly on a part-time basis in the United Kingdom) has meant that women's low paid work has been protected, relative to men's, throughout successive recessions. More recent studies have supported this finding (Rubery and Tarling 1988; Walby 1989).

The notion of disposability can be extended, however, to mean not just women as a category compared with men in a recession, but individual women being more susceptible to redundancy when compared with men in similar work. Breugel (1979) did find limited empirical support for this version of disposability, in the manufacturing sector.

Other critiques of the reserve army thesis have drawn attention to its focus on women's role in production to the exclusion of attention to their role in reproduction (see, for example, Anthias 1980). This fundamental criticism of Marxist-feminist approaches more generally is developed below.

Despite the difficulties with the reserve army thesis, it is enjoying something of a new vogue in popular terms as demographic changes once again herald a welcome for women in the labour force. Allusions to war-time efforts to provide state care for children are echoed in current employers' attempts to facilitate women's return to work despite their domestic commitments. This theme is discussed in Chapter 6.

(2) *Deskilling and the labour process.* Notions of deskilling and the

labour process have their origins in Marx, but elements were also to be found in the writings of Taylor in 1911 (1964). Taylor's thesis was that the scientific management of work and reduction of the skill component of jobs as a mechanism of control over the labour force could increase productivity, keep wages low and so maximise profit. One of his major tenets was that it was essential to disassociate the labour process from the skilled worker. In other words, by breaking the labour process up into a series of unskilled tasks, workers could more easily be replaced, and would have their bargaining strength undermined. Managerial monopoly control of knowledge of the labour process was essential.

Taylor's model (characterised as 'Taylorism') was not in much evidence in American industrial practices (Grint 1991), but his ideas clearly influenced the development of assembly-line production systems, mass production and the resultant isolated, alienated, if relatively well-paid workers. The first such production line for a mass market was introduced as part of a unit cost-cutting strategy by Ford, the American motor-car company in 1913, the company's name becoming forever associated with that style of production and work organisation. Wood and Kelly (1982) found Tayloristic techniques implemented within a range of strategic frameworks in cultures as diverse as the Soviet Union, Japan, the United Kingdom and Italy.

Braverman (1974) has been highly successful in drawing attention to the changes in the labour process in pursuit of capital accumulation. This is manifested in shifts within occupations, industries and sectors as a result of work organisation and the introduction of new technologies, and in changes in the distribution of labour *between* occupations, industries and sectors. Writing on the changes in the labour process at each level has been one of the most developed areas of labour-market scholarship (see Knights and Willmott 1986, *inter alios*).

Braverman (1974) developed Taylor's ideas on capitalism and deskilling, and sought to fit women into the analysis. He predicted further deskilling as an outcome of the struggle between capital and labour, and anticipated that women would take up the majority of these unskilled jobs. He expected many household tasks to be taken over by the private sector, thus releasing women for further engagement in economic activity, and leading to a convergence in male and female economic activity rates as men were thrown out of skilled jobs. Neither of these predictions have materialised in the way in which he described them, although there are certain strengths to his arguments which have been very influential.

Taking the second prediction first, this fell because while the nature of women's domestic labour may have changed, expectations about the level of servicing have changed too (Kleinberg 1983). As a consequence, the amount of time spent by women on domestic labour, although reduced, has not reduced so significantly (see Morris 1990; Schwartz Cowan 1989). There has been no major shift in the domestic division of labour as a result of women's increased economic activity (Brannen and Moss 1991; Gershuny *et al.* 1986; Morris 1990).

Moreover, with respect to Braverman's first prediction, employers have not, on the whole, taken the route of deskilling to control the workforce and keep wages down. As Chapter 8 shows, some German state-of-the-art high-tech companies, for example, have developed more along what might be described as Post-Fordist or flexible specialisation lines. This means reducing the division of labour and using training to create a core of multi-skilled workers who can undertake a range of tasks. It implies flattening the authority hierarchy and developing team working, rather than isolated working. It involves capital seeking out niche markets, and developing new lines quickly, rather than being constrained by assembly-line production, which is expensive to set up and adapt. Post-Fordism also brings an emphasis on high-quality and high-value products, rather than mass-produced items with built-in obsolescence. The thesis, as outlined by Atkinson and Meager (1986), proposes that in addition to a 'core' workforce which is multi-skilled or polyvalent (functional flexibility), there is a peripheral workforce that provides numerical flexibility: it is engaged as needed – for example, through sub-contracting or overtime arrangements.

There are considerable debates about whether Post-Fordism and flexible specialisation systems are in fact replacing assembly lines, particularly in Britain (see Pollert 1991). There are numerous issues surrounding the flexibility debate, not least of which is whether employers can be said to have 'strategies' (Rees, G. *et al.* 1991; Wood and Kelly 1982), whether it can be empirically tested, whether it takes account of women's employment patterns satisfactorily (Walby 1990) and indeed, whether it is actually new (Pollert 1987). The criticisms are both at a theoretical level and in terms of its lack of empirical foundation.

The findings of Chapter 8 suggest that in the highly specific German blue-chip, technologically advanced companies studied, there are indeed changes such as those broadly described that are affecting the occupational life chances of workers, and from which women as well as men should benefit. There is little evidence of such changes being widespread in Britain. Indeed Lovering (1990) argues that Britain's version of Post-Fordism mobilises gender, race, age and class inequalities as key axes of segmentation in the labour market. Even in the German case studies, these factors underlay the opening up of opportunities more generally.

Dual labour-market theory

Some of the ideas in the flexibility debate can be traced back to versions of dual labour-market theory. This originally developed from economists in the United States and was principally concerned with explaining the very different kinds of pay and terms and conditions enjoyed by workers in the 'primary' and 'secondary' sectors (Edwards *et al*. 1975; Piore 1975). Those in the primary sector are assured of career prospects, reasonable security and favourable conditions: those in the secondary labour market, by contrast, are likely to be part-time or temporary or on a short contract; the jobs are less stable and do not accrue fringe benefits. When recruiting staff for primary- or secondary-sector jobs, employers are thought to have sex- and race-stereotyped ideas about suitable candidates. In effect, primary and secondary labour forces are constructed using social attributes.

Although the theory was originally applied to race segregation in the United States, Barron and Norris (1976) imported it to the United Kingdom and adapted it to account for gender segregation. Employers are described as using the female gender as a shorthand identifier for a worker with low-level labour-force attachment who can accommodate being laid off if necessary, will not expect a career trajectory, and will be willing to accept less favourable terms and conditions. Men, by contrast, are identified as the kind of workers suitable for primary-sector employment; they will be 'lean and hungry', anxious to get on, and have a family to support. Gender is clearly not the only construct so used to allocate workers; race and other characteristics are important.

Rather like human capital theory, this argument also has tautological dangers and has attracted much attention and criticism (Beechey 1978; Dex 1985). Criticisms have focused on the undifferentiated treatment of women as a group, and the insufficient account taken of the relationship between women's role in the home and that in the labour market. Inadequate attention has been paid to the role of unions in structuring labour markets, it is argued, and colluding with men to define 'skill' and exclude women (Cockburn 1983; Coyle 1984). The theoretical developments have not been empirically grounded in Britain: indeed, this was a major criticism of Barron and Norris's paper. Dex (1985) argues that one of the best-known British studies to examine dual labour markets, by Blackburn and Mann (1979), which might have tested Barron and Norris's assertions, largely excluded women. Others, by economists and sociologists, while including women in the analysis, have not provided sufficient empirical grounding for the theoretical ideas.

Dual labour-market theory has been developed to a more sophisticated level in labour-market segmentation theories (for example, Roberts *et al*. 1985). Essentially, the complexities of patterns of employment and pay are being analysed with race and gender either as important variables in their own right or at least taken into account, even if only partially (Dex 1985).

Radical feminist approaches

While Marxists and Marxist feminists take class relations as their starting point, radical feminists focus on the concept of patriarchy to explain all aspects of women's lives. Rather than prioritising the relationship between the bourgeoisie and the proletariat, radical feminists highlight the power relationship between men and women, or, more specifically in Brownmiller's (1976) work, between husbands and wives.

Hence, although Marxist feminists would argue that capital is advantaged by women's unpaid domestic labour, radical feminists see the prime beneficiaries as being men, as a category. This helps to explain male-dominated unions and employers excluding women from paid work, and seeking to control the terms by which they enter.

The main focus of patriarchal relations, however, is in the family, which is regarded as the key instrument of oppression and the site of its cultural reproduction. As a consequence, radical feminists have concentrated their attention more on the family and the private sphere, analysing rape (Brownmiller 1976), reproduction (Firestone 1974), and 'compulsory heterosexuality' (Rich 1980), rather than the public sphere and the labour market. If the private sphere is the main site of male domination, then this leads naturally to the slogan 'the personal is the political'. Radical feminists see patriarchy as trans-historical and unchanging: men's need to oppress women is primary, therefore patriarchal relations are fundamental.

Although the concept of patriarchy has been extremely important in the development of feminist thinking, there are criticisms of radical feminist approaches because of the exclusive reliance upon it as an explanatory vehicle. Essentially, change over time, such as the increase in women's participation, remains unexplained, as do the experiences of different women. For women in some ethnic minorities, patriarchy may not be felt to be as oppressive as class relations or racism. Both postmodernists and black feminists have attacked radical feminist theory for emphasising the commonalities experienced by women to the exclusion of differences (Weedon 1987). There are also criticisms by Segal (1987) of 'essentialism' and reductionism: certainly, in the work of Firestone (1974) there are elements of biological determinism.

The main criticism, however, is from Walby (1990), who identifies the problem as being reliance upon only one base/superstructure: she argues that patriarchal modes of production need to be examined in articulation with other modes, such as capitalism. It is this 'dual systems' approach which is considered next.

Patriarchy and capitalism: dual systems theory

Dual systems theory, which has its origins in socialist feminism, maintains that there are two separate systems interacting in all societies, a sex-gender system and an economic or mode-of-production system, the current forms of which are patriarchy and capitalism respectively. Patriarchal and class relations combine to oppress women. The main focus of attention in dual systems theory is the articulation between these two systems, which can change over time. There are various versions of the nature of the relationship between the two: Eisenstein (1979) argues that patriarchy and capitalism are separate systems which have fused together; others, such as Cockburn (1983:8), see them as separate but in continual interaction. Hartmann (1979b) identifies the two systems as having identical interests; for example, they both benefit from the nuclear family as a household form and from women's unpaid domestic labour within it. Walby (1986), however, suggests that at times – for example, during labour shortage such as wartime – the interests of capital and patriarchy may in fact conflict. The advantage of the dual systems approach is that it accommodates the existence of patriarchy in economic systems other than capitalism, but its form is seen as changing and dynamic, so that shifts and changes can be taken on board.

Walby (1990) describes the changing nature of patriarchy since the nineteenth century, and argues that there has been a shift from private patriarchy to public patriarchy as women have increasingly moved into the public sphere. She maintains that, whereas in the nineteenth century women were simply excluded from public life, in the twentieth century they are merely segregated. Walby (1990:20) defines patriarchy as: 'a system of social structures and practices in which men dominate, oppress and exploit women'.

This implies rejection of the notion that every individual man is in a dominant position and every woman in a subordinate one, Walby argues, thereby accommodating the experiences of different women within the model. She also claims it is a rejection of biological determinism, another criticism levied at earlier theoretical formulations. Walby conceptualises patriarchy at the most abstract level as a system of social relations; beneath that she identifies six structures which, she claims, are necessary to account for the variation of gender relations. The limitation of previous versions, she maintains, is that they have tended to focus on only one of the six structures, and therefore cannot account for spatial or temporal variations. The six structures she identifies are (1) the patriarchal mode of production – namely, housework, with a producing class (women) and an expropriating class (men); (2) patriarchal relations in paid work; (3) patriarchal relations in the state; (4) male violence; (5) patriarchal relations in sexuality; and (6) patriarchal relations in cultural institutions (for instance, the media, education). Walby (1990) argues that, although there are reductions in the degree of some specific forms of inequality, in effect the nature of patriarchal relations is simply changing. The inter-relationships between these structures determine individuals' experiences of patriarchy.

This formulation, and elements of dual systems theory more generally, appear to be helpful in understanding the persistence of segregation in work, although there are again criticisms, particularly in the degree to which the relationships between class and gender are adequately explained (Murray 1990). Crompton and Sanderson (1990:17) assess the explanatory power of patriarchy as useful but more limited than the claims that are sometimes made for it. Throughout the empirical chapters of this book it is clear that a narrow focus on work practices, or, indeed, the family or education system in isolation, do not account for the segregation described in a range of workplaces. Rather, the effects of patriarchal relations in a number of sites, reinforced by the state, confirm and reproduce women's restricted access to a labour market that is organised in a way that privileges both capital and men.

The following chapters focus on women in a variety of labour-market settings and at various stages in their life cycle. They expose some of the impact of the interaction between capital and patriarchy, and demonstrate the significance of the three recurring themes of the book, the ideology of the family, the material realities of women's lives, and exclusionary mechanisms operated by men.

Chapter 3

Schoolgirls' occupational 'choices'[1]

For Mary Wollstonecraft, thought by many to be the first British feminist theorist, the road to emancipation and liberty for women was through education. In *A Vindication of the Rights of Woman* (1967), first published in 1792, she argued that education would reduce the differences between men and women as they both realised their full potential for rationality. Any psychological differences between them would be eroded and eventually disappear. She wrote:

> A wild wish has just flown from my heart to my head and I will not stifle it, though it may excite a horse-laugh. I do earnestly wish to see the distinction of sex confounded in society, unless where love animates the difference.
>
> (Wollstonecraft [1792] 1967)

Many liberal feminist campaigns have been centred on attempting to improve equality of access to education since that time. Until the nineteenth century, access to further and higher education was effectively denied women (Delamont 1989); since then there has been a slow but accelerating process of evolutionary change, gradually improving women's opportunities.

Such reform, however, does not challenge the basic structures of those institutions. Initiating equal opportunities measures usually begins with collecting and keeping statistical records to monitor the proportion of women on courses and in the hierarchy, with a view to improving the ratios. Neither monitoring, nor even pointing out the small proportion of women students enrolled on certain courses or promoted women teachers or lecturers or professors, challenges the legitimacy of those systems. As Dorothy Smith writes (1987:26), equality of opportunities is only one aspect of the problem, we need to look at how women are

> located in the processes of setting standards, producing social knowledge, acting as 'gatekeepers' over what is admitted into the system of distribu-

tion . . . participating as authorities in the ideological work being done in the education process.

It is, however, much more difficult to conduct a thorough critique of educational systems and structures and to implement changes that would successfully neutralise the existing impact of malestreamism that underpins them. Given that educational organisations are themselves liberal institutions, it has been much easier for both feminists and liberal reformers alike to address the issue of equality of access.

The tripartite system of education introduced in 1944 was intended to introduce equality of access irrespective of class, but Halsey (1977; Halsey, Heath and Ridge 1980) observed that the system had failed to produce *equality of outcome*: there were still many more children from middle-class backgrounds going on to further and higher education in the early 1960s. This observation was influential in the decision to introduce the comprehensive system. Class, of course, persistently remains a chief determinant of access to higher education. The same observation of inequality of *outcome*, as applied to girls and women, can be made today, both in terms of numbers attending courses, the numbers being paid while they train (rather than having to attend night class), the numbers in higher education places, and so on.

Gender is an enormously powerful determinant of *type* of course selected, in school, in youth training placements (see Cockburn 1987), and in further and higher education. Whereas the history of liberal reformism to date has concentrated on equality of *access* for girls and women, the 1980s were characterised by a series of initiatives, usually pilot, experimental or demonstration projects, that attempted to ensure equality of *outcome*. In other words, they were designed not simply to allow girls into certain subject areas, but to facilitate them to emerge in roughly equal numbers. Despite the efforts of many of their proponents, however, these projects also, in part, legitimised an education system which failed to produce equality of outcome.

That such initiatives are one-offs is in itself interesting. It suggests that the girls in some sense need 'special treatment', perhaps to compensate them for some deficiency in their socialisation, or over-socialisation into being girls: it smacks of a deficit model (see Atkinson *et al.* 1982; Bernstein 1971). The onus is on the girls to change, just as many positive action measures are about making women more 'like men' (see Chapter 6). It also leaves untouched the basis of the education system, which plays a part in the reproduction of sex-stereotyped option choices. And finally, it does not commit educational bodies to implementing wholesale changes to the systems on the basis of the results of the projects: indeed, many are not even evaluated.

It has been persuasively argued by Brenton and Russell (1989) that the introduction of demonstration projects more generally – for example, to combat poverty – can act purely as a political expedient: their very existence suggests that the 'problem' is being addressed, when the focus of such actions is on the symptoms. The systems that produce such inequalities remain inviolate. When new programmes of action are introduced, they inevitably have to be innovative; they cannot repeat successes of earlier pilot projects in holding at bay, dispersing or assisting people in surviving the effects of poverty. Even where evaluation reports recommending policy changes emanate from the research, implementation is piecemeal at best.

Pilot projects or demonstration projects can, then, deflect attention away from the real causes of inequality by focusing attention on the shortcomings of the 'victims' and re-legitimising the system that produces them. This is clearly a recipe for reinforcing the status quo. In the 1980s, a series of initiatives and pilot projects were launched to persuade girls to consider science, technology and engineering as careers. Other initiatives were directed at women, and were geared towards attracting them to engineering. Many of these were funded by both the Department of Education and Science (DES) and the Department of Trade and Industry (DTI). The 1990s, by contrast, given the demographic changes, are already emerging as the decade of special initiatives designed to encourage women returners back to the labour force and to groom women middle managers for senior management (see Chapter 6).

However, these initiatives have been limited in their effectiveness. The education system has been widely recognised as not simply preparing young people for the labour market with appropriate knowledge and qualifications, but as socialising them into sets of expectations about their future roles in the family; hence school is experienced differently by people from different classes, races and genders. There has been a growing awareness in the education world of the tenacious persistence of gender as a predictor of option choice. Issues surrounding gender equality of both opportunity and outcome have resulted in concern about the dearth of role models, sexism in school literature, and in attempts to ensure that all pupils experience broadly the same curriculum (Delamont 1990). This approach is in the liberal tradition of attempting to ensure that pupils are offered and experience the *same* education in the *same* way, irrespective of ascribed characteristics, such as gender and race. Such traditions have informed the mushrooming of these special initiatives targeted at girls in order to attract them into more valued, and therefore better-rewarded careers in science and technology. Despite these initiatives, girls persistently 'choose' from a narrow, prescribed range of gendered course options and jobs.

Holland (1988) argues there is a fundamental contradiction for girls in their location in systems of production and reproduction. To what extent do expectations about future patriarchal relations in the home define and delimit aspirations for credentials and careers, and how is this shaped by class and the reality of local labour-market structures? This chapter examines the notion of 'choice' facing schoolgirls and explores the taken-for-granted assumptions which inform those choices. It draws upon a number of studies of schoolgirls' aspirations to explore the salience of anticipated roles as wives and mothers on option choices made in the mid-teens. More specifically, it focuses on working-class girls' frames of reference in making choices that will restrict the range of opportunities open to them in the future.[2] The determinants of choice which emerge emphasise the importance not only of anticipated roles, but also sets of expectations about the division of labour within the home that they are likely to experience. The strength of stereotypes about men's and women's jobs and men's and women's roles in the family emerge as stronger than any initiative designed to broaden their field of aspiration.

Awareness of sex stereotyping in schools has clearly grown enormously over the last few decades, particularly since the 1975 Sex Discrimination Act. Boys and girls can no longer legally be disbarred from sex-stereotyped options, although some schools in Wales have been found still to restrict choices on the grounds of gender (Delamont 1990), and indeed, one school in West Glamorgan was prosecuted for so doing in 1989. School-books are monitored more effectively for blatant sexist and racist stereotypes. Although many local education authorities already provided such a service through the Youth Employment Service, the 1973 Employment and Training Act *required* them to provide a vocational guidance service to young people attending educational establishments, and a placements service for those leaving them. This offers an opportunity for boys and girls to be informed about a whole range of choices, not just those traditional for their gender. However, the extent to which individual careers services and officers within them actively address the issue of gender stereotyping varies considerably.

On the surface, then, there have been legal provisions which enable wider choices to be made, and a growing awareness of gender issues. However, a limited increase in sensitivity to the issues can lead to complacency, and numerous studies have documented the complexity, subtlety and sheer opaqueness of sexist and racist practices that percolate education systems (see Foster-Carter and Wright 1989). Indeed, one study of a teacher's use of sex-role theory in a lesson on equality showed how he ended up giving the pupils the exact opposite message from the one that was intended (Baker and Davies 1989). Understanding and eliminating some of the more obvious sexist and racist practices can inhibit the development of a more thorough approach to deconstructing and removing more complex sexist and racist systems, structures and practices that permeate the everyday life of the institution.

This chapter draws upon two empirical studies, both based in South Wales, to explore girls' ideas about their future in terms of option choices and life planning. It examines the limitations of special initiatives designed to broaden girls' horizons in the light of the material reality facing them, particularly those of working-class girls with few expectations of academic qualifications. The girls' determinants of choice are outlined, in particular the impact of an expected career break, the strength of stereotyped images of job gendering and their commitment to locality. But first, the social construction of option choice, and the special initiatives which have sought to widen that choice, are discussed.

CHOOSING OPTIONS

The social construction of option choice

One of the major difficulties in breaking down the patterns of gender segregation in the labour market lies in the fact that young girls themselves overwhelmingly appear to 'choose' sex stereotypical options, training courses and occupations. Many of the special measures that have been designed to open up access to non-traditional areas flounder because of this. There is then the danger that these persistent patterns of 'choice' are interpreted as constituting evidence that there is no need to address the issue further – because the girls themselves demonstrate no demand for access to 'typically male' jobs. But how real is this 'choice'? To what extent are such 'choices' based upon a realistic understanding of the mechanisms of the labour market and the sexual division of labour in the home? To what extent do girls feel they have choices to make?

Structural changes in the education system have had unfortunate side-effects as far as girls' socialisation is concerned. The introduction of the comprehensive system meant the disappearance of considerable numbers of single-sex schools. This had the immediate effect of removing many role models in the form of women head teachers, and reducing women teachers' prospects of promotion (Orr 1985; Wilce 1983).

Moreover, there is clear evidence that girls are more likely to opt for science subjects in all-girl schools (see Deem 1984) or where single-sex teaching for science operates in co-educational schools (see Sarah, Scott and Spender 1980; Whyte *et al.* 1985). It is unclear, however, whether this is a result of the fact that the school is single-sex, or whether it is the outcome of a combination of factors such as class and ability (see Connell *et al.* 1982). Girls' schools are increasingly found only in the private education system or in elitist direct grant and grammar schools. Indeed, the single-sex schools that remain in the state system often lack the facilities necessary to teach subjects that were seen as the preserve of the other gender: boys' schools may well not have a kitchen to teach domestic science, girls' schools will almost certainly not have a metal-work and woodwork room, although now they are required to teach Craft, Design and Technology. There is some

Table 3.1 Gender spectrum of examination passes: percentage of pupils leaving school with GCSE/GCE/O Levels/SCE grades (A–C) and CSE Grade 1, Great Britain

| Subject | 1980–81 | | | 1988–89 | | |
	Girls	*Boys*	*All*	*Girls*	*Boys*	*All*
English	43	33	38	52	38	45
Mathematics	27	31	29	34	38	36
Biology	19	12	16	21	14	17
French	19	11	15	17	15	16
Chemistry	10	15	12	14	18	16
Physics	8	20	14	10	23	17

Source: Derived from DES (1983) *Education Statistics for the UK: 1983 Edition*, Table 13, London: HMSO; and DES (1991) *Statistics of Education for the UK 1990 Edition*, Table 33, London: HMSO

evidence that resources for introducing the Technical and Vocational Education Initiative (TVEI) in schools have been used to purchase equipment to fill this gap in single-sex schools (see Venning 1983).

Although technically some barriers have been removed, gender is still highly deterministic of option choice, just as class remains a powerful variable in access to higher education. Simply allowing boys and girls to take options not associated with their gender has had little effect. Girls are still more likely to pursue 'arts' subjects at school and in further and higher education, while boys are more likely to select Mathematics and Science. Mathematics has been described as acting as a 'critical filter', closing off access to a whole range of subjects in higher education that lead directly to well-paid careers. There have been consistently more girls than boys achieving better results in GCSE at school in English, Biology, French and History over the last ten years, while the reverse is the case for Mathematics, Physics, Geography and Chemistry (Central Statistical Office 1991: Table 3.15). While the gap is closing, as Table 3.1 shows, gender sustained its impact on subject choice throughout the 1980s.

Regional patterns show higher staying on rates in Scotland (where of course the education system is different from that in England and Wales) for both boys and girls, but gender differences in attempting and passing public examinations remain stable throughout England, Scotland and Wales (Equal Opportunities Commission 1990). More detailed accounts of gender segregation in education are available elsewhere (for example, Abbott and Wallace 1990; DES 1991; Raffe 1988; Skeggs 1989). All the figures show that although the gap may be diminishing over time, gender is still a major determinant of which options are taken.

The plethora of action research projects and practical initiatives aimed at breaking down sex-stereotypical choices in the 1970s and 1980s included the Girls into Science and Technology Project (GIST), the Girls and Occupational Choice Project (GAOC), the Equal Opportunities Commission/Engineering Council's Women into Science and Engineering (WISE), the Schools Council Reducing Differentials Project and the Girls and Technical Education project (GATE) (Chisholm and Holland 1986; Delamont 1990). More recently, the Women's National Commission has been promoting a series of Women's Training Roadshows designed to introduce a wide range of educational, training and occupational opportunities to women and girls around the country (see Delamont 1990; Pilcher et al. 1988a, 1988b, 1989a, 1989b, 1990a, 1990b). However, the impact of these initiatives has been marginal. None of them can be expected, on their own, to counteract the raft of socialising agents which inform option and career choices. Such choices that are made tend on the whole to be bounded, being made within the confines of gender-appropriate destinations.

Does it matter that 'Girls won't be boys', as a *Times* columnist expressed it: 'If either sex does have a natural disposition towards or against any particular occupation, should we try to change it?' (Butt 1990:10).

'Natural dispositions' are inherently unlikely to be the explanation for gendered differences in career choices. After all, in Denmark, dentists tend to be women; in Egypt, engineers are often women.[3] Maccoby and Jacklin's (1974) celebrated review of 1,400 studies concluded that there are no innate psychological gender differences: environmental factors are a more powerful explanatory tool for observed differences in orientation. Recent attempts to establish innate differences remain problematic (see Megarry 1984). Far more likely causal factors include socialisation processes which perpetuate patterns of division of labour in the home and market place that are convenient for the maximisation of profit. The school can be seen as an agent in the transmission of appropriate skills and attitudes for the reproduction of both the next workforce and people to service it: this socialisation clearly embraces acceptance of patriarchal as well as class relations. The ideology of gender and of the family underpin the workings of the education system in both obvious and more hidden forms. Skeggs (1989:104) reviews education reports which

> have influenced the structure and development of education, all . . . (of which) indicate how schooling is a gender-related experience in which a different form of social control and pedagogy operates for women and men based on the anticipation of their future primary positioning in the family household.

The rise in the 1970s and 1980s of youth unemployment and the New Vocationalism further channelled women into traditional domestic and labour-market positions (see, for example, Pollard et al. 1988). The schemes that were introduced to cope with unacceptably high rates of youth unemployment were intended to address the problem of lack of appropriate work socialisation. The delivery of those schemes – Youth Opportunities

Programme, the Youth Training Scheme (YTS) and so on – also socialised young people into patterns of social relations of production highly stereotyped along class and gender lines (see Brelsford *et al.* 1982; Cockburn 1987). There are indications that for some unemployed teenage schoolleavers, motherhood was adopted as an alternative to a place in the labour market, so fulfilling one at least of the dual expectations of a woman's adult role (see Griffin 1985; Rees, T. and Winckler 1986; Wallace 1988).

David (1983) shows how in the 1980s there was a shift away from a concern with equal opportunities in education and towards a preoccupation with emphasising the ideology of the family. Concern about the growth in numbers of single-parent families, divorce, working mothers, teenage mothers and so on led, she argues, to schools putting more stress on moral education and preparation for parental responsibilities. The model of family life that underpins such education is the standard white nuclear family with a traditional gendered division of domestic and paid labour – the clear concern of the government that schools should not 'proselytise' gay lifestyles lends some support to this view. This inevitably beams out different messages to young men and women in schools about the seriousness with which they should take their future careers: it emphasises to boys that they will have a family to support, and it offers to the girls the corollary, a disincentive to invest in further education or training for a career, given that that career is likely to be interrupted. The traditional emphasis in schools on cookery, domestic science and needlework for girls prepares them not simply for motherhood, but for a particular pattern of domestic division of labour (Prendergast and Prout 1980). Like Willis's (1977) lads in England, and Valli's (1986) girls' experiences of anticipatory occupational socialisation in the United States, young people are thus prepared for a version of reality that renders decision making obsolete.

It is too early to predict what effect the national curriculum being phased into British schools as a result of the 1988 Education Reform Act will have on the gendering of option choices: on the face of it, making gender-loaded subjects common to all pupils should help to neutralise them, in the sense of diluting their association with one gender or another. Similarly, the insistence upon cross-curricular teaching may help to dissociate subjects and gender. Some feminists would argue, however, that no subject can become 'neutral' nor can there be a meaningful concept of equality: simply having more of one gender or another taking that subject does not mean that they are experienced in the same way.

In addition to ensuring that pupils are taught the 'core' foundation subjects, family values are enshrined in personal and social education in the national curriculum with an emphasis on moral education, health education and preparation for parenthood and adult role in family life (DES 1989). But, as David points out, 'the goal of equal opportunities in work life could not be achieved without a reduction of sex inequality in family life' (David 1983:151). The fundamental contradiction remains.

Equal opportunities are on the agenda of TVEI, but there is no evidence that it has radically altered educational practices in such a way as to challenge gender stereotyping, and early reports suggest it has not been successful in affecting cross-gender option choices. Millman and Weiner (1987) argue that little progress has been made, while Berry et al. (1987) suggest that while it may be widening boys' interests somewhat, girls retain traditional perspectives. By the late 1980s, only one girl in fifty on TVEI was opting for technology subjects and one in forty for information technology courses: while these represent increases on previous trends, they still fall far short of TVEI's equal opportunities aspirations (Manpower Services Commission (MSC) n.d.).[4] Dale et al. (1990), in a riveting account of TVEI which they describe as the most important educational innovation of the post-war period, claim that despite being one of the original criteria for the scheme, equal opportunities remains 'among the most difficult and controversial' areas (p. 137). They confirm that girls are reported as not opting for non-traditional areas of the programme, and in some areas, the numbers taking Craft, Design and Technology-based courses actually decreased, while boys are moving into TVEI business and catering courses.

The relationship between educational qualifications and destination in the labour market remains strong. There is little evidence of the breakdown of gender segregation, however, with the exception of some well-qualified middle-class girls entering the professions, for whom class seems to compensate for gender. The proportion of girls from private schools entering higher education at 30 per cent (DES 1986), is substantially greater than that from maintained schools, at 6 per cent: the proportions for boys are similar, at 36 per cent and 7 per cent.

The relative impact of class, gender and race on educational experiences is difficult to disentangle. Black girls, for example, share experiences of racism, a Eurocentric curriculum and a white British (for the most part English) perspective on history and geography at school, but have different patterns of achievement relative both to boys of the same ethnic origin and to white girls. Asian and West Indian girls achieve fewer educational qualifications than white girls, although a fairer comparison would be with white girls of the same class. West Indian girls have more qualifications than West Indian boys, while Asian girls have fewer than Asian boys (Arnot 1986). But such global patterns mask the kinds of complexities revealed in Fuller's (1980) research, which shows how a group of West Indian girls were simultaneously resisting the normative culture of their educational institution but adhering to the culture of valuing qualifications as a passport to better jobs. Regional cultures, too, can have an impact, as the vast differences in regional attainment patterns suggest (Central Statistical Office 1991, Table 3.13).

Despite these complexities, it is evident that the vast majority of girls, particularly but by no means exclusively working-class girls, the unqualified and those from ethnic minorities, are likely both to end up in typically female work, and to bear the major responsibility for domestic commitments. Moreover, Green's (1989) study of boys taking domestic science, and the work of Cockburn (1987) amongst others, have demonstrated how even when individual girls and boys 'choose' non-traditional courses or placements, they daily encounter pressures to make them conform, and most do so. Such studies have helped to highlight the more subtle pressures that operate through peer-group culture and from well-meaning gatekeepers who influence option choices.

Griffin (1985), in particular, has shown how option choices are made at a time when personal development and the construction of a sexual identity is at a highly sensitive stage: to opt for a 'male' course threatens to compromise that identity. Indeed, Cockburn (1987) shows that girls who chose engineering placements on YTS were simultaneously accused of being 'boy mad' and 'lezzies'. Given girls' perceptions of their dual task of finding work and finding a partner, such pressures are not easily withstood.

Initiatives designed to widen choice

There have been a range of initiatives designed to widen choice; this section focuses on just five.

1 Girls into Science and Technology (GIST)

GIST was one of the first schools-based action research projects to address the issue of gender stereotyping in attitudes towards science and in option choice. Teachers in eight mixed comprehensives co-operated in attempting to improve girls' interest in and achievement in science while collaborating in a research programme. The teachers largely designed their own initiatives to stimulate pupils' interest in science, and the effects were monitored. Two control schools were also monitored where no special action took place.

The results of the study have been widely disseminated (see Kelly 1987; Kelly *et al.* 1984; Smail *et al.* 1982; Whyte 1985, 1986, *inter alios*). The general conclusion is that the initiatives were effective in changing attitudes, rather than behaviour. The project was highly significant, however, in that it demonstrated the extent to which 'female under-achievement in science and technology is at least partly socially constructed by the school' (Whyte 1985:79).

This represented a shift away from identifying the 'problem' as one of girls' motivation towards attempts to change the nature of school science to one that is 'girl friendly'; that is, one that will appeal to girls as well as boys.

2 Girls and Occupational Choice (GAOC)

This action research project was designed to develop curriculum units to break down sex-stereotypical patterns of occupational choice for boys and girls. A thousand 11- to 16-year-old first and third years from three London schools participated. The research showed that the gap between aspirations and expectations 'closed off' occupations of a non-appropriate class and gender (Chisholm 1987; Chisholm and Holland 1986). In other words, young people were clearly informed by their perceptions of their likelihood of being offered a particular job in a way that took on board sex and class appropriateness. Girls more than boys were likely to blame their own inadequacies for being unable to fulfil their aspirations (Holland 1988). Moreover, the jobs they chose were described by Holland as servicing the female image or working with children, hence reinforcing the role of women.

3 Women into Science and Engineering (WISE)

Jointly sponsored by the Equal Opportunities Commission and the Engineering Council, the WISE year (1984) and other initiatives were designed to encourage women to take up science and engineering, and employers to employ women in these fields. The emphasis was, however, very much on women needing to take up the challenge that these professions had to offer, rather than on the industries concerned needing to organise themselves in such a way as to make it easier for women, while still in a small minority, to enter and feel comfortable in such a male culture.

WISE itself was not formally evaluated by researchers. However, in a study of women engineers Newton and Brocklesby (1982) demonstrated how the significance of cultural difficulties in working in engineering far outweighed any problems women experience with the work itself. Women reported being treated as special, as not being expected to achieve the same as men, as having to prove their competence. Some felt they had experienced difficulties in relating to women in typically female jobs, while some of the younger men dealt with the issue of the women engineers' gender by denying it, and treating them as 'one of the lads' (Newton and Brocklesby 1982).

4 Engineering Industrial Training Board (EITB) Technician Scheme

The Engineering Industrial Training Board launched a series of initiatives during the 1970s and 1980s to encourage girls and women into the profession in response to anticipated increases in demand for engineers brought about by developments in technology, and because of forecast labour shortages. A major concern underlying the initiatives was to 'correct' the image of engineering as dirty, physically demanding work: it was assumed that this erroneous image was the impediment to women offering themselves for recruitment. The Insight programme, started in 1979, was designed to attract high-calibre girls studying Mathematics and Science into engineering. Other initiatives too, like the WISE programme, were geared towards marketing engineering as a career.

5 Women's Training Roadshows

The Women's National Commission, part of the Cabinet Office set up to advise the government on issues relating to women, plays a central role in the co-ordination of Women's Training Roadshows, which are locally organised one- or two-day multi-media events designed to encourage girls and women to contemplate a range of training and career opportunities that are normally the preserve of men. The nature of the events varies, but they tend to offer exhibition stalls by employers and training providers, career workshops and a range of activities and films. Sponsorship is provided by national and local industry. There have been over a dozen such Roadshows so far, and they have had a multiplier effect: increasingly local authorities are organising their own.

The Cardiff Roadshow, which is the focus of one of the studies drawn upon in the next section, was organised by a committee led by the late Gillian Powell, Professor of Biochemistry and EOC Commissioner for Wales. It was held in University College Cardiff (now the University of Wales College of Cardiff) over two days in June 1987. There were seventy role-models, including an airline pilot, a taxidermist, a bank manager and several engineers. There were also fifty women careers officers running small group workshops for schoolgirls, an exhibition hall, computer workshops, videos, games, computers, balloons and badges. About 2,000 secondary schoolgirls from South Wales attended the Roadshow, in addition to many local women.

The very existence and the experiences of these initiatives draw to light the fact that gender socialisation in option and career choices is deeply ingrained. Such initiatives, by themselves, can only have a marginal effect, and that effect is more likely to be on attitudes than on behaviour. They underline the impact of teachers' attitudes, but also emphasise the all-pervasive strength of the cultures of femininity and masculinity in both schools and the workplace.

DETERMINANTS OF CHOICE

'Choosing' a future

A young woman's entry to the labour market is determined by a complex set of processes. Some of these are external: for example, employers' recruitment practices and patterns of work organisation, the actions of trade unions, beliefs about what jobs are 'skilled' and how they should be rewarded, local labour-market opportunity structures, and transport provision. Some factors relate more directly to the woman herself, except that these characteristics are common to so many women. If a woman has children, for example, then her freedom to sell her labour becomes constrained by issues such as child-care facilities, pay relative to child-care costs, hours and so on. If she has a husband or co-habiting partner, then his position in the labour market has a bearing on her employment (Dilnot and Kell 1987). Other factors have to do with the impact of her particular blend of ascriptive characteristics such as age, class and race: all of which shape and constrain channels of recruitment and promotion, and thereby influence 'choice'. A woman's own cultural capital, her networks and knowledge about the local labour market and training provision, her existing and predicted domestic responsibilities and her qualifications, experience and aspirations, are all important. Her commitment to her family of origin and the locality may affect her preparedness to move for training or employment opportunities.

Choices made in school and on leaving school have to be located within this mesh and the pupil's understanding of them. Of all determinants, it is clear that gender, class and race significantly affect what option and career choices boys and girls think are appropriate, and that this knowledge informs those decisions (see Kelly 1978; Ryrie, Furst and Lauder 1979). The main difference between boys' and girls' perspectives remains the contrasted sets of expectations they have about the impact of their future role in the family.

This section focuses on just a few of these factors, leaving others for consideration elsewhere in the book. It looks at those which have more to do with the woman herself, particularly working-class young women. It is not, however, entirely helpful to disaggregate external and internal factors, as the external circumstances that prescribe young women's choices also inform them.

The rest of this chapter draws upon two research projects, both located in South Wales, to explore these issues further.

The studies

1 Evaluation of Cardiff Women's Training Roadshow[5]

The Cardiff Women's Training Roadshow (CWTR) evaluation included observation of the event itself and interviews with organisers, careers officers, stall holders, teachers and role-models. The main focus of the study (and of this chapter), however, was on the career plans and perspectives of the girls who attended it. Six months after the event, the research team sampled 500 of the 2,000 girls in six contrasted schools in different parts of South Wales to take part in group discussions and complete a questionnaire. The overall intention was to discover what they remembered of the event and what effect, if any, it had had upon their option and career choices. The girls' views of their future, and the determinants of their option and career choices will be one of the concerns of this chapter.

2 The Southall Two Generation Study[6]

The second study was conducted by Juli Southall (1990). Southall traced the cohort of thirty working-class girls with whom she had left a South Wales school in 1973. From material she collected from in-depth interviews with the women, now in their early thirties, she was able to reconstruct their life and work histories. She then compared these with the life and career plans of the 1989 cohort of girls leaving the same school. Her main focus was to assess whether the raising of the school-leaving age to 16 in 1974–75 and the legislative changes between the two years, 1973 and 1989 (the 1975 Sex Discrimination Act, the 1970 Equal Pay Act, and the 1973 Employment and Training Act which *required* local education authorities to provide a careers service) resulted in the girls' planned trajectories being any different from the actual experiences of the women.

The studies revealed four important factors which had a bearing on option and career choice: the anticipation of a broken career, the strength of job gendering, a desire to remain in the area, and low aspirations and confidence levels.

A Anticipation of a 'broken' career

The major difference between girls and boys in their expectations about the future is that girls are far more likely to anticipate having to combine work with domestic responsibilities which will impinge upon the terms and conditions on which they are able to engage in the formal economy. Girls, particularly those who do not expect to acquire formal qualifications, are more likely to 'plan' or at least foresee a working life which will accommodate exits and entrances, and allow part-time working. For more qualified girls, teaching and nursing have remained attractive, in part at least because work in these professions has been perceived as being organised to recognise women's patterns of labour-force participation, determined by unequal degrees of responsibility for children. Both professions have adapted to take account of these patterns: a third of nurses leave and are replaced every year. Supply teachers can be regarded as a reserve army of labour and as a manifestation of the education sector adapting to the flexibility required by its largely female workforce, albeit to the detriment of the supply teachers' own careers. However, such flexibility is at a cost: being able to take time off and perhaps return part-time almost certainly means losing prospects of promotion and can even mean demotion (see Main 1988).

Some innovative careers services invite young people to complete a 'life and career plan', mapping out where they think they will be in labour market and personal terms at various junctures in the future, and to identify anticipated significant events in the years to come. The concept of individual career action planning is gaining momentum. A 'Career and Life Planning' exercise was used in the CWTR by fifty women careers officers with nearly 2,000 secondary schoolgirls in groups of about fifteen. The girls were largely from third, fourth and sixth years, as fifth formers were involved in exams during the two days of the Roadshow. For many of the younger girls in particular, it was the first time that they had come into contact with the careers service: interviews are not normally held until the fourth form (although some may have received guidance during their option choices at the end of Form Three). Many found it strange to think of the future as something that they had any control over: life is something that 'just happens to you'.[7] However, as a whole, the girls enjoyed the opportunity to discuss their futures in a group seriously; the opportunity to do so varies widely from school to school. We observed many of the sessions over the two days, and conducted interviews with most of the fifty careers officers. Their observation, which was reinforced by our later work in the schools, was that the girls' views of their occupations were clearly influenced by their anticipated domestic roles:

> 'Most of the girls I see are only looking for a stop-gap between school and marriage. It was the same with the girls here today.'

> 'The only group consensus I was aware of is that girls are born to marry and have families.'

> 'The lesser able group were all thinking in terms of marriage except one. The more able said the husbands should share 50/50 in domestic chores, and wanted to know about crèches. The less able group talked of marriage and were not relying on husbands for help but their mothers.'

A very broad observation made by the careers officers was that the academically inclined girls were more likely to see career and motherhood as simultaneous activities, whereas the less academic saw them as sequential.

Juli Southall, herself a senior careers officer at the time, used the life and career planning technique with a cohort of 16-year-old girls from the comprehensive school located in a working-class area that she had attended as a girl (Southall 1990). The findings were remarkably consistent with those of the CWTR evaluation in that the girls anticipated a broken career. Southall's study compared the actual number of years the women from her

Table 3.2 Economic activity and domestic commitments: a comparison of women's experiences and girls' predictions

Activity	Women experienced (Average no. of years)	Girls anticipated (Average no. of years)
Studying	2.9	2.4
At home	2.6	2.1
Full-time work	9.9	10.2
Part-time work	3.0	0.9

Source: Calculated from Southall (1990)

own cohort of school-leavers had spent in full-time and part-time employment, and at home looking after children in the fifteen years since they had left school, with the number of years the cohort of 1989 16-year-olds *anticipated* spending in each of these categories over the next sixteen years. The results are shown in Table 3.2.

It should be noted that although the women spent more years studying than the girls anticipated doing, some of the women had returned to education quite recently; most had not continued with their studies after leaving school at 15 or 16. They were the last cohort to leave school before the raising of the minimum school-leaving age in 1974–75. Moreover, the school, which had been a secondary modern, was then in its first year as a comprehensive for 11- to 16-year-olds: the women were the first cohort to take GCE O levels at the school. There was still no sixth form: to continue with studies meant travelling to another school. For the later cohort however, a sixth form was available within the comprehensive (which is now for 11- to 18-year-olds).

A number of differences are observable comparing the two cohorts. GCSEs had replaced O levels by the time the girls came to take their examinations. Although they left school with more qualifications than the women, fewer had passes equivalent to the O-level grades achieved by the women. More of the girls intended staying on at the school for longer. The girls intend to spend more time in the labour market working full-time than their predecessors actually had. The number of girls intending to return to full-time work after having had their children was greater than the number of women who had returned to full-time work. The women had on average 1.4 children, exactly the same figure that the girls anticipated having. Southall reports that the girls were optimistic about finding child care: 'hire a nanny or put in a crèche'; 'they go to nursery/ they go to school and get very good and never get into trouble', 'my mother can look after them'; and, perhaps most optimistic of all, 'let my husband look after them' (Southall 1990:74). The women's actual experiences of making child-care arrangements had proved rather more problematic.

But despite these changes, Southall's overwhelming finding was that the girls had 'chosen' to go into exactly the same, low-paying, low-skilled occupations in the same narrow range of typically female industries as those which their predecessors had 'chosen' sixteen years previously. Clerical work was identified by eleven of the girls as their first choice: it was also the occupation followed by the largest group of women (eleven). Caring work and retail accounted for most of the other girls' choices and women's actual jobs. The girls' career 'choices' take account of an anticipated career break, even if it is expected to be shorter in duration than that of the previous generation. Southall argues that the girls expect

> more years of full-time employment punctuated by a definite 'career break'. The women's group, once leaving their first period of full-time employment, tend to return to part-time and lower status work. They appear not to have enjoyed the luxury of a definite 'career break' from their original jobs, but to have been 'active' – if in less well paid, part-time work, for most of the available years.
>
> (1990:83)

The anticipation of a broken career clearly remains a potent force in shaping, or rather restricting, schoolgirls' career choices, particularly those from working-class homes. It devalues the entire exercise of option and career choice by setting a framework of a narrow range of jobs from which the girls can then exercise choice. Those choices are to be made from a short list of jobs in industries that have adapted to women's domestic commitments from the perspective of facilitating the employment of such women, through the hours available, flexible working arrangements and so on. But they have not, on the whole, truly taken on board women's needs by building in opportunities for promotion within those occupations and industries for people who take career breaks or who wish to work part-time. This is well known to the girls, and their level of aspiration is clearly informed by it.

B The strength of job gendering: making sense of women in men's jobs

Cockburn's (1987) work has demonstrated all too graphically the strength of job gendering on young people's consciousness. The study of the CWTR highlighted the potency of such forces graphically.

We conducted group interviews with the 500 girls in our follow-up study in year groups of about fifteen to a group, for thirty-five-minute sessions. In the group discussions, we posed the following celebrated conundrum, and invited the girls to explain it. The story goes that a man and his son were driving along and became involved in a serious road accident. The father was killed and the son rushed to hospital where it was decided that he needed immediate surgery. The surgeon duly comes into the theatre and glances at the face of the boy before operating, and says, 'My God I can't operate on him – that's my son!'

Surprisingly, few of the girls had heard this conundrum before and knew the solution. They demonstrated creditable skills of lateral thinking in trying to decipher it. Explanations offered included the hypothesis that the boy was an identical twin separated from his brother at birth; that he was an adopted son, that he was a 'milkman job', that the 'father' was a religious or step-father rather than a blood relative, that it was a case of mistaken identity because of the severity of the boy's injuries, and so on. A mere thirteen girls out of the 500 managed to work out that the surgeon was, of course, the boy's mother.

In similar vein, the girls were asked six months after the Roadshow which of the role-models they could remember. There were spectacular examples of role-models' jobs being translated or computed into ones that women were more likely to do: it was as if the girls did not believe the evidence of their own eyes. So, the woman bank manager (the only one in existence at the time in Wales), was recorded as being a bank clerk, the woman airline pilot (the only one so far employed by Danair) was reconstructed in memory as an air stewardess, as was the woman who trained air-cabin crew. The chemical engineer was asked three times whether she really was an engineer, and when she asked why they asked, received the reply, 'it's because you've got a handbag!' These examples of girls struggling to accommodate images of women undertaking 'men's jobs' illustrate the difficulties that special initiatives face in not simply persuading girls to accept that there are such women (without two heads, and indeed, with handbags) but that they themselves might entertain the idea of becoming one of them.

C 'Keeping close': the impact of locality

Numerous studies have argued that local youth labour markets are highly important in determining young people's aspirations (see Brown and Ashton 1987; Bynner and Evans 1990). For less academic girls in particular, moving away to seek work is not considered, and therefore option and career choices are limited by what is available locally.

The local labour market for each of the six schools in our study varies, but they comprised two from the Valleys, two from the Vale of Glamorgan (the coastal strip between Cardiff and Newport) and two from the Cardiff area. Cardiff scores highly on the Durham University quality-of-life indices, while the Vale is a largely rural area where there are some transport difficulties for young people. The South Wales Valleys do not score highly on standard indices of quality of life: while there are wide open spaces to be enjoyed, many acres of them are on sharp inclines. The main industries of coal and steel have been decimated. Social and economic indicators reveal that the Valleys comprise an area with persistently high unemployment, despite the 'economic miracle' and efforts of the Welsh Office, Welsh Development Agency and local authorities to attract new industries. An ageing housing stock, relatively poor infrastructure, communications and transport links render the Valleys relatively unattractive to the outsider, including potential residents seeking cheap housing and the inward investor. Nevertheless, the residents on the whole remain fiercely loyal to the area, as was witnessed by people preferring to remain and be unemployed after the pit closures of the 1970s (Rees, G. and Rees, T. 1984), and as evidenced by the overwhelming support for the 1984–85 miners' strike, where pit closures would mean (and subsequently have meant) the end of economic viability for many villages. For different reasons, then, in terms of quality of life or attachment to area and family, we expected the girls, particularly the less academic and those from working-class backgrounds, to be reluctant to move from the area.

To what extent does the desire to stay in the area limit girls' willingness to take up training and job opportunities elsewhere? The careers officers who took part in the Roadshow noted a difference between Valleys girls and others in terms of the difficulties they faced. Employers were more likely to specify that a boy was required for vacancies; Valleys girls were more likely to have 'traditional' attitudes towards work and marriage, and moving away was more problematic for them. A school careers officer in one of the valley schools remarked: 'The girls are more interested in local things, they don't want to leave (Town X) compared with the boys, that is the 4th and 3rd years, the 6th will.'

We explored attitudes to moving away through 'Karen's dilemma'.

'Karen's dilemma'   We presented the 500 girls in our study with a 'dilemma' in the questionnaire they completed, where a character had to choose between staying or taking up a desired job opportunity elsewhere. Of course, it is not possible to extrapolate the extent to which the choices made by the girls on behalf of our fictional character actually match up to decisions they might make on their own behalf. This is particularly so as it is clear that pupils have triple standards about sex roles; that is, adolescents have very stereotypical ideas about what is appropriate for peers of the opposite sex, more flexible ideas about peers of the same sex, and relatively unstereotyped notions about what activities they themselves can engage in (Guttentag and Bray 1976). There remains the gap, of course, between such attitudes and actual behaviour: nevertheless, the 'dilemma' produced interesting results.

The quandary posed as facing 'Karen' was this. She wants to be a nanny, but there are no such jobs in her area. She sees an advertisement in a local paper for a job as a nanny in Brighton. It is a good job, but to take it up she will clearly have to leave home. What should she do?

This dilemma was not dissimilar to one that thousands of young women

Table 3.3 Moving away: advantages of taking the job*

Rank	Advantages	No.	%
1	Doing a job she wants to	213	42
2	Have more money/be well paid	174	34
3	Freedom/independence	90	18
4	In a job/not on the dole	74	14
5	Gain experience/maturity	72	14
6	Would have a career	66	13
7	Make new friends	44	9
8	See more of the countryside/ in nice area/ near seaside	38	7
9	Enjoy children	20	4
	Total no. of responses	791	

*Note: Respondents could give more than one answer.
N=500
Source: CWTR Study

from previous generations in the South Wales Valleys have faced in the past. During the inter-war years in particular, the Juvenile Transference Scheme aided the movement of young people from depressed regions to those where there was a demand for work. For young women, this inevitably meant taking up domestic service in the relatively prosperous South-east of England, both in wealthy families and in the growing number of hotels in the coastal resorts. In the early 1930s in particular, the number of girls moving under the scheme to go into domestic service outnumbered the boys making for the areas where new industries were developing (see Rees, G. and Rees, T. 1982). These included the Midlands, Oxford and Slough (prompting the apocryphal epitaph on the gravestones of the Valleys, 'Not dead, but gone to Slough').

The choice of a typically female occupation was deliberate, to focus attention on leaving home rather than choosing a non-traditional job. The girls were asked to describe in writing:

1 what the advantages and disadvantages of such a job would be for the school-leaver,
2 what 'Karen's' parents would think, and
3 whether she should apply for the job.

On the whole, the respondents appeared to take the issue seriously and wrote full answers. Overall 91 per cent of the girls felt that Karen should apply for the job; only twenty-nine of the respondents (6 per cent) felt that she should not, although they all saw both advantages and disadvantages. These are shown in Tables 3.3 and 3.4 respectively. The percentage columns show what proportion of the girls volunteered each response.

Table 3.4 Moving away: disadvantages of taking the job*

Rank	Disadvantages	No.	%
1	Be homesick/miss her family	236	46
2	Have to leave home	176	34
3	Miss her friends	174	34
4	Be lonely there/not know anyone	107	21
5	Have to find accommodation	66	13
6	Brighton far away	49	10
7	May not like job	37	7
8	Have to cope on her own	30	6
9	Poor pay/financial difficulties	23	4
10	Live in a rough area/strange place	22	4
	Total no. of responses	920	

*Note: Respondents could give more than one answer
     N=500
Source: CWTR Study

Table 3.3 shows that over two-thirds of the perceived advantages (69 per cent) were in terms of the job itself and the advantages that it would accrue, rather than in terms of possible benefits of moving away. The remaining third were on the whole to do with personal development factors derived from being away from home.

The girls were far more forthcoming in identifying disadvantages than advantages. Table 3.4 suggests that missing the family is an overwhelming disadvantage of moving away; it accounts for over 80 per cent of responses volunteered. Others relate to 'Karen' being on her own (13 per cent) and potential job-related problems (6 per cent).

Parental steering into class appropriate education, training and career choices is clearly a powerful factor, and was first documented by Jackson and Marsden's (1962) seminal study of working-class boys and girls in grammar schools. Table 3.5 clearly demonstrates that parents are expected to have negative attitudes towards 'Karen' moving away: 58 per cent of responses are negative, compared with 36 per cent that are either positive or somewhat reluctantly supportive, and 6 per cent that devolve responsibility for the decision entirely to 'Karen'.

The careers officers at the Roadshow saw parents as having an important influence, but mostly in a negative sense:

Barriers? I think parents are one barrier. Up in the Valleys girls are supposed to go into offices. And when you give the careers talk to a group of girls they laugh when you mention the building trade, and if you say 'why not?' the reply is 'what would my mother say?'

Barriers? I think parental opposition is the biggest problem. Over the

Table 3.5 Moving away: girls' views of parents' responses*

Rank	Anticipated parents' responses	No.	%
1	Upset/disappointed at her leaving	131	26
2	Not like it but let her go	94	18
3	Pleased/supportive	79	15
4	'Karen's' happiness matters most	64	12
5	Try to dissuade her	62	12
6	Willing to let her go	46	9
7	Say it is 'Karen's' decision	37	7
8	Say 'Karen' is too young to leave home	36	7
9	Pleased she is independent	29	6
10	Worry about her	24	5
	Total no. of responses	602	

*Note: Respondents could give more than one answer
N=500
Source: CWTR Study

years I have interested a few in engineering and they go home and come back and say 'I'd rather be a hairdresser'.

The girl expressing an interest in hotel and catering work identified parental opposition as a barrier. Her father (having had some sort of experience in catering) had told his daughter that such work was not 'the right job for a girl'.

However, for careers officers to identify parents as a barrier is part of a well-trodden field of deferring responsibility for sex-stereotypical career choices. Delamont (1990:104) underlines the importance of initiatives being directed at all relevant audiences, not just girls: 'Teachers blame parents, pupils and the labour market; parents blame schools, pupils and employers; employers blame schools, parents and young people; young people complain about adults. No group admits it can change the *status quo*.'

We asked the girls about their occupational intentions and found that Valleys girls were more likely to answer in terms of traditional jobs (65 per cent) compared with Vale of Glamorgan or Cardiff girls (40 per cent). They also answered more in terms of locally available jobs.

This section has sought to demonstrate that girls see more disadvantages than advantages in moving away, on the whole. They may be likely to be reluctant to travel or uproot themselves for training or job opportunities. For Valleys girls in particular, where the range of jobs is limited and where traditional attitudes influence employers, parents and girls themselves, this will have a particularly restricting influence upon choices. Honess's (1989a, 1989b) work on young people in South Wales revealed the extent to which the local opportunity structures affected school-leavers' feelings about

Table 3.6 Hoped for and expected destinations after leaving school

Destination	Hoped for		Expected		Differential
	No.	%	No.	%	%
University or polytechnic	73	35	144	30	–5
Full-time job	150	30	81	17	–14
Training in a college	107	22	110	23	+1
Studying GCE	58	12	57	12	0
Part-time job	22	4	46	10	+6
Start a family	14	3	16	3	0
YTS	12	2	30	6	+4
Help at home	4	1	9	2	+1
Don't know	8	2	46	10	+8
Other	17	3	14	3	0

Source: CWTR Study, N=500

themselves. Valleys girls in particular revealed a high degree of self-blame for their poor employment prospects. But, while many of the Valleys girls describe their home town as a 'dump', few expect to leave it.

D Low occupational aspirations and confidence

> I'd like to be a vet but I expect I'll be a mother.
>
> 8-year-old girl (quoted in Holland 1988:136)

Expectations of marriage and motherhood have a profound impact in structuring girls' occupational aspirations. In the early 1960s, Joyce (1961) reported that of 600 14–16-year-olds asked what their job would be in the future, 48 per cent replied in terms of marriage. While girls may now expect to work and be married, our study demonstrated that girls were still influenced by their expectations of future roles in the family in their occupational aspirations and 'choices'. We asked them what they hoped and what they expected to be doing after leaving school.

Table 3.6 shows that the biggest gaps between aspirations and expectations occur for higher education and full-time employment. The findings support those of Holland (1988). The schoolgirls were asked about their specific occupational aspirations. Although the range was wide (forty-six occupations were identified, and no single job mentioned by more than 10 per cent), less than 3 per cent were in non-traditional female areas. Predictably enough, the most popular were secretarial work (10 per cent), nursery nursing (9 per cent), hairdressing and beauty (10 per cent) and teaching (9 per cent). A further 10 per cent who were academically able and for the most part middle class, chose professions such as medicine, dentistry, law and accountancy.

Expectations of family responsibilities impeded decision-making processes about careers for some girls at a Valleys school very early on, as the careers teacher in one of the schools illustrated: 'Most of the girls tend to stay locally. Some of the Easter leavers have babies or are expecting them now. If they've got low level aspirations, it's it, isn't it – they see it (having a baby) as a way of independence.'

CONCLUSION

I first started research on the labour market in 1976 with a study conducted with Denis Gregory on young unqualified people on an MSC Work Experience Programme placement with a South Wales firm (Rees, T. and Gregory 1979). During the course of the interviews I was shocked by the low aspirations of the young people of both genders, but particularly those of the girls. I was struck too by the way in which the young women found so alien questions which asked them about their hopes for the future, their plans, their dreams. That may have revealed more about my own naïvety or relatively privileged background than about them but, in any event, the experience triggered off a growing interest in the constraints inhibiting such girls' ability even to fantasise about the future. Over a decade later, I was again talking to young women in South Wales about their futures, in one of the studies described in this chapter. Again I was struck, in some working-class Valleys schools in particular, by the slight surprise with which questions about career or life plans were greeted, as if it were a novel but potentially interesting idea to plan, or even to feel sufficiently empowered to make decisions, to make choices. The notion that their futures had anything to do with them, in the sense that they could actively influence outcomes through choices, was clearly alien. Life is something that happens to you. This reflects findings of other studies of young people in depressed labour markets both in the South Wales Valleys (Rees, T. et al. 1981) and elsewhere (Coffield et al. 1986).

The 'fixed point' for so many working-class Valleys girls was the certainty that because they would become mothers, and would spend some years looking after their children, there was no need to think seriously about a career or training or qualifications. The sensible option was a job that allowed you to return to work part-time: by definition this would be a 'woman's job', and one that would be unlikely to demand qualifications. A second 'fixed point', clearly not unrelated to the first in either labour-market or family terms, was an assumption that they would be economically dependent upon a man. Wages were expected therefore to contribute to, rather than support, a family. A third assumption to emerge was that the girls would stay near home, close to the family of origin. All this clearly implies that such choices that are to be made are narrowly constrained by what local employers are offering in unskilled work to which employees can return part-time.

Girls' assumption about their future role in the family, and what that leaves over for participation in the labour market, clearly has an overwhelming effect not simply on what choices are made, but whether choices are effectively made at all. Initiatives that are designed to encourage girls into fields currently the reserve of men have tended to ignore the other side of the equation. There have been no initiatives on the same scale designed to encourage boys to take a more active role in child care. Unless patriarchal relations in the family as well as in the workplace are altered, girls' choices, particularly of those with no qualifications, will remain so constrained that asking them about their visions of their futures will continue to engender surprise.

Gender stereotyping in education is a highly complex process, and clearly cross-cuts with the impact of race and class in determining option and career 'choices'. The notion of choice is a false one, because for so many girls those choices are constrained not simply by their own constructions of their future role in the family. They are bounded by the manifestations of class and patriarchal relations in the structure of local labour-market opportunities, the attitudes of local employers, teachers and careers officers, parental and peer group pressures, and knowledge of occupations appropriate to gender, class and race.

It can be argued that working-class boys living in local labour markets with impoverished opportunities too have 'false' choices to make. However, the key difference lies in the set of expectations that girls, and everyone else, hold about their future labour-force participation patterns, and the devaluing effect this has on the seriousness with which the whole process of 'making choices' is regarded. The knowledge of the limitations of that choice is one that girls are well aware of, by the time they reach third form. It influences not only their 'choices', but their whole approach to studying in schools and their ideas about themselves, their capabilities, and what is 'allowed' and not 'allowed' to them. While special initiatives are designed to open girls' eyes to opportunities in male-dominated fields, they are unlikely to attract them of their own accord. Far more thoroughgoing measures of destereotyping and desegregation in the school, in the workplace and in the home would be needed to bring about any dramatic changes. The fundamental contradiction between women's role in work and the home is not addressed in such special initiatives, they merely accentuate it.

Chapter 4

Women returners' training 'choices'[1]

In the *Guardian* newspaper in January 1991, there were several pages of job advertisements for 'women returners'. After many predictions of labour shortages, and despite the recession, employers as diverse as Canada Life and Manchester City Council were at long last vying with one another to attract women with eye-catching headlines, such as 'Are you a potential returner?' and 'Returning to work: some talk about opportunities, others create them'. They were followed by more advertisements from training organisations: 'Re-train for a caring career as a qualified chiropodist', and, reminiscent of the teacher shortage in the 1960s: 'Returning to teaching? We are offering a Return to Teaching Course. . .'. Although the recession threatened to dampen the effect, and albeit with a whimper, the demographic time bomb had exploded.

Not since the Second World War have women apparently been in such demand in the labour market. The demographic down-turn in school-leavers has meant that while the number of jobs in the UK economy is predicted to increase by 1.7 million in the 1990s, the projected growth in the labour force will supply only half that number. The biggest source of new labour is seen as coming from women currently without jobs and not seeking paid work; those who, for the most part, are currently engaged in looking after children and/or the home. The proportion of such women has been diminishing over the years, but the *Labour Force Survey* (Department of Employment 1990a) showed that in the spring of 1989, there were 4.6 million such economically inactive women: they constitute just under a third of the 16–60 age group. The majority of them (59 per cent) are at home with domestic commitments.

The Government has been encouraging employers to recognise that they will need to recruit women returners; it claims that they 'must recognise that women can no longer be treated as second class workers' (Department of Employment 1988:8). Moreover, it is emphasised that this will mean certain changes:

To encourage women to return to the labour market employers will need to take account of their particular needs. For example, sufficient flexibility is needed at all occupational levels to enable women to combine paid work, at a level commensurate with their skills, with domestic responsibilities.

(Training Agency 1990:16)

A plethora of employer-led schemes for child care and flexible working has erupted, particularly in tight labour markets such as the South-east of England. But to what extent is the renewed marketability of mature aged women likely to contribute to a breakdown in both horizontal and vertical job segregation? Are the shortages in management and skilled jobs, for example, going to be filled by women returners? Or will employers simply be more successful in packaging low-paid, low-skilled jobs in such a way that they accommodate rather better women's domestic commitments? Will work organisation processes and practices be adapted to create new forms of ghettoisation for maternal figures, or will the skills of women returners be valued and used in the market place?

There are some grounds for optimism. Two key issues on the agenda for the 1990s are training and child care: both are crucial for women returners. Women overall have much less access to higher education than men, and are relatively less likely to benefit from training funded by their employers, particularly that of more than three days' duration (Training Agency 1989a). The National Economic Development Office (NEDO/TA 1989) predict that there will be an overall decrease in the number of low-skilled jobs, and that employees will need to have both more high-level skills and greater 'flexibility'. This clearly implies a greater all-round need for training, both for those seeking work and for employees. While TECs and LECs may not have many women on their boards, it is clear that most, particularly in tight local labour markets, have what they describe as the 'special training needs' of women on their agenda. In the context of high unemployment, the difficulties faced by women returners in securing employment commensurate with their abilities was not an issue: the number of initiatives offering training to returners were few and far between, and finding funding for such schemes was a perennial problem. But in order to be competitive, as NEDO (NEDO/TA 1989) predicts and as the pages of the *Guardian* now testify, employers need a more skilled workforce and they need it at a time of overall labour shortage. There should be far more training opportunities for women returners in the future.

The war-time rhetoric regarding the benefits to babies of nursery care has resurfaced, and the Government has encouraged schools (albeit largely unsuccessfully) to open their doors to children for after-school schemes. Workplace nurseries have been fostered through changes in the tax law (see Chapter 6). It is clear that continuing child care (not just provision for the pre-school age group), is beginning to be recognised as a policy issue, although whose policy issue (that of the Government, the local authorities or employers) is still a matter of debate.

While research on women returners remains sparse, there are now at least some studies from which lessons for policy provision can be learned. There are also the experiences of those who have tried, with varying degrees of success, to design courses for returners. This chapter draws upon both in seeking to explore the problems and processes of 're-entry'. It focuses on specifying women's training needs, and contrasting them with training opportunities open to them. The chapter argues that in order to be effective, training provision needs to start from the requirements of returners to assist them to make a successful transition to the labour market. Expecting women returners to slot into a training system not designed for their needs will perpetuate both skill shortages and the under-utilisation of women's skills and abilities, confining them to dead-end jobs.

However, the development of opportunities to learn substantive skills in an appropriate setting is, in fact, but one small part of the package of requirements for transition. Other factors which have a crucial role in that process of returning include *confidence building* and accommodating continuing *child-care* commitments. Moreover, to be effective, training provision needs to take on board the fact that many women have very poor access to *resources* they can use for themselves: this restricts their ability to pay for training, or indeed, even to get to it. Finally, it is argued, employers' recruitment practices, and in particular their use of social attributes as criteria, and their mobilisation of informal networks and internal labour markets to recruit and promote combine to offset the supposed advantages to a returner of having undertaken a course. Training for returners needs therefore to open up both knowledge of and access to appropriate *networks and information* about how individuals are selected for jobs.

In recognition of the need to recruit and retain older women, an increasing number of employers are engaging in career-break schemes and retention strategies: these are discussed in Chapter Six. This chapter focuses on women returning to the labour market who may well not be returning to an old employer or previous line of work: more than half of all returners are thought to take up a new type of work with a different employer. It examines the training needs of and training provision for women returners, drawing upon a number of empirical studies. The lessons and experiences of two case studies of attempts to set up courses for women returners predicated upon perceived returners' needs are drawn out. In the first, in which I was heavily involved, an attempt was made to fit a customised training package in non-traditional skills into a further education institution, using MSC funds. It was far from being entirely successful, but it was a revealing experience in highlighting bureaucratic resistances to 'making a special case' for what was regarded as a one-off, exotic course for a modest number of 'housewives'.

The second, much more successful attempt (in which I was not involved) stepped outside the existing framework of training provision to provide a women-only training workshop. The South Glamorgan Women's Workshop (SGWW), one of the longest running women-only training workshops in the United Kingdom, is portrayed here as a case study of effective, tailor-made training for women returners. It was set up by a group of women in Cardiff in 1984 with support from the European Social Fund (ESF) and South Glamorgan County Council. It targets women disadvantaged in the labour market (through, for example, lack of qualifications, poverty, ethnic origin and disability) and trains them in electronics, computing and complementary studies. Work experience placements with local employers are arranged. An on-site nursery provides child care (a high proportion of trainees are single parents), and the hours are arranged to allow for other child care and domestic responsibilities to be accommodated. No fees are charged, but there are no training allowances either.

An evaluation of the Workshop charted the trainees' needs and documented the process of returning to learn and earn, in 1986.[2] More recently, Freda MacNamara, an ex-trainee of the Workshop herself, traced nineteen of her own cohort to examine its impact on them five years on (MacNamara 1990).[3] The lessons about policy and practice relating to women returning to work, and in particular their training needs from these studies of the Workshop, are brought out in what follows.

Both examples, in my view, highlight the mismatches between returners' needs and training provision. They illustrate the frustration that many groups of women, predominantly in the voluntary sector, have experienced in similar attempts elsewhere. Although the climate may be changing, and older students and trainees may be looked upon increasingly favourably given falling numbers of school-leavers, there is as yet little evidence that providers are designing courses which take on board the reality of the position of women returners. As a consequence, their transformative effect will be limited.

The androcentricity of training provision, and in particular the difficulty for both training funders and providers to adjust to the clear needs of a growing number of 'clients', is demonstrated in these accounts. The prioritisation of male training needs, and the shaping of funding and provision around assumptions that only fit, at best, most men, reflect the same kind of sex-typing which govern patterns of work organisation. Employers have often been criticised for lack of flexibility: they assume that employees are available for overtime, have access to private transport or are sanguine about using public transport after dark, and so on. Much the same criticisms can, of course, be made of training providers. Given that women have less access to employer-funded training, such a mismatch between women's needs and provision helps to cement patterns of job segregation by gender.

The concept of the returner is of course not unique to the United Kingdom but, given the lack of child-care facilities, women are more likely to take a break and to return to work part-time here than in almost any other EC member state. Patterns of women's labour-force participation in the post-war period and the relationship between periods of economic activity and the life cycle in the United Kingdom were described in Chapter 2. It is worth reiterating here, however, that 'only four per cent of non-participants have never worked and over a third have held a job within the previous five years' (Metcalf and Leighton 1989:2). Periods out of the labour force are becoming shorter over the years (Martin and Roberts 1984).

Training is clearly a key element in the return to work, particularly if downward occupational mobility is to be avoided, and if employers are to make the most of their human resources. Gendered patterns of occupational segregation show a tenacity that resists change even in the context of new technology and labour shortage (see Chapter 7). But if employers need to change their patterns of work organisation and selection criteria, so too do training providers. Moreover, training for women returners is only part of the solution.

RETURNER-CENTRED TRAINING: TWO CASE STUDIES

Of all the barriers facing women wanting to return to work, lack of skills and on-going child-care commitments are the most widely voiced and the most difficult to overcome. Respondents interviewed in three different parts of the country in surveys commissioned by the Training Agency (TA) (as was), all reported a demand for training (Hardill and Green 1990; Healy and Kraithman 1989; Sargeant 1989). Hardill and Green's study of women in Benwell and South Gosforth, two areas highly contrasted on socio-economic criteria, found that two-thirds felt they would like to learn a new skill or up-date existing skills on a course. Indeed, training was considered by their sample to be more important than child-care facilities in aiding their return to work. Healy and Kraithman (1989), in their study based in north Hertfordshire, found that 73 per cent of potential women returners felt they needed additional training to re-enter the labour market. Sargeant (1989) recorded an enormous demand for job-related training among potential returners in her study of the Bristol Travel to Work area: only 7 per cent were not interested in training, and some of those did not intend to return to work or were well qualified already. The vast majority of Honess's small group of would-be returners in Gwent, too, responded positively to the offer of a workshop training programme or detailed consultation in respect of their future career plans (Honess 1990:20).

However, the difficulties which this chapter emphasises as facing women returning to work, such as their continuing child-care commitments, their low level of confidence, their lack of resources, inadequate information and networks, also confound their attempts to return to training as a first step. Providing courses that address some of these issues is far from straightforward, as the following case studies illustrate.

1 The case of the construction skills course

In South Wales in the early 1980s, training opportunities designed specifically for women returners were restricted to a few Wider Opportunities for Women (WOW) and New Opportunities for Women (NOW) courses. Other courses for which returners were eligible, such as Training Opportunities (TOPS), did attract women, but in highly sex-typed subjects: women appeared clustered on courses on secretarial skills and hairdressing, they rarely ventured across the threshold of Skills Centres, nor were they to be found on courses directed towards the long-term unemployed in significant numbers.

Early initiatives to attempt to widen the opportunities available for women were taken by the Equal Opportunities Commission in Wales Second Chance Education for Women Committee, which was made up of people for the most part in further and higher education concerned to increase opportunities for women returners. It was recognised that potential returners might be unaware of opportunities available within training and education institutions; indeed, that those unfamiliar with such organisations might not know how to approach them and might be intimidated by them. A leaflet was compiled listing education and training institutions in the area and giving the name of a contact person guaranteed to be 'user-friendly' to would-be returners. Drawing on the experiences of a successful course for women returners in an Adult Training Centre in Gwent, the leaflets were distributed to places such as health centres, mother and toddler groups, libraries and shopping centres. Informal networks were also used, and no handbag-carrying member of the committee ever left home without ensuring that it was well stocked with a ready supply of leaflets.

The Committee was well aware, however, that the training courses on offer in many of the colleges and training centres were not necessarily geared towards the needs of women returners. In 1985, the committee pooled their experience to develop a course that would help women to move out of typically low-wage female work into the construction industry, which at the time was enjoying a relatively prosperous period. Despite the complete absence of any construction skills among members of the committee (the established Piagetian approach of 'cerebral hygiene'), an introductory course was designed, with considerable assistance and support from regional officers of the Union of Construction, Allied Trades and Technicians (UCATT) and the Electrical, Electronic, Telecommunications and Plumbing Union (EETPU).

The intention was to design a course that allowed women a 'taster' of a variety of subjects, such as electrics, carpentry, plumbing, painting and decorating, bricklaying and so on. It was envisaged that such a course would facilitate women wanting to attend a conventional Skills Centre course for further training in one of the subjects, both by increasing their confidence, and by ensuring that they were already equipped with more than a rudimentary knowledge. They would become versed in the naming of parts, and would develop skills in, for example, handling their body weight in such a way as to compensate for any relative lack of strength needed to handle tools designed for the superior strength of men.

The course was designed not simply to facilitate women interested in opportunities in the construction industry to gain the confidence to undertake further training: the intention was that some, at least, might be able to move directly to related employment. They might take up traditionally female jobs, such as secretarial work, but in a building firm, or in building materials supply and distribution, where a specialist knowledge of construction might be attractive to and rewarded by employers.

It was well recognised that even having had the initial training on this course, with or without further training, it would be difficult for the trainees to get jobs in construction because of their gender, and because they were unlikely to be slotted in to the networks through which such jobs are allocated. Moreover, they would lack work experience, they would have no one to vouch for them. And of course, the hours worked in the construction industry (apart from knocking off early on a Friday afternoon), are incompatible with child-care commitments.

Rather fancifully, perhaps, the group nurtured the notion that some of the women, restricted both in their likelihood of securing a 'start' (our knowledge of construction industry discourse came on apace) and by domestic responsibilities, might be interested in setting up co-operatives of home maintenance and consumer-durable 'district nurses'. South Wales has a high proportion of owner occupation, as a legacy from the coal industry, but many houses are over 100 years old and are falling into disrepair. There is also a growing elderly population, and socio-economic indicators consistently reveal the Valleys in particular as areas of multiple deprivation. Such an area, to our minds, created a market opportunity for 'diagnostic repair work', of both houses and of ageing consumer durables. Loft insulation and window replacement were also seen as potential activities that women trained on the course might undertake.

The importance of avoiding substitution and deskilling were well appreciated, but it was felt there were high call-out charges for what can often be routine tasks, and there was a shortage of skilled tradesmen, for whom such work was not particularly attractive. We felt we had identified a gap in the market. Where the 'district nurse' was unable to operate, or indeed even to diagnose the fault, the 'general practioner' or if necessary, the 'brain surgeon' would be called upon, as appropriate. Networks with traditional 'time-served' craftsmen would thus develop. Business might start to flow in both directions. Role-models of women wielding wrenches would be succoured. Elderly people or women living alone, nervous of male strangers calling to the house, might prefer tradeswomen. While it is clear that adopting the nurse/doctor model would potentially introduce gender stereotypes and segregation that already exist in medical settings into the construction and home-repair industry, it might at least provide a foot in the door, and there could be opportunities for progression.

After some protracted negotiations, the MSC indicated that it would be prepared to sponsor such a course under the TOPS scheme, and three members of the committee toured the appropriate departments of South Wales colleges to identify one that would provide a women-only construction course which incorporated arrangements which we deemed necessary to appeal to women returners. These included women-only training; training across a number of departments; ideally, women tutors (although it was recognised that these might be difficult to find on the existing staff); hours to accommodate domestic responsibilities, and confidence-raising sessions. Moreover, it was considered essential that the ambience was welcoming: girlie calendars were out.

Although the relevant departments in the colleges we approached were enthusiastic about allowing, indeed encouraging, women across the threshold, particularly given the dowry of a TOPS budget, difficulties inevitably soon arose when it came to attempting to challenge their androcentricity, not to say sexism! Our desire for an inter-disciplinary course created further problems. Nevertheless, a college that offered to run the course was eventually decided upon, despite various fairly dramatic compromises having to be reached.

The next set of problems emerged when we attempted to apply hard-learned lessons about how best to publicise courses for women returners. It became clear that the MSC was too large an organisation to change its methods of disseminating information and recruiting people for what was in effect, in the context of TOPS provision within the locality, just one very small course. The main method of disseminating information was through Job Centres which, while frequented by the registered unemployed seeking work, are not on the whole visited by women at the beginning of the process of thinking of returning to work or training. The Job Centre nevertheless was used by the MSC as the main source of information about the course, although it remained passive rather than active in attracting trainees, and displayed posters exclusively of men working on building sites throughout the recruitment period.

Despite all these difficulties, the course attracted some local publicity which resulted in women signing up for the course. Three cohorts of women were trained. An application to the MSC for research funding to evaluate the course and its impact was turned down on the same grounds that were used in refusing to adopt different methods of advertising the course: it was too small to warrant it. A small-scale study was undertaken, nevertheless, by members of the working party, and the experiences of the trainees were found to be disappointing. No hands-on experience was offered (tutors 'did not want the trainees to get their hands dirty'); the tutors were both male and patronising; the hours were 9 to 5 with no provision for domestic responsibilities; there was no child care; and so on.

Although the committee's original aspirations for co-operatives may have been hopelessly idealistic and unrealistic (and again, arguably, patronising), the members found the experience of trying to launch the course and the trainees' accounts of it compelling in underlining the inappropriateness of much training provision and funding from the perspective of women returners as consumers, and also in demonstrating that there was a demand for courses for returners, even in construction skills.

2 South Glamorgan Women's Workshop

The SGWW was set up by a group of women after tremendous struggles in Cardiff in 1984. There was some overlap with members of the Committee involved in the construction course, so those experiences were taken on board, but the working party included a local county councillor, Jane Hutt, who was instrumental in ensuring that it secured the support of South Glamorgan County Council. This meant that ESF funding could be sought, with the local authority supplying the matching funding that ESF requires. A building near the main train and bus station was converted to a training workshop which included an on-site nursery and catering facilities.

The SGWW offers training in electronics and computing, areas chosen because of a reading of likely future job opportunities in the changing labour market. The course is arranged so that two groups of women attend in school hours for half the week each: Wednesday lunchtime is the change-over time. The Workshop is used for other activities at half term and during the school holidays. While there is no training allowance paid to trainees, which creates severe financial problems for some, there are no charges either for the training or the nursery. All the staff are women. Attention is paid to what was called initially 'social and life skills' training, but later described as 'complementary studies'. This part of the course includes confidence building. A development officer arranges work experience placements with local employers, some of which evolve into offers of employment.

The Workshop is run by a Management Committee which comprises some women from the working party that originally set it up, some newcomers, and trainee and staff representatives. Sub-committees are responsible for different aspects of the Workshop's activities.

The main target groups identified by the original working party were single parents, unemployed women, those with no or few formal qualifications, and those wanting to return to work after a long period at home. A stipulation for the ESF funding was that trainees had to be over 25 and unemployed. The recruitment process designed to reach such women focused on a community-based outreach programme, using women's networks but also going beyond them to reach more isolated women. Open days were held both at the Workshop and in community centres. Newspaper articles and advertisements, and radio and TV coverage proved effective channels of communication, but word of mouth has also been crucial, and posters in public buildings were effective in the early years. Word of mouth has clearly grown in importance with the growing number of ex-trainees acting as informal recruiters, but at the same time, the Workshop has become much better known over the years.

Motivation is regarded as a key factor in recruitment, more so than existing formal qualifications. Of the first cohort recruited, over 50 per cent had never considered any other training course and could not identify many of those on offer at the time, such as TOPS: they had never heard of the MSC. Of those who had considered other courses, the Workshop was chosen because there were no fees, it had free child care, was part-time, was located in central Cardiff and required no formal qualifications.

The socio-economic characteristics of the trainees match those the working party originally had in mind. The proportion from ethnic minorities and those with disabilities increased gradually over the years. A high proportion of trainees are on benefit.

The activities of the SGWW have expanded considerably since its inception, but the basic formula for attracting, recruiting, selecting and training women disadvantaged in the labour market proved successful from the beginning. After-care support is provided – for example, through continued access to places in the nursery as available – when ex-trainees secure jobs: this has been made possible through extra funding. The Workshop has also developed courses for schoolgirls during school holidays and evening classes. Asian women have been encouraged into the Workshop by an Asian worker and the provision of specially designed short courses: they have been successful in overcoming concerns about sexism and racism in training systems. Some have then gone on to join the main in-take of trainees for the full year-long course.

The SGWW has attracted considerable attention from both UK and European organisations, including the Government and the European Commission. It is a member of IRIS, the EC Network of Training Schemes for Women, and receives regular visits from Government ministers and other VIPs, and requests for information. Despite this, funding has remained a major, annual headache. Although other organisations including companies such as AB Electronics and Laura Ashley have supplemented the long-standing support from the ESF and South Glamorgan County

Council, resourcing remains piecemeal, and applying for funds is a full-time job. Moreover, recruiting female trainers in computing and electronics is difficult (see Chapter 7): this is exacerbated by the need to keep budgets low to attract funding, and the co-operative principles which operate within the Workshop combine to depress tutors' wages compared with elsewhere. Finally, the staff are clearly overburdened; pressure to keep costs low entails a level of commitment that individual people cannot be expected to sustain for more than a few years. This latter point highlights the importance of 'training for trainers'. Such courses for trainers are thin on the ground and yet there is growing demand for women tutors in manual crafts, computing and business skills who are also equipped to deal with the particular sets of problems that women returners bring with them. The Edinburgh Women's Training Workshop used ESF funding to train trainers before launching their workshop.

Despite these on-going difficulties, the SGWW is clearly effective in transforming the life chances of the trainees, who are specifically selected for being disadvantaged in the labour market. The evaluation, which followed the first cohort through the Workshop and into the labour market, showed that six months later, 63 per cent were in paid employment (about half in part-time work), 10 per cent in full-time education or training and 27 per cent were still looking for work (Essex *et al.* 1986a). Continuing child-care responsibilities meant that some women were having to wait until their youngest child started school before being available for work on a full-time basis. These figures are a snapshot at a particular time, however; the transition back to the labour market for women without formal qualifications in a local labour market that was, at that time, experiencing high unemployment is clearly a protracted process. Of the nineteen trainees who left the Workshop in 1986 who were interviewed by MacNamara in 1990, nine were in full-time employment, six in part-time work and four engaged in further training. More telling than the figures perhaps are the comments of the trainees, given below.

Both studies, and others (Hardill and Green 1990; Healy and Kraithman 1989; Murphy and Mullan 1989), illustrate the importance of developing skills and confidence for assisting a return to the labour market. These experiences are drawn upon in the following sections.

WOMEN RETURNERS' TRAINING NEEDS AND TRAINING PROVISION

Women as a group are less likely to have had access to certificated further and higher education and vocational training than men (Clarke 1991). They constitute well under half the student body in higher education: 46 per cent of all undergraduates and 31 per cent of all postgraduates in 1987–88 (calculated from DES 1991: Table 36). Within higher education, they are of course overwhelmingly found in social science, arts and humanities subjects.

Although they remain in further education post-16 in larger numbers, women are less likely to have received training leading to a qualification. They were awarded 29 per cent of BTEC and SCOTVEC higher diplomas and certificates, and 40 per cent of all further education BTEC first and national diplomas and certificates in 1987–88 (DES 1991: Table 36). A recent large-scale survey of employees revealed that, whereas about the same percentage of women and men reported that they had had training within the last three years, women were less likely to have been funded by their employer, and the training that they had received was more likely to be of shorter duration (Training Agency 1989a:50). The study showed that women with children in particular were not likely to have been paid by their employer for training of more than three days' length, and they were more likely to be asked to commit themselves to staying on with their employer after training.

Women have less access to training overall for a number of reasons. They constitute the vast majority of part-time workers, who tend not to receive training. They are less likely to be in supervisory, managerial or professional positions, where people are most likely to be in receipt of initial and continuing training (Rigg 1989). Finally, women predominate in specific occupations where there is little training (beyond that being increasingly introduced because of new technology – see Chapter 7), such as retail and clerical work (see Chapter 2).

The net effect is that women who take time out of the labour market are likely to have had relatively little training as well as no recent work experience.

Training provision in the 1980s

Clearly, women returners have enrolled, and remain free to do so, on any of the existing courses provided by the whole range of public and private education and training institutions, and many do. At the same time, it is noticeable that courses specifically designed for returners are oversubscribed, and they tend to meet the needs of those women in particular for whom, for whatever reason, standard provision is not suitable. The reason may have to do with cost, location, level, hours that conflict with domestic responsibilities or entry requirements. It may simply be that a returner does not have the requisite study skills or confidence to cope with the demands of a course. It may be that the range of courses on offer is bewildering, or that the educational institution looks daunting.

So, what training opportunities are there specifically for women returners? There have been significant changes in the range and focus of customised courses in recent years. In the 1980s, tailor-made courses were pioneered in the main by voluntary organisations (for example, the SGWW and the East Leeds Workshop) and specific individuals in the education sector (notably Ruth Michaels of Hatfield Polytechnic); they took advantage of the ESF funding and Section 47 of the Sex Discrimination Act 1975 which allows for women-only training. A major focus of such courses tended to be low-level information technology or manual trades. The Pepperell Unit of the Industrial Society also provided (and still provides) short training courses around the country, commissioned by organisations or employers. These concentrate more on taking stock, making decisions about return routes, assessing training needs and paying some attention to assertiveness training. It is noticeable that the TA in all its guises throughout the 1980s channelled very little resources into women-only training, despite the demand indicated by the success of ESF-supported initiatives. Equally, it is clear that much of the initiative for pioneering courses or providing support (for example, the Women's Training Network of workshops and the Women's Returners' Network) come from women themselves.

In the 1980s, the TA (and the MSC before it) did not prioritise training for women returners. WOW and NOW were the only central government-funded, designated women-only training courses to run in the early 1980s. They were short courses offering some training and a taster of a range of work-experience placements. WOW received 0.01 per cent of all funding on training in its first two years, rising to 0.02 per cent in the final year, before being dropped (calculated from Department of Employment 1990b: Table B3.1). Women fared well in TOPS but trained for women's work (Payne 1991). Professional Updating for Women courses are addressing the needs of well-qualified returners, but are available only in five English higher education institutions so far. Indeed, even as late as 1989, the TA's major research project on *Training in Britain* (see Centre for Corporate Strategy and Change 1989; Deloitte, Haskins and Sells 1989; Rigg 1989; Training Agency 1989a, 1989b) scarcely mentions the issue of women returners.

ESF funding

The availability of ESF funds specifically earmarked for training women over the age of 25 led to the mushrooming of courses in the United Kingdom. It was used both by the TA to fund NOW and WOW, and by voluntary groups and local authorities. However, it came with strings attached. The rules of eligibility meant that trainees had to be registered as unemployed before signing up. But in the United Kingdom, to an extent not matched by any other European member state, eligibility criteria exclude many women who might regard themselves as unemployed, and might be actively seeking work, but because of their relationship with a man, are not entitled to benefit, and therefore do not 'count' as unemployed (see Cragg and Dawson 1984; Essex *et al.* 1986a; Martin and Roberts 1984).

The ESF guidelines for applications asked for predictions of what percentage of the trainees would be likely to gain employment at the end of the course, and this was clearly an important criterion in the decision as to whether or not it would be funded. It created difficulties for courses designed for areas of high unemployment, and where female activity rates were low. It also posed difficulties for courses designed to train women in non-traditionally female work, where discriminatory factors were likely to impede their recruitment into training-related work. The stipulation also failed to take into account the measured process of return; employment immediately after the course had finished was an unlikely outcome, the course was just the first step on the road.

It was this last issue that proved the most difficult. While relatively few women returners' courses have been the subject of a rigorous evaluation, one finding that consistently emerges from the assessments that do exist is that, irrespective of class, race, locality or nationality, women returners overwhelmingly are found to be suffering from low levels of confidence, and need time to prepare for a return to work. Moreover, an initial course inevitably needs to focus upon the development of confidence to a greater or lesser extent, with the effect that the allocation of time for the transmission of substantive skills is necessarily limited. Such courses are but first ports of call. Comparing them with other kinds of courses (with the exception of those geared towards the long-term unemployed where there are certain parallels), inevitably renders returner courses seemingly expensive and not cost-effective.

It is clear that the criteria for funding women returners' courses need to be different, and to reflect the purpose for which they are designed. They act not simply as a route to employment but often as a first stepping stone to further education or more specific skills training. Further, the immediate outcome may simply be a more confident person who has the courage to break out of an unsatisfactory relationship where she may be the victim of domestic violence: this has certainly been one outcome of some returners' courses. It may be someone with the confidence to take a more active role in the local community, gathering experience, before entering the labour market some years later. It may be someone who enters a mundane, non-training-related, low-skilled part-time job either as a preferred option, or as a dry run, a stop-gap before trying to move into something more demanding. All these 'outcomes' are contributing to improving the stock and quality of human resources that the labour market may ultimately, if not immediately call upon. Both the providers of such projects and evaluators identify these as satisfactory and acceptable results, given the starting point of many women returners. This means that the ESF criteria for 'success', which means 'measuring' outcome almost immediately after the completion of the course, and solely in job or further training terms, are simply not appropriate: it may be some years before the benefit to that trainee, and indeed the labour force, can be seen in employment-related criteria. And yet, as returners testify, without that first step, they may never make that transition.

The ESF also requires courses to be evaluated in terms of their cost-effectiveness. This again is problematic when applied to courses for women returners. Confidence building takes time and is extraordinarily difficult to measure. Child-care provision makes the per capita costs of such training extremely high, compared with other courses. The 'low outcome' of courses, particularly those which specifically target women disadvantaged in the labour market, would automatically appear not to be cost-effective compared with skills courses for relatively unproblematic school-leavers. Such criteria are relevant and, in terms of accountability for the public purse, essential. But oranges should not be assessed in accordance with their ability to satisfy criteria designed for evaluating leeks.

ESF funding may have facilitated courses for returners but it has its own drawbacks. Its method of payment, in arrears, has caused horrendous cash-flow difficulties, for voluntary organisations in particular, rendering some near bankrupt at times. The fact that the timetable for approval of applications does not coincide with that of, for example, Urban Aid, has made the business of trying to satisfy the stipulation of matching funding from another source unnecessarily complex.

Despite these difficulties, the ESF has been of crucial importance in developing training for women in the United Kingdom. In 1985, the United Kingdom received 31 per cent of the sum spent on women's training by the ESF: it was the largest beneficiary (Whitting and Quinn 1989). The rules for ESF funding constantly change: the latest initiative from Brussels is a (new) New Opportunities for Women (NOW) scheme which includes funding for child-care measures: the budget is set at ECU 120 million (approximately £72 million at August 1991).

Training in the 1990s

Whereas the 1980s were characterised by voluntary organisations and a few educational institutions developing courses for returners with support from the ESF and some of the more radical local authorities, the 1990s has seen a wholly different development. Private manpower consultancy companies, such as Blue Arrow and Dow Stoker, have developed a market niche in short courses for women contemplating a return to work, assisted by initiatives such as the BBC/Department of Employment's campaign to encourage returners in 1990 (Bamford and McCarthy 1991). They tend to focus upon developing information networks, devising first steps and brushing up on confidence, rather than in specific skill training. Blue Arrow's seventy-six branches each have a Return to Work Counsellor to advise on prospects for training and careers, and to give advice on child care. Employment Training (ET) offered in the region of 15,000 places for men and women unemployed for two years or more in the early 1990s, and provided up to two months training in labour-market-related skills. Single parents have been able to have child-care costs offset. Access to ET courses has been through Job Centres, however, which many returners would not necessarily think to consult. Moreover, some women are not eligible to receive unemployment benefit, which is one of the criteria for eligibility to ET (Whitting and Quinn 1989).

Women's training workshops and networks in information technology and manual skills, in particular, are located firmly within the voluntary sector. The TECs have identified women returners as a group in need of special provision to a greater or lesser extent, determined by the tightness of the local labour market, but it is too early to judge the nature of the provision that will be made, or the extent to which both TECs and LECs will respond to training needs as specified here.

The experiences and studies of women returners demonstrate that returners most in need of training are those least likely to have qualifications or previous training, so ideally there should be no or few entry qualifications for courses for returners. They frequently experience study-skills problems; they lack recent experience of studying. Study skills should be part of the curriculum. The returner course should be seen as a first step: attention needs to be paid to routes of progression. At the same time, it is clear from studies that the substantive area on offer is of less importance in attracting returners than other features, such as flexible hours or child-care provision.

Women returners will undoubtedly benefit from the effort currently being expended in developing access courses more generally, and attempting to seal the joins between access courses and further and higher education. Current proposals to modularise courses in further and higher education and facilitate trans-binary progression are good news for returners. Educational institutions are on the whole increasingly receptive to 'mature age' students in the wake of the decline in the number of school-leavers. To be effective however, they will need to take on board women returners' needs, which are now discussed.

RE-ENTRY TO TRAINING: PROBLEMS AND PROCESSES

Women's experiences of training as a first step back to the labour force are clearly varied; however, there are four problems which occur most frequently. They tend to have a low level of confidence, they need child care, they have poor access to resources, and are disadvantaged by impoverished information and networks essential to securing well-paid, secure jobs.

1 Confidence

At a conference held in CEDEFOP, the European Commission's Centre for the Development of Vocational Training in Berlin in December 1988, researchers on training for women from all the member states unanimously agreed that extremely low levels of confidence of women who present themselves for training was the most important training issue for returners: the particular skills imparted were wholly secondary to the initial need to build confidence. People lacking in confidence are not at their most receptive. Courses for reasonably confident people already exist in each member state: women without that confidence are in effect excluded from such opportunities for training. Lack of confidence is probably one of the factors in many women's willingness to accept demotion on return to work, the tendency to opt for typically female work, and the choice of part-time as opposed to full-time work (although domestic responsibilities are clearly crucial here).

There can be no doubt about the efficacy of returner courses in improving confidence levels as perceived by tutors and trainees at least, even if methods of measurement remain understandably crude. Bird and West (1987:191) found returners on their course needed a 'boost of confidence and a positive self-image in order to challenge both the domestic division of labour and exploitation in the workplace'. Murphy and Mullan (1989:6) report that trainees from both the Camden Training Centre in London and the IT Studies course in Jordanstown, Northern Ireland 'spoke eloquently about the growth of self-confidence and ability to communicate effectively as being just as valuable as the development of skills in Information Technology'.

There are various aspects of returners' courses that can assist in boosting confidence. The most crucial is the fact that most are women-only. Although trainees are not necessarily particularly attracted by that feature – indeed, some are suspicious of it – they nevertheless come to value it (Essex *et al.* 1986a:18). Both Wickham (1986) and Cockburn (1987) have argued that women need their own space for training, especially in new technology skills. MacNamara (1990) reports that all her cohort of trainees at the SGWW felt that if men had been there, they would not have felt so relaxed about using 'male tools and instruments'. Individual trainees said:

'I was going through a divorce and would cry at the most strange times. I only got through it because of the other women's support.'

'It was my "island", a place where I could be myself, believe in my abilities.'

'I know I gained the skills to use the computer, but they would have been no good if I hadn't been confident in myself.'

(MacNamara 1990:48)

All MacNamara's respondents stressed their increase in confidence: 'it was without doubt one of the most important factors which enabled women to progress to employment or to further training' (p.51). Women-only training projects address the issue of confidence building as part of the curriculum (see Essex *et al.* 1986a and 1986b; Murphy and Mullan 1989). Indeed, 'social and life skills' is now a requirement stipulated by the ESF for such courses. In response to trainee demands at the SGWW, this element of the course increasingly focuses upon assertiveness training and preparation for working in modern offices. In a course run by the University of Ulster in Jordanstown, trainees reported:

'I am much more assertive. I am a person to be respected. I felt used as a person before. This course has developed me. I can relate better to others.'

'I have much more self-knowledge and am more at peace with myself.'

'Did an enormous amount for my confidence . . . I'll take on anything now.'

(Murphy and Mullan 1989:17)

In the SGWW, places were allocated for trainee representatives on the Management Committee and various sub-committees. The experience of being involved in a decision-making structure improved the trainee representatives' confidence and developed useful skills that could be used in working life. The experiences were not entirely unproblematic, as Essex *et al.* (1986a) reveal: although the trainees overwhelmingly supported the principle, in practice the representatives found speaking on behalf of the whole cohort difficult; their lack of experience of committee meetings put them at a disadvantage, and some were unclear as to what was going on, despite attending meetings. Nevertheless, as an additional experience, it was felt to be effective in improving confidence.

Having female tutors has also proved important in bolstering confidence, both in their capacity as role-models, and because they are deemed less intimidating. Cockburn (1983) demonstrates the power of job gendering which means that many people feel uncomfortable seeing women with 'gender inappropriate tools'. MacNamara's cohort stressed the importance to the development of their own confidence of having women tutors:

'I was frightened of the computers but no-one put me down, a woman tutor gave me support, she didn't laugh.'

'I didn't feel daft, asking a woman tutor which bit of wire went where.'

'I couldn't have coped with a male tutor. I would have felt intimidated.'

The development of confidence is by now well recognised as an essential issue to be tackled by women returning to work (Bargh 1991), even for highly qualified women (Jackson 1991). Healy and Kraithman (1989:3) are of the view that 'any and every training programme should include aspects for general up-dating, confidence building and personal development'. Much of the focus in returners' courses has been in learning to recognise skills and achievements that are not normally valued. Some courses are seeking to credit such achievements formally through Accreditation of Prior Learning schemes. Courses then go on to assist in decision making about the future.

However, courses run for returners in the private sector in the 1990s have developed a special interpretation of how confidence levels can be boosted: this centres upon personal appearance. A market niche has been identified by free-lance and private companies in 'image consultancy'. Color Me Beautiful is one such company whose market has expanded rapidly in response to the growing demand for confidence boosting techniques among courses for women returners (and indeed for women in middle management). There are 50,000 image consultants in the United States, apparently, and Color Me Beautiful has 2,000 consultants worldwide, including 250 in the United Kingdom and 400 elsewhere in Europe (Spillane 1991). In Britain they are particularly thick on the ground in the South-east of England. The company provides training for free-lance consultants at a cost of about £2,000, and then sells them the franchise on their name, techniques and products in a specific geographical area. The image consultants are then, according to local conditions, able to charge about £45 a session per individual for colour coding and advice on wardrobe, make-up, and so on.

The session includes identifying which 'season's' palette of colours suits the woman best. A suede-bound Filofax with swatches of the most suitable colours is presented to the client at the end of the session: this is to be used as a guide while shopping for clothes. Group sessions on grooming and its importance are given to courses of returners. The stated aim is to help women to improve their confidence by enabling them to make the best of their appearance at all times: a habit that is easily eroded during years of child-bearing and -rearing: 'Mid-career, middle-aged women returners often signal under-confidence and look like someone's mum the minute they walk through the door' (Spillane 1991:140).

It is interesting that the image of womanhood that is deemed to bestow confidence is one which eschews mumsiness in favour of middle-class professionalism: at once highly feminine and overtly attractive to men (make-up at all times is essential, trousers forbidden, accessories desirable), and smart (suits, high heels). It is the female version of male business apparel, with some glamour thrown in. There are clear echoes here of the apparel of the 'sisters in suits' in Australia (Sawer 1990, and see Chapter 8). Looking smart yet chic is to be taken very seriously, to enhance the confidence of the individual, and to assist recruitment and promotion. More than one image consultant has assured me that wearing lipstick at all times (arguably an overtly sexual signal) is positively correlated with getting promoted. Color Me Beautiful's message is that it is the first impression created through appearance and non-verbal communication that can win jobs in interviews, rather than what is said (Spillane 1991).

There are interesting issues here about whose image of femininity it is necessary to invoke in order to bolster confidence, and to reassure those responsible for recruitment that women applying for jobs (particularly those in fields normally associated with men, or at a level which few women reach), are in a sense 'conventional', adhering to the culturally expected norm of wanting to be attractive to men, rather than being either 'mumsy' or 'man-hating feminists'. Essentially, the message is about conforming with stereotypes of successful women in work which in turn are modelled upon successful men, but made to look attractive to men in a feminine way.

Child care

Participation rates over the life cycle are largely determined by women's access to affordable child care, and the structure of opportunities in the local labour market. Both Metcalf and Leighton (1989) and the Confederation of British Industry (1989) identify inadequate child-care provision as the major reason for women's relatively low participation rates. Indeed, both suggest that if satisfactory child-care facilities were available, many economically inactive women would return to work tomorrow. Moreover, recent studies of women returners have shown that many women who would choose to stay at home with their children, even were child care available, see their period at home as a temporary one: they fully intend to work when opportunities permit or when they judge that they, and the family, feel ready for it (Hardill and Green 1990; Healy and Kraithman 1989; Sargeant 1989).

The issue of child care is discussed in some detail in Chapter 6; here it is simply important to stress that on-going responsibilities for child care are clearly identified not only as a major barrier to women returning to work, but also to their ability to take up training opportunities. As a consequence, returning to work is often a long process, where training is undertaken as a first step in anticipation of the youngest child's starting school within a year or two.

Even when all the children are in school, however, as Honess's (1990) study of potential women returners emphasises, the care for sick children remains an issue. The TUC *Under Fives Charter* calls for ten days' paid leave per annum for illness, hospital treatment or other family crises; this would clearly relieve considerable pressure on parents and all who have elderly dependants too.

Training for women returners needs, then, to allow for the fact that, on the whole, women have sole or main responsibility for children and that this lasts well beyond the pre-school stage. This means providing or funding child care for the under-5s, arranging the hours to suit school hours and terms, and allowing for some flexibility in the event of sickness. The CBI survey (1989) found that in order to attract women back to work, flexibility of hours was more important than level of starting salary.

Many SGWW trainees said that they would not have been able to attend the workshop without the on-site nursery. None thought that the nursery interfered with her training – an argument often used against provision on the premises. They felt that it gave them peace of mind to know that the children were close at hand, and that they could see them at lunchtime (Essex *et al.* 1986a, 1986b). A nursery is expensive and does not address the after-school needs of older children; however, in the view of the SGWW trainees venturing back to work, it is distinctly preferable to any other arrangement.

Poverty

The literature on the feminisation of poverty (for example, Glendinning and Millar 1987) demonstrates all too clearly women's relatively poor access to resources, particularly when they are dependent financially either upon a man or on the state. Pahl's (1989) work has shown how even within families where resources are not short, the distribution of those resources within the unit is rarely even, with some women in reasonably comfortable households experiencing poverty. Women live longer, and yet inherent sexism within pension schemes means that they have less access to adequate pensions. Women whose marriages end are likely to come off worse than their ex-husbands, not just in the United Kingdom but elsewhere – for example, the United States (Weitzman 1985) and Australia (Graycar 1990).

Women in the United Kingdom earn on average less than three-quarters of male wages. They are less likely to have access to private transport. Even in households where there is private transport, women are less likely to be able to use it for their own purposes. The net result of these factors needs to be taken into account when planning training for returners. Training in non-typically female work leads to jobs where wages are higher. Given many women returners' relative lack of access to resources, fees inhibit access; training allowances would facilitate the more disadvantaged to come. Ready access to the training centre via public transport would also help.

Most of these criteria were satisfied by the SGWW: the exception was access to training allowances which were not included in the bid for financing in order to keep the cost down. However, satisfaction of all the other criteria meant that those women most disadvantaged in the labour market, who in effect were excluded from other training opportunities, were able to attend the workshop. Three-quarters of the first cohort and half of the second were either solely or partly dependent upon social security benefits. Just over a third were single parents. Ten per cent were from ethnic minorities and several were disabled. Two-thirds had left school at the minimum school-leaving age, and over a third had no educational qualifications whatsoever (Essex *et al.* 1986a). The SGWW and workshops like it continue to recruit women who, due to personal circumstances and lack of cultural capital that could be used as currency in the labour market, are trapped in poverty.

Job information and recruitment networks

At a number of important junctures, disadvantaged women returners tend not to be plugged into the necessary networks to aid their access to training and return to work. In the first instance, they may not to be in touch with those standard repositories for advertisements about courses that might be suitable for them, such as Job Centres. Secondly, having been on a course for returners, they may then not necessarily be aware of next steps, and routes to further training or employment. Finally, it is evident from a wealth of literature that women returners are at a distinct disadvantage not only because of employers' segmented work structures and discriminatory recruitment practices (see Collinson *et al.* 1990; Crompton and Sanderson 1990), but also because network mechanisms used by employers to identify suitable employees are gendered.

The use of Job Centres by the TA for disseminating information about courses relevant for returners, including ET, has proved inappropriate. Healy and Kraithman (1989) found that their respondents had a very low level of awareness of training opportunities: the highest proportion (13.3 per cent) had heard of ET, but hardly any had heard of other relevant courses available. Some 83.3 per cent of their sample identified newspapers as the best means of contacting women with young children, followed by leaflets (64 per cent) (Healy and Kraithman 1989:27). The experience of the SGWW illustrated that efforts need to be made to circulate information through channels that ensure that it is likely to meet the target group: again, local media proved the most effective. The list of courses compiled by the Women Returners' Network (1987), which is being linked into the slowly expanding Training Access Points system (computerised lists of courses accessible through terminals), and the increased efforts being made by educational institutions and training providers to attract mature students should help to increase awareness about opportunities, but the most educationally disadvantaged will still have difficulty in discovering what is available and what is suitable.

Most returner courses are introductory, pre-vocational and geared to assist in making choices about the return to work. Skills imparted tend to be of secondary importance and low level. It is clearly essential that counselling is provided to ensure progression from returners' courses on to further training or employment, and they increasingly provide this. It is particularly important, however, to seek to assist returners on to further training, given the segmented nature of the labour market (see Chapter 7). It may be easier to enter the organisation further up the hierarchy armed with appropriate qualifications than to get training and promotion within the company.

The use of internal labour markets to attract applicants to jobs in effect restricts opportunities to people associated with existing employees. Networks of existing employees are therefore crucial. Such networks tend to reproduce job gendering. Women's networks ensure that the kinds of jobs to which they have access, through (for example) being 'spoken for' by a friend or relative, will be exclusively in typically female, low-paid, low-skilled work. A series of studies in South Wales (but also elsewhere: see Collinson *et al.* 1990; Grieco 1987; Jenkins *et al.* 1983) serve to illustrate this point. Women's rates of economic participation have traditionally been low in South Wales (see Winckler 1987). In many manufacturing plants, recruitment is by families: there are 'waiting lists' of vouched-for nephews and sons-in-law. Rees, Williamson and Winckler (1990) conducted a study of 300 companies which demonstrated how social attributes (which of course included gender and race) were deemed more important than skills in recruitment. Morris (1984) found that redundant steelworkers from Port Talbot who managed to find employment subsequently tended to be those who shared networks with people in employment. The gendering of such networks was illustrated by Callender (1987), who showed how women in a South Wales valley made use of other women to hear about and secure suitable vacancies in casual and part-time work. The use of such networks by employers and employees not only perpetuates the segregation of the labour force by gender and race; it also provides powerful social control mechanisms within the plant.

Many jobs in the local labour market involve little in the way of skills, so it is more expedient for employers to pick someone who will 'fit in' with (that is, resemble) existing employees. Because other jobs involve training that is specific to that company, it is less crucial that prospective employees have undergone relevant training. Even for women returners who have received relevant training therefore, this will be cancelled out by their inappropriate social attributes. This includes their age as well as their gender.

Bird and Skinner (1989:17) report on the impact of ageism in employers' recruitment strategies, with specific reference to mature women graduates. Local employers in Bristol were very impressed by the quality of trainees on a new technology training course run for women graduates, but admitted to operating selection and recruitment policies that included upper age-limits of 30 or 35 at most, for entry to relevant computing or new technology grades. Bird and Skinner quote reasons given by other employers engaged in a milk round for graduate recruitment and participating in a survey for the Association of Graduate Careers Advisory Services, as follows:

get enough conventional graduates, no noticeable demand;

problems with mobility, salary, supervision by younger people, team fit;

absorbing into established programmes a difficulty, salary expectations, only seek out in shortfall situations;

late degree is not a high flier, management potential and mobility problematic;

long term potential might be unrealised before retirement therefore wasted.

(quoted in Bird and Skinner 1989:18)

While some favourable comments were made about the virtues of maturity, of the eighty-two employers surveyed, sixty-seven held negative views about older candidates.

Just as the criterion of seniority contributes to women who take a career break being at a disadvantage, so 'age for wage' structures make women returners expensive and undesirable compared with younger applicants. Rigid hierarchies and recruitment strategies inhibit the access of returners to jobs commensurate with their skills.

How are women returners to break this vicious circle? Developing alternative sets of networks and having the opportunity for a foot in the door to demonstrate their 'ability to fit' is clearly one method. The SGWW has developed a set of relations with local employers that provide 'work experience placements'. This can have the effect of both familiarising trainees with up-to-date work practices, and of alerting employers to the capacities of people whom they might otherwise not have considered. Much the same rhetoric operated within the YTS and its forebears with reference to young people whose social attributes were the subject of discrimination.

CONCLUSION

Between 1988 and 1989, over three-quarters of a million women returned to the labour force, but only two-thirds found a job (mostly part-time work): the remainder, who tended to be the younger returners, were unemployed (Department of Employment 1990a). And yet in the future, significant reliance will be placed on women returning to a labour market that will require a workforce with more skills than ever before. In order to take up this challenge, both education and training providers, the TECs, LECs and employers themselves will need to widen their doors.

In this chapter I have tried to illustrate how much the same barriers that impede women's return to work restrict their opportunities for education and training, and yet women not only have fewer qualifications and a lower skill level than men, but they also face particular sets of difficulties when seeking to remedy this. Returners' previous experience can deter them from considering further or higher education: the Taking Liberties Collective (1989) have provided a particularly angry set of testaments from working-class women of their experiences of a male-dominated education system. The training infrastructure is geared towards training men, or women without domestic responsibilities: the provision of courses, funding arrangements, criteria for judging cost-effectiveness and so on ignore the reality of the material circumstances facing women returners. Those growing numbers of courses that are designed for returners run the risk of channelling them into low-skilled, part-time work where they will stay, unless routes of progression are in-built. Segmentation in training structures reflects segmentation in the labour market. Both reinforce existing patterns of gender segregation. Nowhere is this more apparent than in training for information technologies, the subject of Chapter 7.

Chapter 5

The feminisation of trade unions?[1]

The 1980s were a decade of considerable change for trade unions in Britain. The decline in union membership since the peak of 1979 (Kelly 1990) has been attributed to shifts in the industrial structure, and the increase in the proportion of the workforce who are unemployed or who work part-time. Legislative changes have reduced and reshaped unions' freedom to participate in industrial action. The locus of power, the collective bargaining system, has been seriously threatened for some unions which have been involved in protracted disputes. But the decade was characterised too by the growth of women's membership of unions, and by the extent to which the issue of gender inequality, both in the workplace and in the unions themselves, received attention. It is now over a decade since the TUC Charter of Action identified ten means of pursuing the goal of equality for women in unions, but there has been limited progress in achieving those aims (Ellis 1988; TUC 1986; Labour Research Department 1988, 1991a; Trade Union Research Unit 1986).

Unions are often described as having become 'feminised' over the last decade, but although the proportion of members who are women has been growing, this has not on the whole been reflected in the number of women in the union hierarchy or by the effective prioritisation of 'women's issues'. This chapter explores two inter-related aspects of the 'feminisation' of unions: participation and activism. It draws upon two major studies carried out for trade unions in the 1980s, one blue-collar and one white-collar, which were commissioned to identify the 'barriers' to women's participation and office-holding in unions. The studies underlined, among other factors, the significance of the complex inter-relationship between men's and women's positions in the union, in the workplace and in the family.

Trade unions still play a significant role in establishing and maintaining the structures and systems by which wage labour is sold, and through which patterns of horizontal and vertical occupational segregation are sustained. They are involved in the business of negotiating and retaining pay differentials related to shared perceptions of what constitutes 'skill': perceptions shared, that is, by trade-union leaders and employers, both of whom tend overwhelmingly to be male. Trade unions negotiate terms and conditions of employment which privilege some workers more than others: they contribute to management decisions about who should go first in the event of retrenchments;[2] they are party to decisions about what kinds of jobs should attract overtime and bonuses, and which can be organised on a part-time basis. Trade-union negotiators have traditionally made similar sets of assumptions to those of employers about women's role in paid work. The 'family wage' is still clung to most tenaciously by some unions, with negative consequences in undermining bargaining power for low-paid women workers. Despite the increase in female membership, equal pay is not identified as a major campaigning issue. Trade unions prop up those very mechanisms in the organisation of work which make patterns of gender segregation so difficult to break down.

Changes in industrial restructuring have led to an increase in the proportion of the labour force which is female. Indeed, the viability of some unions is now seen as depending not only upon women's membership but on their active involvement. The issue to be faced by unions is whether women are to continue merely to be incorporated to support the edifices of work organisation which so patently disadvantage them, or whether unions will change both their own organisation and that of the workplace so as to reduce the impact that gender has on occupational life chances.

The key dilemma, then, is whether the concerns of unions' changing membership are to be prioritised in the policies adopted by those unions, or whether those new members are simply to be used for boosting numerical political weight in order to campaign for more traditional priorities which benefit a specific group of members. There has, of course, been a shift from participative or collective models of union democracy, based upon discussions and debate, to representative or 'parliamentary' forms, preferred by the Conservative administration and personified in the postal ballot system which was given a legislative boost in the 1980s. Now office-holders have to be elected regularly rather than appointed for life, and members must have the opportunity to vote in a secret ballot before strike action is taken. This legislation was enacted by the Government out of a belief, shared with both some Marxists and some feminists, that union leaders were out of step with members. This issue is at the heart of the current debate about trade-union democracy (see Fosh and Heery 1990). The specific concern here is the gendered nature of union representation. The growth in female economic activity and union membership has not been matched by increases of a similar order in female representation in lay union decision-making hierarchies. Their interests may indeed conflict with those of the leadership. There is growing evidence to suggest that women have a different set of priorities, reflecting the disadvantage they experience in the labour market – not just as a result of a system which penalises people who take career breaks or who work part-time, but as a result of patriarchal relations, one of the most visible manifestations of which is sexual harassment. The growth in female union membership has led to an increase in the extent to which such issues are regarded as legitimate union concerns, but only in some unions, and in some cases only at national level, whereas it is at branch level that many of these issues need to be tackled.

Would having more women active in the union mean a shift in priorities of that union? Recent research by Heery and Kelly (1988) on the impact of female full-time officers suggested that female representation did 'make a difference' to the prioritising of issues such as 'equal pay, childcare, maternity leave and sexual harassment in collective bargaining' (p. 502). This suggests that if more women were active in the union, these issues might be given more priority. Full-time women officers are also more committed to encouraging female participation among lay members (Heery and Kelly 1988; Ledwith *et al.* 1990).

The extent to which the TUC and individual unions have attempted to increase female membership cannot be doubted (Labour Research 1991a). Some unions have sought to understand why it is that those new members do not then join the bureaucratic machinery, but the seriousness of those endeavours has been variable, as has the alacrity with which the implications of the findings have been acted upon. Some of the studies, both those conducted internally and those commissioned externally (including the ones reported upon in this chapter), make it clear that there are sets of structural constraints which impede women's participation in the union similar to those which restrict women's access to senior positions in the workplace. Those constraints are rooted in the patriarchal relations which govern the workplace as well as the family and which restrict women both directly and indirectly. To alter those relations would mean fundamental changes. On the whole, the response of unions to the barriers facing women's participation has been to try to facilitate women taking on the 'triple load', of union, work and family responsibilities.

It should be remembered that women represented by a union enjoy better pay and terms and conditions of employment than those who are not (Martin and Roberts 1984; Yaron n.d., cited in Labour Research 1991a). Moreover, women full-time employees are now as likely as males to be union members: but part-time workers are only half as likely to join as full-time workers: this shows that it is hours rather than gender that is the significant factor (Witherspoon 1986, cited in Millward and Stevens 1986). Nevertheless, there was a significant increase in union membership among part-time workers in the late 1980s, and unions such as USDAW are targeting them more consciously (Labour Research 1989). Despite the increase in women members, the major issues of pay inequality, gender segregation in occupations, improvements in terms and conditions of employment for part-time workers, sexual harassment and workplace childcare provision, all of which are of great importance to women unionists, are not yet the main campaigning areas for most unions with a majority of women members. Times are changing, however. The demographic changes which have suddenly made women the focus of employers' recruitment and training strategies have increased, too, the attention that they are receiving in the trade-union movement. The TUC unions are drawing up a 'Charter of Women's Rights at Work', and in the words of Norman Willis, the TUC leader, 'Every policy, every service, every demand of the trade union movement has to be examined in the light of the needs of women' (Norman Willis, addressing the 1989 Women's TUC Conference).

This chapter explores structures impeding women's participation in unions – some of which are as a result of unions organising principally for the benefit of men, while others are due to the way the family and domestic division of labour are organised in a way which privileges men. The surveys it draws upon were conducted with colleagues in the Social Research Unit of the University of Wales College of Cardiff and the Research Departments of the National and Local Government Officers' Association (NALGO), a white-collar, public-sector union, and the Union of Shop, Distributive and Allied Workers (USDAW), a largely blue-collar, private-sector one, in the early 1980s.[3] For both unions, surveys were conducted of both members and activists. The NALGO survey of over 5,000 statistically representative members remains one of the largest and most comprehensive of such surveys. While the membership survey conducted for USDAW encountered some methodological problems described below, a sample survey of 607 branch secretaries revealed interesting insights into their views on women's participation in branch affairs. The surveys examined the position of women in the union and in the workplace from a number of perspectives. They sought to explore the barriers to women's participation in the union, and in so doing, documented the inter-relationship between women's position in the family, the workplace and the union. They illustrate the parallels between the factors inhibiting workplace and union careers, and show the impact of stage in the life cycle on trade-union participation. They, and other more recent surveys like them conducted by other unions, informed policies for positive action which are still developing.

The case studies were commissioned by the two unions because of their concern for equal opportunities, and their commitment to identifying ways of increasing women's participation. Both have moved on in terms of developing policies to facilitate the removal of 'barriers' to that participation. In USDAW, for example, a Women's Officer has been appointed; in NALGO, equal opportunities officers have been introduced at both regional and branch level, and in both unions special training has been introduced to address needs identified by women members. Other measures, too, have been introduced by both unions; indeed, at a national level NALGO can be described as being at the forefront of unions developing equal opportunities policies that have also taken on board ethnic origin, handicap and sexual orientation issues too. Although the surveys are in a sense historical, they nevertheless remain significant given their scale. Most studies of women and unions offer more invaluable in-depth, qualitative data but are restricted to one or two branches (see, for example, Charles 1986; Cunnison 1983; Nicholson *et al.* 1981).

The first section of the chapter sets the scene by briefly outlining patterns of change in employment and trade-union membership in the last decade. The case studies, which comprise national surveys of activists and members, are then described. Three issues which emerge from the empirical work are then addressed: the structure, organisation and discourse of branch meetings as the locus of trade-union democracy, the parallels between careers in work and in the union, and the relationship between members' concerns and activists' priorities. The conclusion reviews the dynamics of gender, power and trade-union democracy.

WOMEN AND TRADE-UNION MEMBERSHIP

The changing industrial structure has created numerous problems for union organisation, particularly among the more traditional craft unions. The shift in employment from manufacturing to services, and the growth in unemployment, particularly among traditional craft workers, has affected blue- and white-collar unions in different ways. Blue-collar unions, whose strength or even very existence has been threatened with declining numbers as plants close, have had to merge and amalgamate with other unions in order to maintain bargaining power. Such merged unions may have little inner coherence or spirit of unity, although they can retain their influence through sheer weight of numbers in the TUC. Organising such multi-employer, multi-workplace unions presents a range of strategic problems of which a major one is communication with members. Meanwhile, the white-collar unions, and in particular those in the public sector where membership increases have been greatest, such as NALGO, enjoy a reasonably straightforward set of employers with whom to negotiate. They can organise workplace, work-time meetings of members, and are able to have union dues deducted from wages at source. White-collar unions have grown from relative insignificance into a powerful base in the union movement, notwithstanding the impact of public expenditure cuts in the 1980s on staffing levels.

The growth in the number of women in trade unions has not, however, kept pace with the growth in female employment overall. Whereas about 45 per cent of the workforce is female, only just over a third of union members are women. Labour Research (1991a) report that only 26 per cent of the 11 million women in the workforce are in TUC-affiliated unions, compared with 47 per cent of employed men. This is partly a reflection of many women working in non-unionised service sector work with small employers, and partly a result of the lower membership rates among part-time workers, the vast majority of whom are women. The Women and Employment Survey found that 51 per cent of full-time workers compared with 28 per cent of part-timers are union members (Martin and Roberts 1984). Many unions, in particular the Transport and General Workers' Union (TGWU), the General and Municipal, Boilermakers and Allied Trades (GMB), and USDAW, are now actively recruiting part-timers. The net result of all these changes is that although the typical image of a British unionist may well be that of a miner or docker on a picket line, numerically, she is increasingly more likely to be a white-blouse clerical worker.

Among the ten largest trade unions, there were five in 1990 which had a majority of women members – in order of size of union: NALGO (53 per cent), National Union of Public Employees (NUPE) (71 per cent), USDAW (62 per cent), Confederation of Health Service Employees (COHSE) (79 per cent) and the National Union of Teachers (NUT) (72 per cent) (Labour Research 1991a). However, as Table 5.1 illustrates, having a majority of members who are women does not necessarily imply a majority of women on the national executive, on TUC delegations or as full-time national officers, even though the trend is clearly moving in that direction. Women comprise 20 per cent of national executive committee members, 23 per cent of delegates to union conferences, 20 per cent of national full-time officers and four out of seventy-five general secretaries (Labour Research 1991a).

There are far more women now among the activists than when Coote and Kellner's rallying pamphlet 'Hear this, brother' was published in 1980. Most of the unions with the largest female membership now have National Women's or Equality Officers and most have them at regional level too. How have these changes been brought about? During the 1980s, all the unions with substantial female membership explored, and to a greater or lesser extent tackled, the issue of women's involvement in the union. While some identified the problem as women themselves and sought to change their behaviour, others have been more reflexive and examined barriers to participation within the organisation itself. These manoeuvres parallel similar concerns to attract and retain women by employers, brought on by school-leaver shortages (Rees 1989a; see also Chapter 6).

The increase in the proportion of women in the workforce has had implications for both blue- and white-collar unions, and for those in the private as well as the public sector. The following case studies of NALGO and USDAW draw out some of the contrasts and the similarities faced by unions across the public/private, manual/non-manual divides.

WOMEN IN A WHITE-COLLAR UNION – NALGO

Trade-union density (the proportion of eligible workers who are members of a union) in British public-sector unions was high in the mid-1980s (at 75 per

Table 5.1 Women's participation in the ten unions with the largest female membership, 1990[4]

Union	No. of women members	% women members	women on National Exec. %	Women on TUC Delegation %	Women full-time National Officers
National Union of Public Employees	430,000	71.3	46.1	36.1	38.5
National and Local Government Officers' Association	398,660 (1989)	53.1	42.0	41.7	31.6
General, Municipal, Boilermakers and Allied Trades Union	267,894	30.8	29.4	19.8	11.8
Union of Shop, Distributive and Allied Workers	251,371	71.3	31.3	26.9	20.0
Transport and General Workers Union	210,758	16.9	7.7	20.6	3.4
Confederation of Health Service Employees	165,900	79.0	50.0	31.6	54.2
Manufacturing Science Finance	140,000	21.4	21.6	25.5	21.4
National Union of Teachers	133,675	72.0	28.6	40.0	42.9
Amalgamated Engineering Union	105,022	14.2	0.0	7.4	0.6

Source: Labour Research Department (1991a), calculated from Table 1

cent) compared with other countries (for example, the United States: 20 per cent; or Germany, 47 per cent) and more than double that in the private sector (Blanchflower and Oswald 1989). NALGO is the largest white-collar union and has grown enormously in recent decades; the new members are largely drawn from women joining the expanding service sector. The industries whose white-collar workers NALGO organises are in those sectors of the economy where women's employment has increased most dramatically, particularly in the late 1960s and early 1970s: local government, health, the utilities, new towns and universities. Over half the members are in local government. It is too early to say what effect privatisation will have on union density in some of the major utilities in the long term or in other parts of the public sector that may be sold off.

NALGO commissioned Martin Read and myself to conduct surveys of members and officers to explore the issue of equality, both in the workplace and in the union (Rees, T. and Read 1980, 1981). The membership survey of a statistically representative sample of over 5,000 men and women was conducted in 1981, which controlled for region and industry. The results revealed that women had become, by a slim margin, the majority of the union membership (51 per cent): they have hovered between 53 per cent and 50 per cent since then.

NALGO members

The differences between women and men in the sample in terms of their position in the workplace were stark. Two-thirds of the women were in typing and clerical grades, while over half the men were in professional grades. This was reflected in the relative rates of pay: over half the men were in the top income bracket compared with 4 per cent of the women. By the same token, two-thirds of the full-time working women were in the bottom income category, compared with just 10 per cent of the men. Some 10 per cent of the women were working part-time compared with 0.4 per cent of the men. A break in service had been experienced by 40 per cent of the women in the survey and less than 1 per cent of the men. Three-quarters of the women whose careers had been interrupted identified children as the cause; the remainder were for other family reasons or brought about by having to move because of partner's change of job to a new location. Some married women in the survey experienced restrictions in their career opportunities not only by being unable to move for promotion but also by having to give up their own jobs because of their husband's promotion.

The tendency on the part of the women to have a break in service meant that the demographic profiles of the men and the women were very different, as Figures 5.1 and 5.2 show. The women largely fell into two categories; young, single or married but child-free, and older 'returners'; both groups were more likely than the men to be either single, widowed or

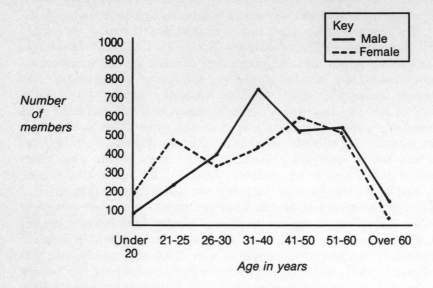

Figure 5.1 Age profile of men and women NALGO members

divorced. Nearly 80 per cent of the men were married (compared with only 60 per cent of the women). Both categories of women were less likely to have children than the men: two-thirds of the men had children, but only 47 per cent of the women did. Moreover, the mothers' children were far more likely to have left home or to be in secondary school than the fathers'. In other words, family formation had little effect upon the men's involvement in paid work, but there was a distinct lack of mothers of small children among the NALGO members. The typical 'NALGO man' matches the television advertisement image of a family man: aged between 31 and 40, married (although we do not know whether or not his wife goes out to work) and with two children of school age. The peak of men between 31 and 40 disturbing an otherwise standard shaped curve of male economic activity (in Figure 5.1) reflects the extra recruitment during the expansion of the public services and the reorganisation of local government and health authorities in the early 1970s (when these men would have been in their twenties).

Many of the older female members worked part-time, and over 90 per cent of them were married, compared with 54 per cent of full-time women members. The pattern reflects exactly female participation rates more generally and illustrates the impact of the career break on the profile of women workers.

Crompton *et al.* (1982) argue that there is a clear relationship between qualifications and career prospects. About the same proportion of men (86 per cent) and women (83 per cent) respondents had some qualifications; however, the women tended to have typing qualifications and CSEs, while

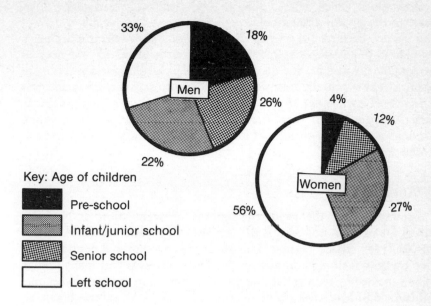

Key: Age of children

- Pre-school
- Infant/junior school
- Senior school
- Left school

Figure 5.2 Age of NALGO members' children

the men had much higher ones. Indeed, the higher the grade, the larger the gap between men and women. While the proportion of men and women with City and Guilds was the same, twice as many men as women had A levels, four times as many men as women had ONC, HNC, degrees and postgraduate qualifications, and five times as many were members of professional organisations. But Crompton *et al.* refer specifically to post-entry qualifications, and in the study it was striking that employers were more likely to sponsor men for training. This was to a certain extent due to discrimination: four women had been refused employer sponsorship for training on the grounds of their gender (before the legislation that made such grounds illegal) and twenty-six on age – an indirect form of sex discrimination. However, a numerically more significant factor explaining the differential between sponsorship rates lay in the fact that far fewer women had sought sponsorship for training. Indeed, 80 per cent of women had never asked for it, compared with 55 per cent of men. The actual refusal rates were similar for both sexes. But for those women in typing jobs and in part-time employment, there would be little realistic possibility of sponsored training leading to promotion. Men were far more likely to have requested a promotion or regrading in the three years prior to the survey, and more men than women were given one, irrespective of whether or not they had requested it. Again, the fact that so many women were in typing and

secretarial work which offered few, if any, chances of promotion con-
tributed to the gender differential.

The survey showed the power of structural constraints on women's
promotion in public-sector employment. Continuity of service, the need to
be geographically mobile, and qualifications all proved important factors in
promotion, but essentially men were more likely to satisfy these conditions
irrespective of their stage in the life cycle and particular family circumstances. Added to which, there was no ladder out of secretarial and typing
work, nor were there opportunities for promotion or training for women in
part-time work.

NALGO activists

The significance for the gendered patterns of segregation of NALGO
members for us here, however, is the fact that they were reproduced in the
union itself, for related reasons. Length of membership and continuity of
service are both factors in union activity. This is an issue that many unions
have now tackled by reducing the length of membership required to become
an office-holder. Moreover, some women who may, with several breaks in
service, have accumulated a substantial number of years' membership, do
not clock up sufficient *continuous* years since their last rejoining to feel they
have enough recent relevant experience and confidence to stand for office.
The NALGO study showed how twice as many men as women had been
members of the union for over ten years, and three times as many for over
twenty years (see Figure 5.3). The women's briefer period of membership
simply reflected their shorter number of years in work since last returning to
work.

The sample of members contained 358 male and 317 female activists (that
is, office-holders), but of these, the men were far more likely to be both a
shop steward/departmental representative and hold one of the key posts on
the branch executive. By contrast, the women were more likely simply to be
branch executive members. Those who held branch officer posts were in the
more peripheral posts, such as welfare officer or thrift secretary, rather than
in key positions. Both the men and women shop stewards/departmental
representatives tended to have been members of NALGO for between six
and ten years. However, as Figure 5.3 shows, nearly half the women
members had yet to serve six years since joining or last rejoining, compared
with only 27 per cent of the men, so there were far fewer women with
significant years of service to act as a pool of potential activists.

How typical were the activists of the membership? While we know that
they are more likely to be men than would be expected if they were
randomly selected, in what other ways were activists different from the
membership at large? The survey showed quite clearly that whereas the male
activists did not differ greatly from the membership in terms of their stage in

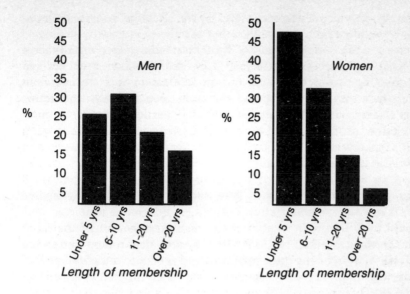

Figure 5.3 NALGO members' length of membership of union

the life cycle and level of domestic commitments, the women certainly did. The male shop stewards/departmental representatives were marginally more likely to be married than the members as a whole, whereas the female activists were less likely to be; indeed, 16.5 per cent of the female shop stewards/departmental representatives were separated, widowed or divorced. Fewer had children, whereas for the men, the proportion was the same as the membership as a whole. So the female activists had fewer child-care commitments than the female membership, a group from which women with young children have already been selected out. Clearly, the only women who felt able to take on union duties were those relatively free from family commitments, including a partner.

Many of the same patterns of gender relations within the union were found to characterise a very different union, USDAW, but there were significant differences too.

WOMEN IN A BLUE-COLLAR UNION – USDAW

USDAW, concerned as it is with shop, distribution and allied workers has as its rationale the organisation of workers in the production of food 'from the field to the shelf'. It organises workers in agriculture, pharmaceuticals, distribution, retailing, hairdressing and other industries. It has amalgamated with a number of smaller unions to retain its position as one of the most powerful voices in the TUC. Some 62 per cent of the members are women (1988–89), the majority of whom work part-time.

Organising groups of members who work in large supermarkets is relatively straightforward, but many other members are relatively isolated and remote and are difficult to serve. Branches can be geographically large and comprise members in a variety of industries. 'Holding' branches and 'section' meetings are devices to help communication with and between members where they are very spread out both geographically and across industries and employers, but they are difficult to organise. Moreover, given the fluid nature of the labour in the industries organised, about a third of USDAW's membership turn over every year. Communication with members is as a result problematic. A statistically representative survey of shop stewards was successfully conducted in 1983 (Davies, Rees and Read 1983), but a membership survey in 1984 both fell foul of and highlighted USDAW'S internal communication difficulties. Enormous problems were experienced by USDAW in its attempts to distribute the questionnaires to members. Graham Markall of USDAW's research department persevered with the task of overcoming these problems and produced a useful report of the study, albeit on a rather smaller scale than originally hoped for (USDAW 1987).

The surveys were commissioned by USDAW to establish the degree of participation of women in union activities and to identify what shop stewards and members saw as the 'major barriers' to equal participation. The first stage was a questionnaire survey of all branch corresponding secretaries (shop stewards) to establish the pattern of women's participation in the union. The response rate was an acceptable 58 per cent (607 of the 1,054 branch secretaries responded).

USDAW activists

USDAW tends to recruit its full-time officers from among lay officials of the union, operating in effect an internal labour market. The access of members to participation in the union is, therefore, clearly particularly important. In the survey, branch officers revealed to us that although women were the majority of members, both in the union as a whole and in about 75 per cent of individual branches, only 27 per cent of the branch committees had a majority of women members. Only a third of those same branches had a majority of women shop stewards. As in the NALGO study, women were in a clear minority in branch officer posts, and those positions that were held by women were in the 'support' roles, in particular assistant secretary or minutes secretary, rather than the key posts. Of those branches which indicated that they sent representatives to the Annual Delegates Meeting, two-thirds of the delegates were men and one-third women. Among the non-voting visitors sent, the breakdown was closer, with 55 per cent being male and 45 per cent female.

The responses on branch organisation revealed some of the difficulties of organising meetings. Only 27 per cent of the branches (136) organised employees of a single employer in one workplace. Seventy-two per cent of branches (434) organised members in several places of work – although they were not necessarily all different employers; this figure includes multi-site employers. Two-thirds of branches altogether covered single employers (single and multi-site branches), while the remaining third were all branches covering several employers. This complex pattern was to prove highly significant for branch meeting organisation, for communication with members, and for the logistics of conducting the membership survey.

The study showed that in some branches, meetings were rarely held. The nature of the multi-workplace branches clearly made organising such meetings problematic. Those that were held were, on the whole, badly attended by both men and women. Some branches covered huge geographical areas: in one case attendance at a branch meeting could involve a round trip of 250 miles! Over half the branches held their meetings off the employers' premises and in their own time. Over 80 per cent of these held their meetings after work or late in the evenings. Only ten branches provided child-care facilities. These factors clearly affect both men and women's attendance, but are likely to have a greater effect upon women given traditional patterns of division of labour in the home, women's relatively poor access to private transport, and greater fear of being out at night alone.

The branch secretaries' returns showed that attendance was considerably higher in single-site branches (over 50 per cent in 27 per cent of such branches) than in multi-site ones (two-thirds of such branches reporting 10 per cent). This pattern was observed for both men and women, but fewer women attended meetings of multi-site branches. Similarly, the venue and timing had a noticeable effect upon attendance. It was much higher at meetings held on employers' premises in employers' time: a quarter of the branches had over 50 per cent of members attending compared with 3.6 per cent of branches where members were attending in their own time. Proportionately more women attended meetings in employers' premises in employers' time, and proportionately fewer those held off employers' premises in members' own time. Over half the meetings held off employers' premises were in pubs, clubs and hotels, venues which women may find difficult to enter on their own; indeed, in some working men's clubs, they would have to be signed in by a man.

USDAW members

For the membership survey, USDAW originally intended that branch officers should distribute questionnaires to named members, randomly selected in a statistically representative sample designed by my colleague, Martin Read. This proved impossible. Branch secretaries had no efficient way of distributing the questionnaires, as they did not necessarily know where the named member worked. USDAW did not hold up-to-date details of address or workplace centrally. A range of strategies was then employed to arrange the distribution and boost the response. Eventually 1,496 (1,104 women and 392 men, that is 73 per cent of women at a time when they constituted about 60 per cent of members) responded in what became a much smaller study than was originally intended, with the statistical representativeness of the response in some doubt as a consequence. The full results are in USDAW (1987). A side-effect of the legislation on union democracy is that unions have now in effect had to computerise their membership records, which should in the future make surveys of this kind much easier to conduct (see Owens et al. forthcoming).

The methodological problems described preclude too much being made of the results. Nevertheless, just looking at the broad trends, it is interesting to note that, as in the NALGO study, women are under-represented at every level of branch activity. They reported a greater degree of lack of confidence than men and identified this, together with lack of skills and knowledge about the union, as a major barrier to further involvement. The women also emphasised problems highlighted in the survey of branch secretaries related to the timing and location of branch meetings – in particular, transportation. There was considerable support for women-only initiatives to allow women to develop skills and confidence. The view was expressed by many women that impenetrable jargon at branch meetings and the domination of branches by small cliques led to their feeling a degree of alienation from the union, although, rather to USDAW's surprise, this view was shared also by some men, albeit to a less marked degree (USDAW 1987).

BARRIERS TO WOMEN'S PARTICIPATION

These studies of two unions have highlighted a number of constraints on women's participation in unions. As a consequence, there remain severe limitations to the extent to which unions can be said to represent women's interests. In the first instance, union activity may well be expected to begin with a process of familiarisation with the organisation through attendance at union meetings. It is clear that women's domestic responsibilities, their break in service, the venue, timing and location of branch meetings, all contribute to differential rates of access to such meetings. The studies challenge the notion that women's relatively low level of union activity is simply a result of 'low work attachment', as has traditionally been supposed. Secondly, these data demonstrate clear links between 'careers' in work, and 'careers' in the union. The same constraints which inhibit promotion for women in one similarly restrict progress in the other. Finally, the fact that women do not have good access to union decision-making hierarchies to voice the concerns they have over systems which privilege men, guarantees the status quo. Such systems limit the extent to which trade unions can be described as 'democratic'. Patriarchal relations in the home, the workplace and the union cut across these three levels and restrict any significant changes in women's access to union power. As a consequence, women's stage in the life cycle, or rather their domestic commitment load factor, determines to a large extent their freedom to participate and become active in union life. However, without that involvement, it is clear that unions are unlikely to address issues which would radically improve women's working lives. These three issues are now discussed in more depth.

BRANCH MEETINGS: LOCUS OF TRADE-UNION DEMOCRACY?

The surveys of NALGO and USDAW showed that attendance at meetings was low for both men and women, but particularly for women, and that rates varied in accordance with the time and venue of meetings: again these factors appeared to affect women more than men. Union meetings generally are notoriously badly attended; it has been calculated that 10 per cent attendance is probably about the figure for attendance generally. Quoracy is a perennial problem unless a union is engaged in a dispute. Poor attendance can of course be interpreted in different ways. It may simply suggest that members are reasonably happy with the way the union is handling matters. Alternatively, it can be because the time and venue are disenfranchising members and in a way that systematically makes it more difficult for people of one gender rather than another to participate.

The Women and Employment Survey (Martin and Roberts 1984) revealed that 20 per cent of the women respondents who did not attend branch meetings were prevented from so doing by the timing of the meetings. If branch meetings are held in the members' own time, the woman member, because of the usual pattern of power relation and domestic division of labour within the home, has to convince not only herself that it is worth her while going, but her partner as well. The USDAW study revealed how pressures from partners were felt to be a particular problem for women working part-time. Men and women have different degrees of access to branch meetings then, given their venue and timing. As one corresponding secretary wrote:

> Despite a majority of women members, USDAW like a great many other trade unions is still a male dominated organisation. It is not enough to say that it is a democratic organisation and women have the same chance as men to get involved. The administration of the union is geared towards male convenience – evening meetings, often in licensed premises etc while men do not have the same amount of domestic duties as a woman. Men have been guilty unwittingly of excluding women from the trade union world, through years of tradition and habit. Women can and should

challenge such male habits by insisting that meetings are held in non-
licensed premises, that if necessary creche facilities are provided etc.

Of course, many women work part-time, and they in particular have
difficulty in attending even those meetings which are in workplace and
work-time if they do not happen to coincide with their particular shift.
Being involved in the union even at the minimal level of attending meetings
represents a proportionately more substantial part of their leisure time.

Transport is clearly an issue when meetings are held off employers'
premises and out of work hours. Even if a household has private transport,
it does not necessarily mean that the woman in the household has access to
it. In low-income households in particular, and for part-time workers, fares
incurred by attending such meetings can be a deterrent (just as travel costs
also restrict women's leisure activities: see Deem 1986).

Having negotiated access to branch meetings, both case studies pointed to
problems experienced by women in particular related to the formality of
branch meetings, and their lack of familiarity with the discourse and
procedures. This in part relates to the break in service; women who have
such a break cannot accumulate experience and familiarity in the same way
as men. It has been argued too that men's methods of organising are more
formal than those of women (Taking Liberties Collective 1989); and that
there is a 'female management style' (Gerver and Hart 1991), to which
women might respond more readily. The Greenham Common peace camp
and women's support groups during the miners' strike have been pointed to
as movements that appeared to operate without the need for hierarchies,
office-holders, standing orders or jargon. In Italy, feminists have described
how, in order to participate in 'masculine' models of union militancy, they
had to deny their femininity: to gain equality they faced internal conflicts
they describe as '*lacerazione*' (lacerations); becoming integrated entailed
feeling 'mutilated' (Beccalli 1984:201). Such Italian feminist unionists
determined to change the unions rather than seek equality within them.

A further explanation for the greater degree of discomfort that the
women in these studies and elsewhere have expressed with the nature of
branch meetings and their ability to participate relates to the power
relations between those men and women members in the workplace. An
USDAW branch corresponding secretary commented:

> Most women feel very inhibited when they have to take part in courses
> with men or stand up among men at branch meetings. I would like to see
> more union courses being run solely for women to try and help them gain
> more confidence and help them feel less inhibited in what can be a very
> male dominated union.

Taking the case of NALGO, it is clear from the data on occupational
position that most of the women were likely to be in clerical and secretarial

posts, and the men to be officers, even senior officers – unlike the Civil Service unions, NALGO represents people from the top to the bottom of the hierarchies in most of the workplaces it organises. Participating in meetings is far more likely to be second nature to far more of the men, as part of their day-to-day work. The women's lack of confidence, and inexperience of such formal meetings, stemmed, in part, from their relatively lowly position in the organisation. Their views would not normally be sought in decision-making processes. For, say, a secretary, to feel comfortable in standing against a senior officer in the same local authority branch for a post on the executive or arguing against him in a branch meeting would take a deep commitment, a forceful personality, and a high level of confidence, or some combination of these. Black and Asian women have also to contend with racial disadvantage in the workplace being reflected in union arenas. The South East Region TUC Women's Committee (n.d.) found a correlation between status of job and position in the union. Women in professional and management jobs were more likely to hold senior positions in the union.

Clearly, after joining a union, attendance at branch meetings is the most basic level of union activity. Nevertheless, it is significant in that some unions make attendance at a certain proportion of meetings a criterion for standing for office; indeed, in USDAW the rule books specified that a candidate for shop steward must have attended at least half of the previous year's branch meetings. The organisation of branch meetings is then the first stage in 'filtering out' women's involvement in the union.

Career in work, 'career' in the union

A number of factors have been identified as explaining why relatively few women reach the upper rungs of the hierarchy in their place of work: these are discussed in other parts of this book. However, some of these factors do not simply impede progress at work, they affect women's access to the higher reaches of the union hierarchy too. There is a nice irony here, of course, as with few women in the union 'board room', there is little prospect of pressure for change in either union or workplace organisation.

The factors I want to focus upon here are seniority and time. In the first instance, the value put upon length of continuous service over other potential criteria in judging fitness to serve is one shared by both employers and unions in selecting people for high office. Secondly, the same time constraints which inhibit women's opportunities to sell their labour because of domestic commitments, most obviously revealed in the extent of part-time working, constrain their ability to participate in and become active in trade unions. This section discusses these two factors in turn.

Break in service

The analysis of the Women and Employment Survey (Martin and Roberts 1984), which like the NALGO survey also had a sample of 5,500 respondents (but all women), demonstrated that a break in service was clearly deleterious to career prospects, in particular if one went back to work part-time (Elias 1988). Our survey of NALGO members certainly identified a few female graduates in the typing pool. However, the point here is that the individual's career in work is related to their 'career' in the union. Most crucially, the break in service has the effect of reducing the pool of women with appropriate trade-union experience from which activists can be recruited. Moreover, because the break in service affects women's position in the workplace, they are less likely to be sufficiently senior to have the confidence to pitch in.

Trade-union activists tend to be drawn from people with considerable years' membership. But, as Coote and Kellner (1980:30) wrote:

> A smaller proportion of women aged 25–34 work than among any other age group between 18 and 55; a smaller proportion of those who do have a job work full time than in any other age group; and a smaller proportion of those who work full time belong to a union than in any other group. The cumulative result of these biases means that one man in two aged 25 to 34 has a full time job and belongs to a union – compared with one woman in 20 in the same age group.

The typical male NALGO member in his late thirties or early forties has had work and union experience for about twenty years, with all the advantages that such experience and concomitant confidence-building and familiarity with union affairs provide. By contrast, when a female NALGO (or indeed other union) member reaches the same age, she may have had little more union experience than the office junior who has just left school – despite an age difference of up to twenty years! We found that most NALGO activists had six to ten years' membership of the union, and relatively few women had clocked up such years consecutively. Moreover, female activists were less likely than female non-activists to have had a break in service.

The (1990) study of SOGAT activists by Ledwith *et al.* found three main groups of women: the single and child-free, mothers who had become active before having their children, who both received support from partners and could afford child care; and the over 40s, who had not become active until their children were independent. The authors maintain:

> They were the ones whose break in work and trade union activity had rendered them 'invisible' at the crucial age when their (mostly male colleagues) were building their careers and 'getting their faces known'. By the time they returned, these women felt it was too late to get to the top.
>
> (1990:121)

Men are advantaged and women disadvantaged by the fact that the relationship between career in work and career in the union is a reciprocal one. Experience and confidence gained through union activity can be beneficial for people's careers. In California, Roby (1987:153) suggests that: 'service as a steward affects the employment of many of those who so serve by providing training in leadership skills and by being a step toward higher level positions in unions, companies and government agencies'.

American literature on trade-union activism in the 1950s suggested that the activist has a higher commitment to work than the non-activist, and is likely to be in a more senior position, earn more, be male and married (Seidman 1958; Tannenbaum and Kahn 1958). A break in service is not simply a black mark because of seniority conventions and the value put upon length of continuous service in themselves, it is traditionally read as indicating a low commitment to work. Main (1988), among others, has done much to turn that view on its head by illustrating how women's attachment to work as indicated by proportion of adult years spent in the labour force, although less than that of men, is clearly demonstrated as high over the whole working life through a series of returns at every available opportunity (see Chapter 2).

Despite the fact that there is little empirical evidence for the notion that women have a lower labour-force attachment, it is frequently put forward to explain women's relatively low rates of union membership and activity. A far more powerful explanation of membership lies in the fact that women often work in occupations and sectors which are not unionised and are in part-time work, which unions have until very recently, on the whole, ignored. Low levels of activity have more to do with exclusion measures, such as insistence upon continuity of service for office-holding, and patriarchal relations in the home constraining women's time and power to participate.

Crowding out: the time factor

There is a growing interest in time as a factor both in the social analysis of everyday life and in feminist theory (Adam 1989). A number of studies have charted the respective amounts of time spent by men and women on domestic work and the relationship between those patterns and economic activity. Women, even when both partners are in full-time employment, spend many more hours a week on domestic responsibilities (Gershuny *et al.* 1986). This inhibits women's freedom to undertake training out of work hours, to do overtime and to put in extra hours that might help with promotion. Again, this pattern is reflected in careers in the union. The fact that women already frequently carry 'the double load' of work and domestic responsibilities means that 'crowding out' explains, in part at least, relatively low levels of union activism. As McCarthy (1977:161–2) wrote:

It is, of course a truism to say that the majority of women are, and always have been expected to do at least two jobs, running a home and bringing up children, caring for elderly relations and all the other home-based activities, which are seen by society as a woman's primary function, with any paid employment, or activity outside the home, as a secondary, 'spare-time' occupation, which can be dropped at any moment. To build in a third activity – active participation in a trade union – requires both the sympathetic understanding and encouragement of a partner, and a degree of organisation, not only of the woman herself, but of everybody else in her life.

It is not simply a matter of finding time, but of persuading other members of the household to co-operate in order for that woman to be 'released'; she must almost seek permission. This is reflected in Roby's (1987:152) detailed study of twenty-six female and nine male shop stewards in California: 'Many of the arrangements the women had for handling their three jobs did not happen automatically, but were the result of their persistently educating and sometimes struggling with their spouses and children.'

The bifurcated age distribution of women in the labour force, where there are young women in their teens and early twenties, then a dip in participation rates during the main childbearing years, followed by a rise again of women in their late thirties and older, is reflected in the profiles of union activists. The NALGO study showed that women activists were more likely to be single or divorced than the female membership as a whole. In the USDAW study, women over 30 especially reported that they met with great pressure from their partners not to get more involved in the union.

Union activity can be enormously time-consuming: it can involve evening meetings, residential courses and conferences and travelling. Any industrial disputes will of course magnify the amount of time that lay officials need to invest. Women rarely have as much access to 'leisure' time as men, and are visibly less active in politics, local government and sporting activities (Deem 1986). It is noticeable that it is those women with a relatively light domestic burden through being child-free and partner-free who predominantly become activists.

Much of women's apparent lack of interest in union activism derives from the fact that all women tend to be compared with all men, despite the fact that there are particular problems faced by part-time would-be activists, and that 40 per cent of women work part-time. These points are borne out by the Women and Employment Survey: 61 per cent of the respondents in work knew there was a union that they could join in their workplace, of whom 41 per cent had actually joined. The full-time workers were much more likely to have a union that they could join than the part-timers (69 per cent compared with 50 per cent); much more likely to belong to a union (51 per cent compared with 28 per cent), attend union meetings (16 per cent compared with 6 per cent) or to hold an office in a union (9 per cent compared with 2 per cent: Martin and Roberts 1984). Employers are unenthusiastic about activism among part-timers if it involves paid time off for union duties, as it represents a proportionately larger amount of their work-time.

The domestic division of labour directly affects women's availability to participate in union activities, which are organised on the assumption that members are free to participate in lunchtimes and evenings (and feel comfortable attending meetings in pubs and clubs in some cases). The only women free so to participate on the whole are those who are single, older or have very supportive families. This clearly restricts the available pool of potential women activists.

CONCLUSION: FEMINISATION AND TRADE-UNION DEMOCRACY

The net result of the impact of the relationship between work and union 'careers' is that women are not heard in the unions as loudly as their numbers of members and particular sets of disadvantage in the workplace warrant. There are clear gender divisions of interest in what should be negotiated. The NALGO branch survey showed how few branches (at the time) had negotiated improvements to national agreements on a whole range of issues that particularly affected women members. This was despite the fact that the majority of the members were women in the union as a whole and in many of the branches.

There is a view that unions should not negotiate on issues that make it easier for women to cope with an uneven division of labour in the home because it establishes more firmly the status quo, rather than challenging it. On the other hand, it is clearly difficult for a union, as a union, to do very much about the domestic division of labour, over and above tackling the issues of women's inadequate pay and occupational segregation, which make women financially dependent upon men, the state, or both in the first place. Nevertheless, the issue here is that because women have less access to branch meetings, and are less likely to have sufficient years' experience and seniority to come forward as activists, even in unions where they are in the majority, then issues of central concern to them will be neglected.

The most obvious example of this is the case of part-time workers. The Women and Employment Survey showed of even just those workers with a trade union at their workplace, full-timers were more likely to have benefits such as sick pay, occupational pension, and training and promotion prospects (28 per cent) compared with part-timers (3 per cent) (Martin and Roberts 1984). And yet trade unions negotiating packages rarely focus on or even include issues of vital importance to part-timers. The neglect of certain members who feel that issues of concern to them are ignored and that the structure of union organisation makes it difficult for their voice to be heard is expressed by the following NALGO woman in the membership survey:

> As a working single parent – and knowing the difficulties of being so, I feel I am in the double bind of being unable to be totally free to engage in political/union activity, but I also feel that people such as myself – an increasing number – need the active support of their unions for the promotion of getting/organising creche facilities/after school/school holiday programmes/job sharing provision with more security for part-timers/longer maternity leave and paternity leave. It is something I believe union executives should be promoting, with support from membership, but not necessarily regular active support. After all, if you've worked all day, it's difficult to attend union meetings at 6 p.m.

Hyman (1989:233) has described how there is a divergence between the interests of activists and the members they represent, because the two groups have different characteristics:

> Typically, activists and officials derive disproportionately from relatively highly advantaged sections of the workforce: male, white, higher skilled, higher-paid, in more secure jobs. Such characteristics – commonly associated with greater self-confidence, familiarity with official procedure, standing with fellow-workers, and identification with work and hence work-related institutions – may be seen as encouraging involvement in trades unionism and a successful 'career' as union activist. Hence hierarchy within the working class is replicated within trade union organisation. In identifying grievances, selecting demands, formulating strategies and determining priorities, the perspectives and interests of the dominant sections almost inevitably exert disproportionate influence.

It is the reproduction of power relations between men and women in the home which is reproduced in the union, but different racial groups also experience patterns of relations in the union which reflect those in the community. And women are restricted in their freedom to challenge those power structures in work, through the union, by those self-same power structures in the home.

Some women do become activists. But as the NALGO study showed, they were less typical of the NALGO members than the men. They were more likely to be full-time, and less likely to have domestic commitments. Similarly, Roby and Uttal found in a study of 158 male and female trade-union leaders in the United States that the presence of a partner and children affected stewards' levels of participation in union activities, but did so in opposite directions for men and for women. They found that, while for women the presence of a partner and/or children lowered their level of participation in union activities, for the men the effect was the opposite; having a partner and children boosted their level of union participation

(Roby and Uttal 1988). To what extent, then, can men whose families support their union activities and women who are able to be activists because they do not have a dependent family be expected to understand, articulate, and prioritise issues of concern to women with part-time jobs and domestic commitments?

This chapter has explored just some aspects of the 'feminisation' of unions and some of the barriers to women's union activism. There are others: Ledwith *et al.* (1990), for example, demonstrate the importance of networks in bringing potential activists into the union hierarchy: those networks are of course gendered. Some of the organisational constraints are well recognised and are being tackled by the TUC and individual unions. USDAW has been particularly active in setting up a women's network. Many unions now routinely provide child care for meetings and have tried to ensure that the venue and timing is appropriate for women with children. British unions have far more reserved seats for women than unions in most other countries. Nevertheless, the patriarchal relations that exist within families and within the workplace are reflected in the unions themselves. As a consequence, pressure from unions on employers to improve women's employment conditions and prospects is likely to be muted.

Chapter 6

Demographic change and positive action measures

The late 1980s and early 1990s have been characterised by increasing concern among employers about the 'demographic time bomb', and a sudden awakening to the scope that women offer as a source of 'untapped potential'. 'Opportunity 2000', launched in 1991 by Business in the Community and the Equal Opportunities Commission, backed by the Prime Minister, John Major, is a rare initiative whereby employers have pledged themselves to promote women within their organisations by the end of the decade. Some made fairly modest commitments, others have been bolder in their specified targets and will need to implement positive action policies in order to get anywhere near them. But what is the nature of this demographic imperative which has been the catalyst spurring employers on to rediscover the talent in their midst? What are the positive action measures designed to harness women's untapped potential? How realistic is it to suppose that the decade will be marked by a significant decline in occupational segregation, and in particular, that more women will get to the top? This chapter explores these issues.

There is considerable confusion as to the nature of the demographic changes among employers. Surveys of employers have revealed that many are under the impression that the labour supply is set to diminish (National Economic Development Office/Training Agency – NEDO/TA 1989). In fact, its *rate of growth* is predicted to decline, but at a time when demand for labour is likely to increase, so that there will be a mismatch between labour supply and demand. The more significant change is that the nature of the labour force will change: the proportion of young people will decline and that of older workers increase. The real demographic challenge is that of contending with an *ageing* workforce (see Figure 6.1). This implies a need to make better use of existing employees, and recruit labour from new sources. It should mean that ascriptive characteristics such as race, age and gender will have less impact in recruitment and promotion processes. The ageing of the workforce clearly has significant implications for the amount and type of training and retraining required.

What are these predictions which have apparently caused such major

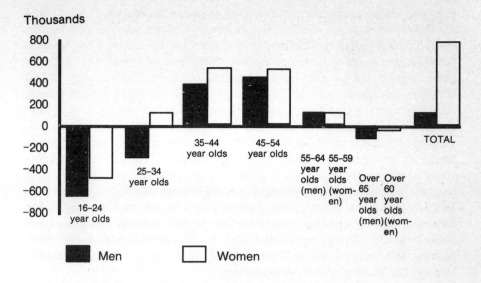

Figure 6.1 Projected change in the GB labour force, 1989–2001

Source: Department of Employment (1990) *Labour Market and Skill Trends 1991/92: Planning for a Changing Labour Market*, Sheffield: Employment Department Group

rethinks on human resource management? The last chapter introduced some of the features which have so far been identified. The Institute of Manpower Studies predict that there will be 1.7 million more jobs in the British economy in the 1990s, at a time when the increase in the labour force is set to grow by only half that number (Metcalf and Leighton 1989). The key element, and the one which has attracted most attention, is that by 1994 there will be 1 million fewer 16- to 19-year-olds entering the labour force than there were in 1984.

These demographic changes will be experienced to a greater or lesser extent throughout the countries comprising the EC, with the exception of Ireland, which will retain the expanding demographic profile of a developing country until the end of the century. Other industrialised nations such as the United States and Japan are also experiencing the effects of a decline in the birth-rate, but to a lesser degree than the EC (NEDO/TA 1989).

How will the labour shortfall be filled? There are a number of potential sources of new workers, including the unemployed, but employers appear to be looking most favourably on women, both existing employees and the economically inactive. Chapter 5 explored the training needs of women returners, who are universally seen as comprising the biggest pool of new labour. Of existing employees, men tend already to be working full-time,[1] and the EC's draft Directive on Working Time will limit the number of hours on shifts, so overtime is a limited solution. Moreover, in the United Kingdom, men already work far longer hours (41.8 per cent work more than forty-six hours) than the EC average (where 23.1 per cent work more than forty-six hours) (1988 figures, Eurostat 1990, cited in Marsh 1991:82). Far more women, of course, work part-time (44.0 per cent in the United Kingdom compared with an EC average of 28.0 per cent). Those women currently working part-time who would prefer full-time employment as their domestic circumstances change, or as employers facilitate their working full-time by addressing the issue of domestic commitments, represent one major source of under-utilised labour. The latent demand for full-time employment among part-timers was explored in the Women and Employment Survey. It was found to be strongest among women working eight hours or less per week (Dex 1988). Existing employees who are underemployed, but who with training could be moved up into higher, more skilled grades, are another source. Retaining women who would otherwise leave for child-bearing and -rearing, or at least ensuring their return, is an alternative strategy for dealing with labour shortages.

Measures are being introduced by some employers designed to both recruit and retain women. The key issue is whether these measures will alter patterns of occupational segregation. Will workplace nurseries, for example, merely help women to carry out the double load, while being restricted to low-paid, low-skilled and undervalued work? Will career-break schemes simply allow women back into the same low-level jobs with no promotion prospects? Or will employers introduce cultural and organisational changes which will enable women to move across into male-dominated manual and technical jobs, and up into professional and managerial positions?

The effect of the demographic imperative on occupational segregation will be tempered by three important factors. Firstly, the demographic predictions do not take account of the recession, which is causing redundancies rather than recruitment difficulties in 'tight' labour markets. The recession is experienced in sectorally and spatially specific ways. Enthusiasm for positive action measures may well be tempered by other concerns.

Secondly, there are predicted changes in the mix of occupations which will be needed. Specifically, there will be a growth in managerial and professional occupations, and a decrease in unskilled and semi-skilled operatives between 1989 and the end of the century (Institute for Employment Research 1990; NEDO/TA 1989) (see Figure 6.2). Employees will need to have both higher-level skills and greater flexibility (see Chapter 2). This clearly implies a need for training over and above that implied by the ageing of the workforce. Some sectors and some employers rely heavily on school or college-leavers for their labour supply; they will need to resort to male workers in their forties and fifties, and to older women, and to rethink their training requirements accordingly. Older workers, for example, are

Per cent

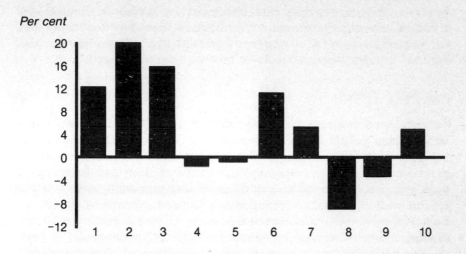

Key
1 Managers & administrators
2 Professional occupations
3 Associated Professional
4 Clerical & secretarial
5 Craft & Skilled manual

6 Personal & protective services
7 Sales occupations
8 Plant & machine operators
9 Other occupations
10 Whole economy

Figure 6.2 Occupational employment projections, change 1989–2000

Source: Department of Employment (1990) *Labour Market and Skill Trends 1991/92: Planning for a Changing Labour Market*, Sheffield: Employment Department Group
Original source: Institute for Employment Research (1990)

less likely to have the familiarity with new technology that school-leavers can now offer (see Chapter 7).

Thirdly, the removal of trade barriers and restrictions on the mobility of labour in the European Community in 1992 means that it is a company's use of human resources, and their skill levels, that will to a large extent determine whether it survives and prospers, or goes to the wall. The competitive edge between companies in the EC, the United States and Japan increasingly hinges on human resource management, as technological levels even out. In this context, using gender as a criterion for recruitment and access to training and promotion rather than ability, however subconsciously, does not make economic sense. For once, the interests of social justice and economic development appear to coincide.

This chapter explores the potential effects of the demographic imperative in shifting some of the fundamental aspects of work organisation that keep gender segregation patterns so rigid. What scope is offered for women to penetrate the better-rewarded male dominated industries and occupations? If a major constraint for women is their financial dependence upon men and the state, will employers' strategies to cope with demographic changes and increased competition mean more women earning living wages?

POSITIVE ACTION

Positive action measures are prompted by a recognition that women as a category face specific difficulties in paid work. These are often perceived as being the result of shortcomings of women themselves, or as a consequence of their having the major responsibility for children. The 'malestreamism' of work organisation and the issue of differential responsibility loads at home are rarely acknowledged or identified as a focus for concern by employers. Rather, positive action measures can, at worst, be seen as employers simply bending in times of stress to accommodate women's 'special needs'. At best, they can lead to changes in practices and value systems which accept the fact that women have patterns of participation which may differ from those of men, but do not reflect their innate level of ability. Again, at worst they merely assist women to bear the 'double load'.

Positive action measures should not be confused with affirmative action, which discriminates in favour of a group that is under-represented in the workforce proportionate to its numbers in the available pool of labour. Affirmative action measures in the United States and Australia have assisted women and members of ethnic minorities to move into the professions. In the United Kingdom, such affirmative action remains illegal. Positive action measures are essentially, then, specific actions which allow women (or any other group) to compete more effectively by tackling structural constraints which restrict them. Single-sex training simply seeks to give women an opportunity to reach the same starting position. It tends only to be available for women returners and in short management training courses, however. Separate training courses designated for ethnic minorities are even more rare (Cross and Edmonds 1983).

The positive action measures considered in this chapter are currently being discussed and introduced by employers in Britain primarily in response to the decline in school-leavers (the bottom of the cycle is in 1993) and the predicted labour shortage. They can be categorised under three headings: (1) strategies aimed to make the firm more *'family-friendly'* (Berry-Lound 1990a), by addressing the fact that women employees may well have domestic and, more specifically, child-care responsibilities which inhibit their availability for work relative to that of men; (2) strategies which address women's *training* needs; and lastly (3) *organisational change*, where employers examine their own recruitment, promotion and work-organisation culture and practices, and seek to introduce changes which would reduce the potency of gender as a determinant of occupational life chances.

Measures designed to accommodate women's domestic responsibilities have grown in the last few years, although not to the extent that the media coverage of them would lead the unwary to expect. While men can benefit from measures which entitle them to more paternity or parental responsibility leave, which provide child care, and offer flexible working, it is clearly women who benefit most, given the uneven domestic division of labour (Brannen and Moss 1991). The family-friendly policies discussed here fall into two broad groups: those which seek to *retain* women employees during the child-bearing years by providing direct or indirect assistance with child care, and those which aim to ensure that women employees who do take a career break, will *return*. Such measures have received support from the EC in the form of various Directives on Equal Treatment, and draft Directives on Parental Leave, Pregnancy and Maternity, and Child-care. The TUC has its own charter on child care, and the Equal Opportunities Commission has proposed a new National Childcare Development Agency be set up under a government department to co-ordinate child-care policy and initiatives (Equal Opportunities Commission 1990). The Government's response to the issue has been indirect, through tax concessions to employees taking up in-firm nursery places.

Positive action training measures geared towards the returner are not on the whole provided by employers: those offered in the voluntary and public sector were discussed in Chapter 4. Employers have largely focused on training to assist women to move from middle to senior management. There are also a few employer-provided training opportunities which recognise that many middle-aged women in particular may have missed out on educational opportunities at school-leaving age and are therefore underemployed: with training they can more easily realise their potential. Examples of both forms of positive action training are given in this chapter.

Organisational or cultural changes, to my mind, offer the most promising route to desegregation. These involve employers examining themselves in some depth to identify structures and practices which amount to systematic discrimination, and implementing changes. Examples of companies that have taken this approach are few on the ground, and it is too early to predict what the effect of these changes will be in the long term. Crucially, it will depend upon whether the company's diagnosis of structural or indeed attitudinal barriers is correct, and whether it is then prepared to act upon its diagnosis. As the excellent dissection of employers' recruitment strategies in Collinson *et al.* (1990) reveals, even employers who regard themselves as non-discriminatory and good 'equal opportunities' employers can be riddled with assumptions and practices which sustain gendering. Explanations offered by the employers for segregation were grounded in the ideology of the family and stereotyping. They tend to see the causes as being rooted in job applicants themselves, in society at large, in customers' preferences and in the prejudices of the existing workforce: the authors found employers had little insight into the effect of their *own* practices and underplayed their power to effect change.

Nevertheless, major companies, particularly those already experiencing 'staff wars' in the South-east of England, the recession notwithstanding, are already competing by offering a 'woman-friendly' packaging of personnel policies. A market is growing in consultancies and do-it-yourself books advising companies on how to become equal opportunity employers (see, for example, Beck and Steel 1989; Berry-Lound 1990b). Some employers have sought to be identified as such in order to recruit high-flying women who anticipate their chances of reaching the top to be greater in such a company. The Equal Opportunities Commission has set up an 'Equality Exchange' of employers who want to learn from one another. There are numerous accounts of firms which have introduced various measures by organisations such as the Hansard Society Commission for Women at the Top (1990), the National Economic Development Office (NEDO/TA 1989), the Institute of Manpower Studies (Rajan and van Eupen 1990) and the Industrial Society (Nevill *et al.* 1990).

This chapter draws upon research conducted by Anna Pollert and myself for the EC's Centre for the Development of Vocational Training (CEDEFOP), based in Berlin.[2] CEDEFOP was interested in identifying trends in positive action generally in each of the member states (for our account of the United Kingdom, see Rees, T. and Pollert 1989). CEDEFOP also commissioned us to document three case studies of employers which had introduced positive-action training for women in the United Kingdom. In this chapter I draw principally on just one of them, the Management Development Course for Women run by the Civil Service College (see Rees, T. 1990b). However, the employers in all three case studies (the Civil Service, British Telecom and Esso UK plc) are also engaged in other forms of positive action, and these are described at appropriate junctures here: I describe the British Telecom training initiative briefly. The positive-action strategies are located within a more general framework of employers' responses to labour-supply difficulties.

EMPLOYERS' RESPONSES TO THE DEMOGRAPHIC CHALLENGE

There are, according to the Institute of Manpower Studies (Metcalf 1989), four main employer responses to their understanding of the changing labour supply:

1 Do nothing.
2 Tighten up recruitment practices, through better liaison with schools, improving the image of the company as an employer, recruiting from further afield and improving pay levels.

3 Substitution – that is, changing the type of worker recruited, the main target being women returners.
4 Making better use of existing staff. This is achieved through looking at the job content, and using training and internal promotion of existing staff, rather than going outside to fill more senior posts.

Clearly these strategies are not mutually exclusive. Nevertheless, so far, the second strategy is proving by far to be the most popular: three-quarters of employers are focusing their efforts on competing more effectively for the diminishing pool of young people, according to NEDO (NEDO/TA 1989). Only one in three are seeking to tap into alternative labour sources, women returners being preferred to either unemployed ethnic minorities or white males. It is clearly the third and fourth strategies that will affect women the most, although improving pay, as is beginning to happen in the retail sector, may mean that some women currently at home could then afford to go out to work.

The strategies of the bigger employers are of course better documented than those of small to medium-size enterprises (see Chapter 2). Many of the smaller employers are unable to articulate a recruitment or training strategy as such (Fielder *et al.* 1991a; Rees, G. 1991); custom and practice determine recruitment patterns, and a need for training is not identified (see Rees, G. *et al.* 1990). It should be remembered that such employers dominate employment throughout Britain.

Spatial specificities

Different levels of spatially specific recruitment markets operate for different kinds of jobs. Whereas an employer might simply 'put out the word' that a vacancy exists for an unskilled or semi-skilled person, advertising in the national press or technical or professional journal is more likely to be used for technical or professional staff. Cutting across this is the condition of the local labour and housing markets. Hence, employers in the South East of England and other tight labour markets are not only more likely to be compelled to consider a range of strategies, but they do not have open to them the option of recruiting from further afield for anything but the top jobs, as people not already in the housing market will not be able to afford to enter, and local authority housing lists operate in such a way as to preclude outsiders from realistically expecting to get housed – especially given the sale of many council properties. Some employers located in labour markets where recruitment difficulties are increasing can avail themselves of labour in nearby areas. This is increasingly evident in South Wales, where employers along the M4 corridor can tap into the ex-mining-valley communities. Moreover, NEDO/TA (1989) have predicted significant variations in the impact of overall national labour-force trends in specific areas. For example, the fall in the number of 16- to 19-year-olds between 1988 and 1995 will vary from 17 per cent in East Anglia to 26 per cent in the North West of England.

The spatial factor also comes into play where recruitment and training policies are devised by a head office based in London, and informed by the acute difficulties faced there, but then are imposed on outlets in regions and localities where the pressure may not be nearly as great. The extent to which regional and even local personnel and training officers have jurisdiction over manpower planning in their area varies enormously, particularly in the private sector. Moreover, accounts of employers' strategies tend to be based on those large enough to employ people whose responsibility it is to devise corporate strategies for recruitment and training. The impact of the strategies at the local level will be highly variable. In essence, clearly, the tighter the labour market, the more likely that some strategy will be invoked, but the precise nature of the labour shortage experienced in terms of skills will have a bearing.

THE FAMILY-FRIENDLY FIRM

Domestic division of labour

Some 15 per cent of British families are now headed by a lone mother (OPCS 1988), but women retain a disproportionate responsibility for domestic work and child care, even when there are two partners and both are in work (Brannen and Moss 1991; Morris 1990; Pahl 1984; Witherspoon 1988). The group which is particularly heavily burdened comprises those women with part-time jobs, who tend to have young children and are either single parents (Dex 1988) or receive very little assistance from their partners (Gershuny *et al.* 1986). As Morris (1990:90) reports, men have increased their participation in domestic work, but not in amounts sufficient to offset women's increased work in the labour market. This extraordinarily robust pattern of division of labour is the cornerstone of feminist interpretations of the relative impact of patriarchy and capital on women's labour market position (see Chapter 2).

There have been a variety of employer manpower strategies which address the fact that women bear the major responsibility for child-care, from workplace nurseries and subsidising child-care costs to career-break schemes. There have, however, been no employer-led moves to facilitate or encourage men to take greater responsibility for children, except for a few cases where paternity or parental leave has been introduced or extended. British employers' tendency to demand longer working hours from male full-time employees than their fellow-European counterparts militates against an evening up of the domestic load (Eurostat 1990).

The relationship between the domestic division of labour, the life cycle and women's economic activity (which is spelled out in some detail in Chapter 2) is complex. A particular feature of the United Kingdom is the high number of women working part-time, which is a function both of the uneven domestic load and the absence of state-provided child care. The level of state provision for pre-school child care in the United Kingdom is among the lowest in Europe: only about 1 per cent of under-5s are accommodated in local authority nurseries (Cohen 1990). The economic activity rate for women with pre-school-age children in Britain is much lower than in other European countries: 30 per cent compared with 50 per cent in France and 80 per cent in Sweden (Cohen 1990). Dex and Shaw (1986) point to the relationship between child-care provision and the pattern of economic activity over the life course in the United States and Britain: the latter stands out as exceptional in low provision, low rate of continuous activity and high rate of part-time work. In France, although the female economic activity rate and the proportion of the workforce which comprises women are similar to those of the United Kingdom, the rate of part-time working is much lower: the provision of paid maternity leave is a partial explanation for this (see Crompton and Sanderson 1990:173–4). Denmark has the only other radically high level of part-time employment among women in Europe (Eurostat 1990), undoubtedly related to the length of the school day, which ends at lunch-time (Cohen 1990).

If women's wages were not seen as a second income, when for a growing group of lone parents they are often the only income source, then child-care subsidies, be they direct or indirect, would not be necessary; the free market would provide adequate child care. As Metcalf and Leighton (1989:5) claim:

> Raising net income from working by 45p per hour would raise participation by between 48,700 and 58,400. If done through a childcare allowance, the Exchequer cost would be between £43 and £79 per new participant per week. Better enforcement of maintenance payments would also increase the participation of lone mothers.

'Family-friendly' strategies in the United Kingdom have tended to focus upon looking after the children, making it possible for women to work by subsidising child-care costs, and by arranging terms and conditions more flexibly. The growing issue of care of elderly dependants has not received much attention here, although it is addressed indirectly through policies such as flexible working and home-working. In the United States, the American Telephones and Telegraph Company of New York has included in staff contracts an arrangement for six months' leave to care either for a new baby or for sick parents. Such 'Eldercare' policies are growing in popularity there (Berry-Lound 1990a). The positive action measures prevalent in the United Kingdom are now discussed in turn.

1 Workplace nurseries

Employers' strategies for child care have tended to focus on workplace nurseries, but they are not necessarily the most appropriate solution. In the first instance, they only address the needs of parents with pre-school children. They do not help women with older children after school, during school holidays and at half term, occasions when children of any age are ill or when scrunched up notes found in their pockets reveal that 'school is closed tomorrow for a training day'. The capital cost of setting up a workplace nursery is considerable even if there is a suitable site. The most successful nursery buildings tend to be purpose-built ones on the ground floor, which incorporate space outside and give good access. It is not very often that an existing employer builds new premises, however, or has land available nearby. Demand for places is inevitably going to fluctuate from year to year: individual children do not stay in the pre-school phase for long. Consortia of employers may share the cost of a nursery, and 'buy' as many places as they need on an annual basis, renting out any surplus places on the open market. Even where such facilities do exist, though, they do not necessarily appeal to all parents with pre-school children. Some dislike the idea of a long daily journey for the child. Others feel that very young children at least need more individual attention, and prefer a child-minder or relative. Some are all too aware of the likelihood of their children catching more coughs and colds through exposure to other children. The language of the nursery can also be an issue, particularly in Wales, and among ethnic minorities.

In practice, women in work already use a wide variety of arrangements for child care, the complexity of which is a testament to their organisational skills. Workplace nurseries will suit some but by no means all. Nevertheless, it should be said that where they do exist and are used, they improve absenteeism, time-keeping and retention rates, and are reported in one case study to improve employee motivation, make employees feel encouraged to apply for promotion and to reduce stress (Truman 1986:18).

Capital costs incurred are high, but running costs are also expensive, which is why a shared nursery is an increasingly popular idea. The IMS has calculated that the average cost per place is £100 per week (Metcalf and Leighton 1989). Employers contemplating workplace nurseries are greatly assisted by the exemption from income tax on the benefit introduced by the Government in 1990 for employees. This allows employer subsidy per place at a rate which means that women should be able to afford them on their wages. A parent earning £12,500 a year and receiving a £2,500 nursery subsidy from the employer will typically benefit by £625 a year, the *Financial Times* has calculated (*FT*, 21 March 1990). British Petroleum was the first big employer to announce plans for workplace nurseries following the March 1990 Budget; the chairman, Mr Robert Horton, commenting that 'We have had a quite appalling drop-out rate for 28 to 29 year old senior professional women' (quoted in *FT*, 21 March 1990).

To put this in context, a survey of 2,000 employers revealed that only 2 per cent had workplace nurseries so far (Blue Arrow Personnel Services 1989). However, there has been a rapid increase in interest, and the number is likely to grow substantially. It has been estimated that there are at present around 100 workplace nurseries in the United Kingdom, 80 per cent of which are in the public sector, mostly in local authorities (Income Data Services 1989). Some Civil Service departments are now experimenting with them to discover whether they are a cost-effective way of retaining and recruiting staff. The first opened in the Department of Social Security in Hertford in March 1990, and six more are planned to follow. Feasibility studies are under way for a further twenty-four, which will look at the scope for both setting up nurseries and extending play schemes. Most of these are in the London area. In the private sector, the Midland Bank opened the first of a planned 300 workplace nurseries amidst much fanfare. There are a growing number of examples of nurseries set up through partnership between the private and public sector (see Association of London Authorities 1989).

2 Subsidising child-care costs

Given the limitations of workplace nurseries in meeting child-care needs, subsidising child-care costs is a promising alternative. Subsidies allow the flexibility of arrangements both across employees, and over the life cycle of existing employees. A variety of versions have been introduced. The company Luncheon Vouchers introduced Childcare Vouchers, redeemable at nurseries and registered child-minders – such a scheme was pioneered in the United States. Another company, Mercer Fraser, has started a similar scheme with the National Childminding Association. Some employers prefer direct child-care subsidies: an increasing number of local authorities are paying allowances that amount to about a third of the child-care costs of their staff (see Income Data Services 1989). However, it looks as if tax-exemption measures on workplace nurseries will not be extended to parents whose employers offer them cash vouchers which can be exchanged for child care with child-minders. It is as yet unclear whether they cover parents whose employers use contractors to operate nurseries, although it is known that places bought in other companies' nurseries will be excluded.

3 Holiday play schemes

The Civil Service has been the prime mover in the United Kingdom in organising holiday play schemes for the children of its employees. Some date back to the 1970s, but it was the 1984 *Programme of Action* (Cabinet Office 1984) on equality of opportunities for women that identified lack of child-care facilities for women as a major barrier to their employment and promotion, and most schemes have been introduced in more recent years. The *Programme of Action* recommended the sympathetic consideration of day-care schemes, in particular holiday schemes, and suggested exploring the possibility of shared schemes with other local employers. Departments help by putting money up front, securing accommodation, meeting costs of equipment and furniture, advising on the appointment of staff and allowing staff to use work time to organise the setting up. Once established, a holiday play scheme covers its own costs, as parents pay for the places. Daily costs range from about £1.50 to £5 per child. In some departments a sliding scale of charges is implemented according to the salary and family circumstances of the parent. So far, about twenty departments have introduced holiday play schemes.

4 Career-break schemes

Career-break schemes were first introduced in the finance sector by the four main clearing banks in the early 1980s in order to retain experienced staff. The take-up has always been low, however: in Barclays Bank, only ninety women and one man took advantage of the scheme during the first eight years or so of its operation, while in the Midland Bank, the figures were seventy-nine women and one man. Part of the reason for the relatively low response at the Midland and Clydesdale Bank is because eligibility is restricted to managerial staff. In the face of staff shortages, eligibility criteria are on the whole being widened. The Banking Insurance and Finance Union (BIFU) wants such schemes to be available to all staff who have two years' service, with a break of at least five years which can be taken in three periods, individuals having the right to return to the same or an equivalent job. BIFU also wants there to be an option to return to part-time work, the break period to count towards pensionable service, and for the employee to be eligible for all benefits upon return (IRS 1991).

The key element of career-break schemes is that employees should be allowed to return to the same grade as that on which they left, with updated annual salary rises. In the Civil Service in particular, historically women's talents were being wasted because they in effect lost any seniority they had earned prior to a career break. While such schemes demand a certain amount of flexibility on the part of the employers to find an appropriate post on the employee's return, in larger organisations, such as the Civil Service and banks, this should not pose too much of a problem. The Civil Service now operates a 'Keeping in Touch' scheme which enables staff on career breaks to maintain contact with their employer and which facilitates their eventual return to work. The aim is to ensure that 'women can regain their career momentum following a career break, and enable employers to retain the services of skilled and experienced members of staff' (Cabinet Office/OMCS 1989:9). Formal 'Keeping in Touch' schemes have been introduced in thirteen government departments, and a further nine are in the process of setting them up. These departments between them employ over 90 per cent of all staff in the Civil Service. The majority of the participants are in middle management grades where resignation rates, particularly among women leaving to bear and raise children, are the highest. Eight hundred members of staff have participated in the 'Keeping in Touch' scheme so far, and ninety-six have already returned to their departments (Cabinet Office/OMCS 1989).

In 1987, the Civil Service introduced a 'Special Leave' arrangement to provide for short periods of paid leave or longer periods of unpaid leave. This might be to care for children, or to accompany a spouse abroad or on a training course. Employment rights are assured and seniority is accrued during the period. The key difference between 'Special Leave' and 'Keeping in Touch' is that the employee is not required to resign upon taking leave, and is therefore more likely to return.

Other public-sector schemes operate in local authorities, most notably in the teaching profession. In the private sector, some employers such as GEC Marconi and Boots the Chemist, although not guaranteeing a job upon return, do undertake to try to offer an appropriate one.

An IDS (1989) study of eight employers' use of career-break schemes found that other employers were contacting them and showing great interest in the schemes. They were cheap, and there appeared to be no great difficulties in operating them. Despite this, a survey of 2,000 employers found that only one in ten companies offer extended leave or career-break schemes, and only a further 9 per cent are considering them (Blue Arrow Personnel Services 1989). Nevertheless, the right to return to work was the second most frequently cited factor that was most likely to persuade women to re-enter the workforce, according to a survey of 243 women who wanted to return to work after having had a baby (Maternity Alliance 1989).

5 Home-based working

Home-based working is being offered by an increasing number of employers. It enables employees both to work and to accommodate their domestic responsibilities, and means that the employer can reduce over-heads by not having to provide premises. Home-working has traditionally been a largely invisible contribution to the economy in official statistics (see Chapter 2), which a number of recent studies have sought to correct (for example, Allen and Wolkowitz 1987; Hakim 1988; Pennington and Westover 1989). Despite the difficulty in calculating numbers, Labour Research (1991b) estimated that there were 300,000 homeworkers in 1985,

70 per cent of whom were women and 74 per cent of whom worked in traditional manufacturing industries.

There is now a growing trend for white-collar home-working, facilitated by new technology. 'Teleworking', for example, enables the link-up between a home-based computer terminal and central system at head office. Home-working is usually associated with highly exploitative work and dis-advantageous terms and conditions – low hourly rates, no holiday or sick pay, low wages, piece-rate payment systems which do not take account of the time needed to set up equipment. Civil Service unions and BIFU are concerned that white-collar home-based workers will create two tiers of employee.

The FI Group was one of the first employers to introduce professional, hi-tech work into the home; but in response to demand from its workforce, it has now introduced neighbourhood work centres to counteract the profes-sional and social isolation of teleworking (Labour Research 1991b; NEDO/TA 1989). Hampshire County Council has employees teleworking from home, and major companies such as ICI use home-based working to retain and recruit highly motivated and skilled women employees. It remains to be seen whether their employees will also find isolation a problem.

The design of houses, particularly in the South East of England, will increasingly need to accommodate office space for home-based workers.

6 Flexible hours and terms and conditions of employment

The UK labour force is characterised by men working long hours and a substantial proportion of women doing part-time work. Many employers now want to extend their hours of operation, both in manufacturing and in the service sector (Horrell and Rubery 1991). Changes in retail, for example, from corner shop and high-street supermarkets to out-of-town hypermarkets mean that shop workers are now needed to work through the night stocking shelves for the morning, and increasingly are required to work on Sundays too. How will these trends combine with the changes in the labour supply, and how will employers react to them?

The 1989 HOST survey found that the use of more part-time workers was the most popular of new working systems being introduced by employers who took part in their survey of 2,000 employers (NEDO/TA 1989). However, the kinds of jobs that it is possible to do part-time are currently restricted. One of the anticipated effects of the 'demographic time bomb' is that managerial and professional jobs may increasingly be available on this basis. Job sharing (where responsibilities are shared) and job splitting (where the duties of a post are divided up) are more likely to be entertained. This would have a significant impact on the underemployment of women, both attracting back those who only want to work part-time, and ensuring that women are more likely to be able to secure jobs commensurate with their skills.

However, only 7 per cent of companies in one survey were introducing job-share initiatives (Blue Arrow Personnel Services 1989). The Civil Service has expanded opportunities for part-time working at more senior levels, but so far this has been largely in response to specific requests from individual employees. Departments are now being encouraged to anticipate demand and consider the scope for part-time working and job sharing, and to bring opportunities to the attention of all staff (Cabinet Office/Office for the Minister of the Civil Service 1988). Job sharing has increased, and there are two women job splitting at Grade 5 level in Customs and Excise in what has been described as a successful experiment. The participants found that job splitting, rather than job sharing, was more effective at that grade. Some fifty-six local authorities have set up job-share schemes covering 2,000 employees (Income Data Services 1989). In the retail sector, Boots have introduced job sharing at supervisory level.

In the Blue Arrow study, flexible working hours were found to operate in a quarter of the employers surveyed, but a third of these only make such schemes available to a small number of employees (Blue Arrow Personnel Services 1989). A further 1 per cent were planning forms of flexibility, such as term-time only contracts, which Boots the Chemist, Dixons (the electrical goods retailer) and Thistle Hotels have already introduced. While many of these initiatives were introduced initially in response to recruitment or retention difficulties experienced in branches in the South East, they have become part of a nationwide policy for those companies. The extent to which the policy is implemented in different localities, however, will be influenced by local labour-market conditions.

TRAINING STRATEGIES

Training is a major component of strategies designed to retain and develop existing workforces. NEDO (1988) advocate training as a means of increasing job satisfaction, motivation and retention rates, and as a tactic for avoiding the expensive and costly task of recruiting. Traditionally, many employers have regarded training as the function of the public sector and prefer to recruit (or poach) ready-trained staff from elsewhere. Changing technological needs, however, are increasingly putting training on the agenda.

There are a growing number of employer initiatives geared towards improving women's skills (see Clarke 1991). Business in the Community are currently documenting particularly innovative ones. Some are aimed at school-leavers, particularly in science and engineering, where in response to the demographic changes employers want to widen the potential source of apprentices or graduates, and so are targeting young women in their sponsorship. Others are examining the existing workforce, and identifying people who would benefit from training and could then be promoted. There are a few examples of training initiatives introduced by employers which have the potential to alter employees' occupational life chances in a radical way.

The first category comprises employers such as the Post Office and Marks and Spencer, who have focused on training women in middle management to groom them for senior management. The Hansard Society Commission on Women at the Top (1990) has documented how in business and in all the professions studied, women were found in diminishing numbers towards the top of the hierarchy. Skinner (1988:157–8) maintains that:

> The proportion of management posts occupied by women has remained remarkably constant over the past sixty years at 18 to 20 per cent of all such posts. Also fairly constant is the percentage of top level posts – at 2 per cent.

She points out that in Hunt's (1975) study, 50 per cent of all work establishments surveyed employed no women at all in managerial or supervisory posts, and her own unpublished research indicates that the proportion of women managers in traditionally female areas such as teaching is declining (Skinner 1988:158).

The Civil Service course (featured as a case study here) was pioneered over a decade ago, and had its roots in a concern with the use of human resources rather than a specific recruitment problem. It is used nevertheless as an example because it has been the subject of monitoring and evaluation, and is similar to the many other courses that are now developing, particularly in the private sector, in response to management shortages. In the United States, such courses have been identified with the need to smash the 'glass ceiling' (Morrison 1987), which women cannot see but can feel impeding their promotion to the top. The Midland Bank has a programme aimed at developing management potential among women and ethnic minorities by offering scholarships on a business diploma course.

The second category is aimed at female manual workers, with a view to training them for skilled work normally undertaken by men. Austin Rover are offering women non-traditional manual skills training. British Telecom's (BT) scheme (the second case study considered), targets women telephone operators for a training scheme designed to transform them into engineers (see Pollert 1990 for a detailed account). Both categories are illustrative of how training potentially can contribute to the breakdown of gender segregation.

Table 6.1 Women in the Civil Service by grades, April 1990*

Grade level	Numbers	% Women
1–4	1,026	5
5	2,800	11
6	5,200	10
7	16,200	12
Senior Executive Officer	23,900	10
Higher Executive Officer	73,100	18
Executive Officer	121,000	40
Administrative Officer	154,400	66
Administrative Assistant	91,600	73

*Full-time equivalents, non-industrial, Home Civil Service. Broadly equivalent grades in the Open Structure/ Administration Group based on a comparison of salary scales.
Source: Government Statistical Service (1990) Key Figures on Civil Service Staffing: 1989–90 Edition, London: HM Treasury

The Civil Service College's Management Development Course for Women

The Civil Service opened its doors to women in 1920, but on discriminatory terms (Walters 1987): married women were ineligible until 1946 (those who married in service were required to leave) and equal pay for the same work was not granted until 1955. According to Fogarty et al. (1981:50): 'the Civil Service made a discernible move towards establishing equality of treatment in promotion between men and women administrators with recruits who came in from the beginning of the 1950s'. Since then, and in particular since the introduction of measures following the Equal opportunities for women in the Civil Service: programme of action (Cabinet Office 1984) in 1984, women have certainly fared better, if not equally. They now constitute just under 50 per cent of the half million civil servants. While they are to be found in all departments, they are in diminishing numbers towards the top of the management hierarchy (see Table 6.1).

The Civil Service Training College at Sunningdale in Berkshire launched what is probably the longest running management training course for women prior to the Programme of Action, at the instigation of an individual member of the College, with considerable support from the trade unions. The demand for the course has ensured that it has not only survived, but expanded. It supplements rather than substitutes for other management courses run by the College (trainees sometimes 'progress' from one to the other), and its purpose is to assist women in middle management to prepare for senior posts. The course consists of a residential week during which trainees receive assertiveness training, learn about management techniques and develop their own Action Plans: this is followed up by two days' review some three months later.

The course has been extremely popular: indeed, about eight such courses are now run each year with twenty-four women on each course. Moreover, some departments now run their own versions of the course. There has been a slow improvement in the proportion of women in the more senior grades, but quite what role the course has had in this is a matter for conjecture. It is evident, however, that the women themselves feel that they benefit from the course (Rees, T. 1990b; Williams 1983), that they develop networks which are maintained for years afterwards (sometimes through weekends spent at hotels), and that the main source of recruits for the course is through 'word of mouth'.

There is clearly a limit to the effect such a course could be expected to have in breaking the 'glass ceiling'. Many of its benefits are seen by tutors and trainees alike to be in personal as much as professional terms: assertiveness, a sense of direction and people-handling skills were identified as the main benefits, and these are clearly useful in both arenas. Nevertheless, Williams (1983:13) found that five of the sixty in his study had been promoted within a year of completing the course, one describing her experience thus:

> I got promoted after the course. I think this would have happened anyway, but the course made me more determined. . . . Personnel asked me what kind of job I would like. Because of the course I was able to make sensible answers. I knew what I could offer and what I wanted.

The integrated approach towards positive action now operating within the Civil Service is one which is clearly beneficial and more effective than single strategies (see Berry-Lound 1990a). Fogarty et al. (1981:280–1) concluded in their study of 1979 that there had been no change from their earlier examination of the Civil Service in 1968: they had then concluded that there are

> understandings, attitudes and mores which are part of the texture of the informal organisation of higher administration and which operate to steer women more than men away from the scenes of important action and hence lessen the likelihood of their being seen as candidates for top posts.

It would be interesting to know whether Fogarty et al. would detect any significant changes in the 1990s, now that the ideological climate towards equal opportunities in the Civil Service is more favourable (Corby 1983) and there is more of a conscious effort to implement change. Does the Civil Service remain an institution geared 'to people who will work continuously from recruitment to retirement' (Brimelow 1981:319)? Is the high premium put on seniority still advantaging only men and those women who, in terms of family responsibilities 'travel light' (Fogarty et al.. 1981:10)? Will more women ultimately reach senior grades? By increasing women's confidence, assertiveness and skills, encouraging them to develop career plans and facilitating the development of networks, the course has benefited the growing numbers of women who have attended it; it remains to be seen whether this will change the face of the Civil Service.

Training women: British Telecom's bridging course

BT employs 232,000 people (1990 figures, Pollert 1990), just under a third of whom are women. It is a highly segregated workforce, women predominating in the telephone operator and clerical grades. BT was faced with difficulties in recruiting engineers in the South East of England, partly as a result of the problems faced by people recruited from outside the area in penetrating the housing market. BT decided to utilise its existing staff, who already lived in the area, to better advantage, in particular women who were of the age that meant that they were likely to have missed out on educational opportunities the first time round because of a combination of their gender and class. Further motivations were provided by the fact that BT had a commitment to developing an equal opportunities profile, and the decline in need for operators and clerical officers because of new technology.

BT arranged for a local college to provide an annual access course (or 'bridging course') for about twenty telephonists and clerical officers to prepare them to go on to a three-year engineering degree course. The first course ran in 1987, and therefore the first cohort graduated from their degree courses in 1991. This initiative, while small-scale, piecemeal and wholly linked in to the necessity created by skills shortages, nevertheless clearly has the merit of potentially transforming unqualified working class women's occupational life chances.

ORGANISATIONAL CHANGE

Why do so few women break through the 'glass ceiling'? There have been numerous sets of explanations offered, which the Hansard Society Commission on Women at the Top (1990:24) summarises as follows:

unnecessary age bars and excessive mobility requirements;

informal selection procedures which tend to be inconsistent, secretive and not open to accountability;

stereotyped assumptions among selectors about the women's career availability and intentions;

unspecified selection criteria which change with the candidate;

the use of word of mouth or old-boy networks to find potential candidates, to the exclusion of women;

prejudice by selectors about what is 'right' for women, in particular that women are suited to their traditional roles as wives and mothers.

Moreover, there is evidence from Collinson *et al.* (1990) and Coyle and Skinner (1988), among others, of these shifting criteria, sets of assumptions, manipulative practices and old-boy networks being in operation in a wide range of fields. They and their contributers document the 'malestreamism' of work organisation. Coyle (1988) reveals how the organisation of work in television, for example, effectively institutionalises male power. Case studies of local government, television, banking, teaching and higher education are presented which illustrate all too clearly the ways in which women are measured up against male standards (rather reminiscent of the 'black personality' deficiency theories of the 1960s) and are inevitably found wanting. The imagery of the discourse of management is imbued with masculinity. It is interesting to note how management training courses specifically designed for women tend to include topics such as assertiveness training, which could be construed as training women to cope with a male environment.

To what extent can employers both identify such barriers to women's advancement within their own organisations and deploy the will and the support to introduce change? There are examples of employers evaluating company practice in recruitment and work-organisation strategies. They are essentially rooted in human-resource management ideas, rather than necessarily born out of a concern with equal opportunities.

Recruitment strategies which allow for little or no internal movement from one tier to another curtail women's progress within an organisation to a greater extent than that of men because they tend to be in the bottom grades. Reorganising work to remove the ceilings which separate the tiers of employees can, potentially at least, help to reduce gender segregation, although employers control who moves up the organisation. Allowing only posts of certain grades to be undertaken on a part-time basis again prohibits many women from using their skills – Barclays is the only bank which allows managers to work on a part-time basis. 'Hands up promotion' strategies, which depend upon employees' own self-evaluation to produce candidates, rather than staff appraisal and encouragement by senior staff, automatically limit the number of women who put themselves forward because of what has been described as the 'Cinderella complex' (Dowling 1982). The specific barrier to women imposed by criteria such as a willingness to move to take up promotion was widespread in the banking sector until relatively recently; some banks now ensure that moving to another branch for promotion does not necessarily mean having to move house. It is still a major problem in other sectors however, and Crompton *et al.* (1982) identified geographical mobility as one of the main impediments to women's progress.

Seniority and unbroken service requirements constitute further barriers. Ashburner (1988) reports that fifteen to twenty years' unbroken service was required before entry to management in banking: this clearly disqualifies women who had a career break and discourages women from considering advancement. Age bars are clearly discriminatory, given the career break.

Application forms which do not ask for the gender, marital status or number of children of candidates can help to reduce the subconscious impact of gender stereotyping on selection boards (just as marking examination scripts by numbers rather than names may remove the effects of sexist and race assumptions), although it is difficult to obscure a candidate's gender from application forms entirely.

Some companies have examined their practices in an attempt to identify sources of indirect discrimination and introduced monitoring in order to understand the pattern of gender segregation within their own organisation. Some have introduced training in equal opportunities policies for recruiters, managers or (in the case of Esso UK and London Weekend Television Ltd) all section heads. Some have hired outside consultants, or held brain-storm sessions. Others, such as Brown and Root (UK) Ltd, have introduced positive action in recruitment. Littlewoods has now changed its selection and recruitment policies. Both Littlewoods and British Rail now set targets for the promotion of women. GEC Marconi targets sixth-form girls in its recruitment strategy.

Esso UK has been discussing five-year career planning for all staff; the Bank of England and Unilever have introduced career planning for potential managers. Cardiff City Council has career planning available to female staff. Mars Confectionery has introduced advertising designed to attract senior women.

Role-models, mentoring and networks are clearly vital in the selection and promotion of senior staff, and these tend to be gendered. Many networks are exclusively male: the Oxbridge colleges which traditionally at least have had such a hold on the senior management of the Civil Service have of course been a breeding ground for such male networks. While some organisations such as freemasonry directly excluded women, others such as the golf clubs and Rugby clubs, may partially exclude them[3]. Places ostensibly open to members of the public, such as bars, remain problematic for women. Not least of the difficulties is the issue of access to time; securing freedom from domestic commitments can be difficult in order to take part in 'leisure activities', such as a drink with colleagues after work, where decisions may actually be being taken. Moreover, psychological literature has illustrated how people feel comfortable with their own kind: men can feel they are on safe ground opening conversations about sport, for example, with other men. Women have to devise strategies to avoid being labelled in stereotypes when mingling with men in traditionally male work (Breakwell 1985).

Most of the measures have been introduced too recently for it to be clear whether they will have any effect on women's opportunities and, ultimately, patterns of gender segregation. It might well be the year 2001 before it would be reasonable to expect to see any effects. It will certainly take several decades for the message to filter back to girls taking their option choices in schools that industries and occupations currently identified as male preserves might be worth contemplating.

CONCLUSION: POSITIVE ACTION OR HUMAN RESOURCE STRATEGIES?

A key question for all positive action measures rooted in the exigencies of a labour crisis is, how long-lasting will they be? Will they fade away, like war-time nurseries, once the demographic upturn is reached towards the end of the century, or will the changes be so dramatic that the British labour force will no longer be so rigidly segregated on gender lines? Will more women in the hierarchy mean that mentoring and networking will have a trickle-down (or -up) effect, despite the inevitable vulnerability of measures introduced in the context of labour shortage? Retention measures and child-care provision seem unlikely to survive another recession, let alone an increase in labour supply. While organisational change will arguably have the longest-lasting effects, the scarcity and newness of examples (not to mention the marketing hype that surrounds or, in effect, constitutes some employers' 'positive action'), mean that it is too early to judge the effects.

While positive action measures may have some impact upon women's access to the labour market, and male-dominated areas within it, those policies that are adopted by employers in response to changing skill needs and the necessity of making better use of human resources more generally may in the long term have more impact upon gender segregation than some of the measures outlined here.

Training measures, for example, that are not specifically directed towards women, but are intended to improve the skills of the workforce more generally, may prove to be of greater significance. Women are more likely to be among the unskilled and semi-skilled and therefore will benefit disproportionately. Moreover, such general upgrading of skills is tied in with corporate strategies to utilise human resources more effectively. This can mean that jobs which historically carried little or no training, and no route into more advanced work, may now be a rung on a ladder. The most dramatic changes in this direction are to be found in the retail sector and in the catering industry, although they are by no means universal.

In retailing, the major supermarkets are attempting to improve customer-care relations and 'total quality management' (TQM). Competition for customers is becoming fierce, so strategies for improving customer loyalty and market share increasingly include training staff in customer relations. At one level this can be seen in check-out staff smiling at rather surprised and harassed customers, and engaging them in conversation; this can be described as a curious attempt to reconstruct the atmosphere of the corner shop in a multi-million pound retail concern. At a more material level, however, stores wish to motivate staff and to encourage them to think of having a career, rather than a 'job' with the company. This is to be achieved partly by offering training and opportunities for advancement. In an industry where training has not been on the agenda for staff, this clearly involves a major re-socialisation. Interviews we have conducted with training and personnel staff in one food retailer[4] revealed a certain antipathy among employees to coming off the shop floor and up to the 'training room' when, as far as they were concerned, they could do their jobs perfectly adequately and were therefore wasting their own and the company's time (Fielder *et al.* 1991a:24). Company uniforms, logos on ties, brooches and so on are utilised to encourage an awareness of the corporate identity and develop loyalty to it. In part at least, these strategies are clearly inspired by the projected shortage of the traditional source of retail workers, school-leavers (and schoolchildren in Saturday jobs before that). But women returners, another source of labour, may well benefit too. There is now a clear route from check-out and shelf-filling to section and department supervising and possibly even into management, in theory at least. There are certainly opportunities to learn specific trades such as butchery and baking. These changes in work organisation may well have some effect on women's prospects by reducing the number of jobs with no training or opportunities for advancement.

Catering is increasingly being contracted out to large concerns where again there is a new emphasis on training as a labour retention strategy (Fielder *et al.* 1991b; Rees, G. and Fielder 1992). One such multi-national business is now seeking to grow its own managerial talent, rather than having to recruit from outside, and divisional and regional managers are responsible for training programmes and career planning systems.

While both retail and catering concerns have developed training as a corporate strategy in the face of South-east-informed experiences, they clearly may well improve prospects for women and men in loose labour markets, if regional and local training and personnel staff carry them through.

Another major area where corporate training and human resource strategies may, as a side-effect, benefit women disproportionately is in the area of training for new information technologies, the subject of the next chapter.

Chapter 7

The new information technologies and desegregation

There have been major changes in the labour market and indeed in daily life over the last decade, as a result of the all-pervasive escalation of the production and use of new technologies. These have metamorphosed the level and kinds of skills required in the workforce, the demand for training and retraining and patterns of work organisation. They have opened up opportunities for working from home and for flexible shifts. They have the potential to change the very nature of jobs that have remained static for decades. Brawn is not the prerequisite for some newly emerging occupations in the way that it was for some of the old ones. Rather, new 'social skills' are required, such as the ability to communicate and take responsibility: these skills are frequently associated with women. Sets of expectations about the appropriate gender for new or evolving jobs should arguably be less entrenched than those for more traditional ones. Moreover, much of the growth in the use of new information technologies has taken place predominantly in the service sector, where women overwhelmingly work. What impact are the growth of and training for new technologies likely to have on gender segregation?

Training is likely to become an increasingly important part of industrial strategies in the 1990s. Employers are already reporting, especially in manufacturing, that a major response to demographic trends is simply to make better use of existing staff (National Economic Development Office/ Training Agency 1989; and see Chapter 6): this clearly implies more training. However, new technologies have their own training imperative. One clear impact of their growth is that there will be an overall reduction in the number of unskilled and semi-skilled jobs. Moreover, identifiable skills shortages are already emerging both in high-level IT skills, but also among business analysts and other professional workers who can use new technologies. Indeed, they have been identified as a main constraint upon the take-up of new technologies in the manufacturing sector (Christie *et al.* 1990). Not only is it vital to address these skill shortages, but it is also self-evident that training allows new technologies to be used to the best advantage. Considerable expenditure is invested by employers in hardware and software to maintain a competitive edge; appropriate training costs are relatively modest.

Changing technologies clearly have implications too for the labour process and for patterns of work organisation. Within this century, there have ostensibly been several major transformations, from Taylorism, to Fordism and Post-Fordism (see Chapter 2). Changes in patterns of work organisation are uneven and explanations for them highly contested. Universalistic theories such as those of Post-Fordism and disorganised capitalism have been found wanting in explaining emerging differences in response to technological change – for example, in contrasted countries. On the other hand, studies of national societal effects propounded by the Aix-en-Provence school (Maurice *et al.* 1986) have been criticised for ignoring both international effects such as globalisation, and regional differences (Thomas and Rees 1991). Both criticisms argue for more specificity in comparative studies of work organisation. The implication is that greater stress should be placed upon the relationship between training systems and training cultures and employers' patterns of recruitment, training and work organisation in order to understand both national and regional differences, and the patterns of gender segregation to which they give rise.

In this chapter, I draw upon three studies in order to explore in a preliminary way some of these relationships, by contrasting strategies of some of the more advanced companies in the forefront of technological development in the old Federal Republic of Germany (FRG), with those of much smaller employers in the United Kingdom, for the most part in South Wales. The FRG has a highly centralised training system, frequently described as arguably one of the best in the world. In England and Wales, responsibility for training now lies with locally based employer-led TECs and in Scotland, LECs. Some of the differences in training systems clearly impact upon local patterns of recruitment, training and work organisation, and the social relations which underpin them.

However, underlying any examination of gender segregation in new technologies is the issue of 'ownership' of technology, the 'masculinisation' of machinery. To what extent is it likely that new jobs, without the baggage of sex-typing, will be colonised by one gender or the other, according to the skill level? Wajcman (1991) has demonstrated how new technologies can reinforce existing inequalities, that their design is informed by class, gender and race relations. Cockburn, similarly, has argued that class and gender relations are merely re-asserted when new technologies are introduced:

> On the one hand capital applies new technologies to class advantage, 'revolutionizing the forces of production' with the effect of wresting back control of production from skilled workers, increasing productivity and maximising profit. On the other hand men *as men* appropriate and sequester the technological sphere, extending that tenure (*not control –*

that remains with capital) over each new phase, at the expense of women.
(Cockburn 1986a:82, original emphasis)

For the most part, Cockburn's assertions are uncontestable when examined in the light of the reality of materialist practices. The solidity of what she describes as the 'hegemonic ideology of masculinism' has indeed already led to a sexual division of labour in the new technologies. The number of women entering computing, for example, has been declining while opportunities in the industry increase. There has been a clear pattern of feminisation of low-level IT skills and exclusion of women from high-level skilled work, despite the chronic shortage of people with such skills. Connor and Pearson (1986:75) report that

> The IT profession is characterized by a low representation of women, although large numbers of women are employed in IT at lower levels on data input and electronics assembly operations. Women typically represented only 1–2% of a company's electronic engineers, although they could be as much as 10% in the larger electronics and telecoms groups. In software jobs, the proportion of women was generally higher, averaging 15–20%.

Of course, the reinforcement of class and gender relations following the introduction of new technology is well documented, not least by Cockburn herself (1983, 1986a, 1986b; Crompton and Sanderson 1990; Knights and Willmott 1988; Lane 1988; MacKenzie and Wajcman 1985; Wajcman 1991). Inevitably, the shifts in use of new technology are complex and uneven; they vary by sector, by size of company, and spatially. Responses vary too. Some employers may train up production workers, well socialised into the company's products, *modus operandi* and corporate culture, and convert them to skilled or even white-collar technical staff. Others will retain a segmented and gendered labour force and rely on 'poaching' skilled labour as required.

However, in the FRG at least, the current speed of technological change and the urgency with which employers need to increase their competitive edge are forcing a pace in changing patterns of labour recruitment, training and work organisation that is having the effect of opening up channels of training and promotion dramatically. Changes in patterns of work organisation in some plants are allowing for much more progression; workers are crossing the manual/non-manual divide, or moving from unskilled or semi-skilled work into technical, trained occupations. What prospect is there that the increased emphasis on training and the opening up of deeply segmented patterns of work organisation will shift the patterns of relations between classes and between the genders? Will the imperative of new technologies be stronger than the dominance of patriarchal relations on work organisation?

More specifically, will training for the new technologies facilitate women to move into more skilled work in the FRG?

In the United Kingdom, the TECs and LECs have identified as their main concern serving the needs of existing employers (or 'customers') in their localities. Some have already expressed misgivings about their responsibilities for training the unemployed and other 'special needs' groups, such as women (although some TECs have sponsored courses for women managers).

Employer and employee attitudes towards training will need to change if they are to benefit from what new technologies have to offer. This is only likely to occur if both can see some tangible benefit to themselves in investing in training, in the context of a culture which for the most part, regards it as an irrelevance. Both employers and employees in the United Kingdom consistently define training as simply the minimum learning necessary to 'do the job'. It may be that the new technologies will provide a scenario where training will be viewed as potentially *transformative* (Rees, G., Fielder, S. and Rees, T. 1991) – both of profit margins or even survival for employers, and of future prospects for employees and the unemployed. However, even in the FRG, where training is much more firmly on the agenda and is recognised as a route to promotion, there are some groups of employees resistant to continuing training opportunities and the prospect of a move into a job which brings more responsibilities.

The chapter begins to explore these changes and their implications for patterns of gender segregation and the training and employment of women. A brief description of the studies is followed by an account of the new technologies, particularly information technologies in the office. The chapter goes on to explore gender segregation and its reproduction through patterns of work organisation, recruitment and training.

The studies

Three studies are drawn upon, all carried out since 1988 and all of which were conducted with Gareth Rees, Sarah Fielder and others.

1 Low-level IT skills in South-east Wales[1]

The first study is of the demand for and supply of low level information technology skills in South-east Wales (see Rees, G. *et al.* 1989). The region has undergone a major industrial transformation with the decline of the coal and steel industries and the growth of Cardiff as an administrative and financial services centre. The Welsh Development Agency has been actively pursuing a policy of attracting inward investment to the region, focusing specifically on banking, insurance and finance, with some success. The growth of the number of jobs in these industries, and the spin-off service-sector jobs such as catering, cleaning and so forth, has had a dramatic effect on women's employment (see Fielder *et al.* 1990). As part of the study, we interviewed training providers and a cross-section of thirty public- and private-sector employers who were heavy users of IT to investigate patterns of use of and demand for employees with low-level IT skills. These were defined as those needed by people in order to be able to (1) carry out basic computer operations, such as word and data processing; (2) use computerised accounts and payroll software, spreadsheets and desktop publishing; and (3) operate computer-aided and computer-controlled systems in manufacturing.

2 Employers' recruitment and training strategies[2]

The second study was also based in South-east Wales, specifically in the Bridgend travel-to-work area, and focused on 'training cultures' (see Rees, G., Fielder, S. and Rees, T. 1991): a parallel study focused on Swindon (see Doogan and Lovering 1991). The Bridgend project concentrated on twenty-seven employers' recruitment and training practices. They were from a variety of industries and from both the public and the private sector. It examined the transformation of strategies as demographic changes brought on labour shortages, or were thought likely to do so in the short-term future. The employers were at various stages of technological development.

3 Employment and training perspectives in the new information technologies in the European Communities[3]

The final study was a review of education and training systems' responses to new technologies in the European Community. As well as a secondary analysis of sources on educational qualification levels and training provision across the Community, in-depth interviews were conducted with employers and training providers in case-study member states: Ireland, the FRG, Greece and the United Kingdom (see Rees, G. 1990). I draw here in particular upon interviews I conducted in the FRG with companies such as AEG, Siemens and Daimler-Benz.

WHAT ARE THE NEW TECHNOLOGIES?

Various historical surveys have documented the employment effects of earlier technological changes, such as the telephone, the typewriter and the calculator (for example, Hartman *et al.* 1986). What characterises the 1990s, however, is clearly the speed of change and the all-encompassing nature of its impact. Senker and Senker (1990) identify three groups of new technologies: information technologies (IT), new materials and biotechnology. IT has been described by the EC as involving the interconnection of technical and organisational innovations in electronic computers, software engineering, control systems, integrated circuits and telecommunications, which make it possible to collect, generate, analyse and diffuse large quantities of information at low cost.

IT has clearly had remarkable effects on most sectors, from Electronic Point of Sale (EPOS) systems in retailing to computer-aided design (CAD) in engineering and construction, and robots in manufacturing, for example. Some modern microcomputers are more powerful than were the cumbersome mainframe computers of the 1960s. The 1990s will see further revolutions in the use of micros and the increased use of more sophisticated forms of networking. Moreover, as Senker and Senker point out, IT has become a part of our everyday life:

> Over the last ten years we have all become increasingly reliant on IT. Even those who recoil from computers depend on satellite weather forecasts and 'hole in the wall' cash dispensers. Our holidays are checked and booked through computer networks and household goods from washing machines to CD players rely on sophisticated microprocessors.
>
> (Senker and Senker 1990:1)

The development and use of new materials such as new plastics, composites, advanced ceramics, fibre optics, advanced adhesives and new metals is likely to escalate in the 1990s. Developments in biotechnology, which Senker and Senker describe as the 'applications of living organisms to manufacturing processes', are still at the research stage but are likely to develop rapidly and bring with them demands for new types of skills.

Not only is the introduction of new technologies reshaping the labour process in both manufacturing and service industries, but of course their production creates new work in manufacturing, marketing and maintaining equipment, particularly in telecommunications, electronics and data processing. Moreover, in order to exploit the benefits of the equipment to the full, staff need to be trained to use it. This is the weak link in the exploitation of new technologies in the United Kingdom. Much new equipment installed in shops, offices and factories is grossly under-used because staff are insufficiently trained – just as many domestic users of new technology tend to use a microwave oven simply to defrost, use only one or two settings on their dishwasher and automatic washing machine and are ignorant of the purpose of many of the buttons on their video programmer.

There are acute shortages of trainers who both understand and are familiar with new technologies and yet are able to teach effectively. Training organisations report that they can recruit the equivalent of car mechanics when what they need are driving instructors (Rees, G. *et al.* 1989). There are also crippling shortages of trainers to train the trainers.

It is IT which is the most advanced of the new technologies and the one with which this chapter is principally concerned. The next section looks more closely at evolving technologies in the office and their implications for work; this is followed by a consideration of new skill requirements and gender segregation.

THE DEVELOPMENT OF NEW TECHNOLOGIES IN THE OFFICE

The development of new technologies in the office has been described by CEDEFOP (1989) as falling into three phases. The first phase was a quest to have more efficient handling of mass production through automation and centralisation; the second focused on a need for better management and a balance between centralisation and decentralisation; and the third was a period of attempting to achieve both the development and maintenance of innovation potential and the operation of lowest cost. Each phase was characterised by different patterns of work organisation and training.

In the 1960s and early 1970s, businesss activity increased substantially and the main aim of IT was to facilitate the handling of large amounts of data; this led to a system of centralised processing. Large mainframe computers were introduced into specialised departments. CEDEFOP (1989) describe how often 'rigid upstream administrative procedures had to be introduced and new areas of Taylorism emerged'. This was the era of rooms of punch-card operators and verifiers, and the separation of information-processing from the users. Training tended to be on-the-job, and merely preparation for low-level work, apart from that for the informatics engineers, who were the only ones to understand the entire system.

The 1970s saw the development of terminals allowing more users to access data sets and the multiplication of local applications for processing. Typewriters with memories appeared, and around 1979, the first word processors. Training during this period centred upon:

> [the] exploitation of tools and software by the users, and [was] controlled by an 'extended elite' made up of computer experts, representatives of work organization and some experts for specialized applications.
>
> (CEDEFOP 1989:22)

In the 1980s, facilities were developed for the integration of different forms of data processing and transmission techniques. It became difficult to distinguish between word processors, which could also manage files and process figures, and microcomputers, which could word-process and had high-quality printers (CEDEFOP 1989). The new IT combines computing and telecommunications in telematics.

As Christie et al. (1990) recall, in the 1970s there were fears that new technology would have 'three malign consequences': massive job loss, deskilling, and widespread opposition from trade unions. None of them has come about. While some job loss has been associated with new technology, as Batstone and Gourlay (1986) report, jobs have also been sacrificed as a result of failure to introduce it. Deskilling was projected as a means whereby employers would attempt to increase their control over the labour process but, in the event, other factors have proved more significant. Rather than widespread deskilling in the most recent technological phase, there are many examples of job enlargement. Trade unions clearly recognise the importance of new technologies in retaining competitiveness and thereby protecting jobs, although the role of individual unions in negotiations has varied enormously: the better-organised ones have been able to have much more of an impact (Batstone and Gourlay 1986). Unions tend to have positive attitudes towards the training implied by new technologies, although this has not always been forthcoming (Rainbird 1990).

What implications do these changes in new technology in the office have for new packages of skills which can be constructed and the social relations of labour? Different phases of technological development have been characterised by contrasting patterns of work organisation, but there are choices which can be made about division of labour and job content. Employers respond in different ways to these opportunities: some, particularly those who understand little of the capacities of either the new technologies or the human resources they employ overlay existing patterns of demarcation and gendering on the new equipment; others use training and the removal of old segmented tiers to create new, less segmented structures.

NEW INFORMATION TECHNOLOGIES, NEW SKILLS AND GENDER SEGREGATION

The impact of the development of IT on the labour market is enormously complex (see Ducatel and Miles 1990; Elger 1987; Fielder *et al.* 1990; Freeman and Soete 1991; Rees, G. 1990; Senker and Senker 1990). Some trends are emerging, however. In the first instance, it is clear that the process of introducing and upgrading IT is evolutionary, not revolutionary. Adaptation tends to be piecemeal. Technologies do not need to be treated as deterministic in governing either social relations or work processes and organisation. The potential for changing patterns of recruitment, training and work organisation evolved during eras of different technologies may be far-reaching, but the extent to which employers introduce and make full use of what IT has to offer varies enormously. Firms which introduce sophisticated technology do so for different reasons: some are concerned to reduce labour costs or to rationalise work, while others use it simply as an instrument to improve productivity, gain more control over their work processes or to improve quality. UK companies on the whole are described as 'still using IT to cut costs rather than underpin their business strategy. . . . Only 39 per cent of a sample of more than 70 companies indicated that they were fully aware of the benefits of IT' (Cane 1990).

Contributors to the labour process debate have accepted Braverman's (1974) emphasis on the importance of geo-political structures on work organisation while resisting the notion of technological determinism, emphasising instead the potential power of workers to negotiate in the control of technology, and of managers to choose between work-organisation strategies (Knights and Willmott 1988). The size of firm, sector and spatial location will all bear upon the extent to which IT is introduced and the motivation for its introduction. These factors in turn have a bearing on the extent to which recruitment patterns, training requirements and work organisation are restructured, and determine the packaging of skills for the new jobs.

Job re-design and new skills

While IT can be, and sometimes is, grafted on to existing patterns of division of labour, it can also offer opportunities to break down barriers between recognised occupations and to enrich jobs. In such situations, workers are expected to be more flexible. The nature of some jobs is changing dramatically: the skills required now are not simply technical. New workers need self-reliance, communication skills, the ability to work in teams and think in abstract terms: in the FRG, these are described as the 'new pedagogics'.

In manufacturing, the need for traditional manual skills and physical strength is giving way to more intellectual characteristics. Workers need to be able to diagnose faults in expensive equipment, carry out routine maintenance themselves, know when to call in an expert. Many employers' increasing concern with quality has been made manifest in strategies of making operatives responsible for maintaining standards – through the 'right first time' principle – thereby replacing direct control with 'responsible autonomy' (Martin 1988). New technologies are affecting the standard patterns of division of labour in the workplace in terms of skill levels. Many jobs which are unskilled or semi-skilled either disappear, or the incumbents have to be trained to take on more responsibility to deal with the new technologies. All this implies not simply a need for up-dating skills, but a lifelong programme of training and retraining, and expectations about moving up in the organisation. This is already being taken on board in many German companies.

The introduction of new technologies in offices, theoretically at least, should open up more opportunities for women at higher grades of work. Clerical work used, of course, to be clearly identified as men's work; it only became downgraded and feminised earlier this century. The 'administrative revolution' in office technological development historically and its effect on the gender composition of office workers has received considerable attention (see, for example, Lowe 1987, on Canada). Studies in the United

Kingdom and the United States have explored the impact of more recent changing technology on social relations and the mechanisms of maintaining control over the labour process: they do not reveal a radical shift of balance in job gendering but instead suggest that both patriarchal and class relations will overlay the new technology (Baran 1988; Barker and Downing 1985; Child 1986; Crompton and Sanderson 1990; Knights and Willmott 1986, 1988; Webster 1986, 1990; West 1982).

Although IT offers potential for job enrichment, in some organisations some jobs are deskilled. IT can further polarise the quality of jobs, between men and women, but also between women of different skill levels. This can be exacerbated when managers are not fully aware of the potential that IT has to offer and are unwilling to take the time to be trained themselves – or to admit to the deficiencies a need for training implies. Vickery (1990) identifies a number of issues critical to the development of an IT strategy which hinge on lack of familiarity with the implications and possibilities of IT on the part of business managers. He particularly points to their lack of understanding of the IT planning process; cultural barriers between business and IT directors; problems in the total understanding of data-base and systems-management issues, and using IT effectively to deliver customer satisfaction (Vickery 1990:15).

Such lack of understanding undoubtedly increases the likelihood that existing gendered patterns of division of labour will prevail. In a highly segregated pattern of use, typing pools become data-entry or word-processing pools, but offer employees less job satisfaction. Such deskilled jobs are demotivating, particularly when coupled with poor remuneration, no prospects of advancement and the risk of repetitive strain injury. Introducing or upgrading IT should ideally involve wholesale job re-design.

Senker and Senker (1990) predict a decline in the number of low-skilled jobs for keyboard data entry. In banking, for example, this function is being taken over by customers themselves (as in withdrawals from cashpoints). In retail, bar-code scanners speed up checkouts and electronic point-of-sales systems can ensure that replacement stocks are ordered automatically from the warehouse as goods are purchased. However, they maintain that while there is some evidence of deskilling of clerical work because of new technology, there are many examples of job enlargement, particularly in the financial services sector. Equally, some senior clerks and secretaries are beginning to assume responsibility for tasks previously undertaken by junior managers. There is no single trend in the social construction of technology which describes patterns of control through deskilling (Elger 1987), rather, a complex mesh of patterns, determined by the strength of unions, the level of understanding of IT by managers, the availability of labour, and the nature and rigidity of traditional class, race and gender divisions in the industry concerned.

In insurance companies and building societies, the use of new technology has enabled more junior staff to take responsibility for discussing clients' needs with them and making 'decisions' about what can be offered to clients by feeding the appropriate information into a computer which, in effect, makes the decision for them, following programmed guidelines. This frees more highly qualified staff to make the more difficult decisions on marginal or complex cases. In turn, although this may mean that fewer such staff are needed, more usually, productivity improves or the range of services is expanded. Branches no longer require such professionals on the premises at all times. Baran (1988) has argued, however, that although some junior unskilled jobs are enhanced through automation in the insurance industry in the United States, others are lost altogether and that the junior professional jobs, which provided a route for occupational mobility for some, are disappearing.

IT has affected most people's working lives in offices to a greater or lesser extent, but the way it is organised can clearly directly affect the quality of job for employees. It can be used in such a way as to enhance productivity and provide more rewarding jobs all round. Senker and Senker (1990:10) describe how this can work:

> Some managers with PCs use them to write reports, but few are prepared to use PCs themselves. Many managers put PCs on their secretaries' desks, delegating a wide range of other computer applications, including diary management, spreadsheet, database, accounting, and electronic mail to them. This phenomenon of senior managers relying on intermediaries to use IT on their behalf has been called 'chauffeured' use. Apart from word processing, PCs are used mainly for databases and spreadsheets, but there are few users who understand how to use these applications effectively. Secretaries who can acquire the skills to use these new applications may be able to take on junior administrative tasks, acting as a personal assistant to their bosses.

However, secretaries are rarely given the necessary training to upgrade their computer skills. This is even true of word processing, where typists find that they have to teach themselves a wide range of skills additional to those used by a traditional typist; for instance, the requirement to organise the storage and indexing of computer discs and their files, and to take responsibility for their safety and security.

The current IT 'skills crisis' is largely in high-level IT jobs such as systems programmers, network controllers and in application system development, for which graduate recruitment of people with technical qualifications is the main point of entry. In addition, there is growth in demand for people to do what used to be called 'hybrid' jobs, which combine business management skills with an understanding of IT: such people are now more usually referred to as 'business analysts'. Philip Virgo (1991) of the Women into IT Campaign (run by major British employers and supported by the Department of Trade and Industry) has illustrated how the main strategy adopted by employers to fill the shortage of business analysts is to convert the technical people (of whom there is already a shortage), thereby fuelling further problems in the future. Moreover, such people were originally hired for their technical qualifications and skills, rather than the personal aptitudes and understanding of business necessary to do the new jobs. They do not universally make a successful transition.

Virgo argues that to fill shortages in both high-level technical jobs and of business analysts, recruitment nets need to be widened. The two main obvious groups are non-technical graduates (for example, arts and social science graduates), and existing staff in secretarial and clerical grades:

> The evidence is that those who can make effective use of a full WP package have little problem learning most of the modern database packages and those who can make effective use of dBase 11 or 111 can learn most system generators without too much difficulty. Taking charge of departmental computing on a Unix Box or an AS 400 is the next logical step.
>
> (Virgo 1991:4)

Both groups – non-technical graduates, and secretaries and clerical officers – are of course substantially made up of women. Virgo argues that computing and IT generally has a bad image as far as women are concerned, and that employers, overwhelmingly male, tend not to associate women with such potential skills or to recruit them. As a consequence, career routes within the organisation for secretaries barely exist, and women arts graduates are unlikely to consider or be considered for IT or business analyst posts.

The Women into IT Project attempts to persuade employers to consider women for such skill shortages, and indeed to 'correct the image' of IT to make it more attractive to women. Very few IT jobs after all involve exclusively technical work: increasingly those skills are part of a package required. However, this is clearly an ambitious task: the relationships between technology, the concept of skill and gender relations are highly complex. The next section attempts to deconstruct some of the strands.

The masculinisation of technology and the gendered concept of skill

Unsurprisingly, despite the scope afforded by new technologies for changing jobs and reducing the amount of segmentation and gender segregation in the labour market, there is little evidence of this happening in the United Kingdom as yet. New patterns of gender segregation are simply emerging in the new technologies: indeed, IT is more gendered now than it was in the 1960s. This raises questions about the power relations of gender, and more specifically, whether technology has been colonised as masculine territory so effectively that even with the imperative of skill shortages, women will in effect remain excluded.

Gender is clearly used as a screening device: the notion that a job has a certain skill level or technological component leads to segmented recruiting strategies, as Collinson *et al.* (1990) have demonstrated all too clearly. Employees themselves recognise which jobs are men's and which women's, and of course collude to a greater or lesser extent. The power of the link between men, machinery and the concept of skill in the eyes of an ex-miner, for example, is demonstrated in an extract from an interview with a training officer of an electronics plant in South Wales:[4]

> young males will do the work which is very similar to the women's work. But it is very difficult to put a forty year old man, who's come out of the pits, on a fiddly little job, especially amongst a group of women, but a young bloke won't bother. It's just a difference of perception over the years. You can attempt to make the jobs more masculine by putting them on machines. It could be even a more simple job than the woman is doing on the line, but as long as he's using that machine, something powerful, he'll assume that that's a man's job and he'll do that.

While it may be acceptable for young men to do 'women's work', rates of pay will ensure that they soon move on to more lucrative jobs (see below). For women who succeed in gaining access to 'men's jobs', the price of being a misfit can be severe. Various studies of women engineers and senior managers have outlined the difficulties of behaving as women in such a setting: they have to adopt one of a set of strategies to survive (see Chapters 2 and 8). Limitations are imposed upon technically competent women in a number of workplaces. As Cockburn (1986b:185) says, 'For a woman to aspire to technical competence is, in a very real sense, to transgress the rules of gender.' In her study of women and men working in three fields where new technology has been introduced (warehousing, manufacture and hospital X-ray), and in the engineering firms which developed these technologies, Cockburn (1985) revealed that gender divisions remain clear-cut. Even where women learned new technologies, men continued to be the 'technologists' and women the low paid 'operators'. She argues that:

> Whatever opportunities the new technologies appear to offer the operator, they do not in themselves enable her to cross a certain invisible barrier that exists between operating the controls that put a machine to work and taking the casing off it in order to intervene in its mechanism. This is the difference between an operator and a technician or engineer. For an operator there is always someone who is assumed to know better than she about the technology of the machine on which she is working. That someone is almost invariably a man.
>
> (Cockburn 1986b:181)

Wajcman (1991:158) argues cogently that technology is a cultural product which is integral to the constitution of male-gender identity. The female-gender identity is the negation of that of the male, and so the stereotyped cultural ideal of a woman, in the ideology of sexual difference, must be technically incompetent. Wajcman (1991) underlines the significance of this technological ownership as a source of power in gender relations.

The association of masculinity with technical competence and control, and its obverse in women, is related to the social construction of skill (Phillips and Taylor 1980), which is then translated to levels of pay: this was discussed in Chapter 2. The technical competence required in 'women's' jobs both at home and in work is often undervalued. Numerous studies have established the gendering of the concept of skill (Beechey and Perkins 1987; Crompton and Jones 1984; Pollert 1981). Most recently, Lane (1988) has shown the importance of gendering in determining what constitutes higher-level competencies in clerical work. Whereas jobs and the skills associated with them naturally come and go with the development of new technology over time, the relationship between 'women's work' and low value being attached to the 'skills' involved in doing it has remained constant.

The means of acquiring skills is an important element of the extent to which they are rewarded. This is particularly the case with high-level IT jobs. Increased credentialism characterises high-level IT work, and the lack of opportunities for progression in training between low-level and high-level work acts as a barrier to women's entry. While IT may be triggering the shake-up of rigid patterns of segmentation in some quarters, that does not on the whole apply to IT work itself. The social construction of high-level IT work is increasingly clearly, exclusively masculine.

TRAINING AND NEW TECHNOLOGIES IN THE UNITED KINGDOM

Training for IT work in the United Kingdom is highly segmented. There has been a significant growth in the numbers of training courses on IT, public- and private-sector provided, for all levels. Courses for low-level IT skills tend to fall into three categories: (1) public-sector providers gearing up young people, the long-term unemployed and women returners for the changing labour market through Youth Training and Employment Training (ET); (2) small, private-sector training providers offering courses on specific software packages; and (3) in-firm training, often on firm-specific software.

In the United Kingdom, a variety of private- and public-sector training providers offer courses that can be described as training in low-level IT skills. In the public sector, these include colleges of technology and further education, ITECs and Skill Centres. The courses on offer can be categorised as initial training pre-employment, training, retraining and updating. The pre-employment courses are almost exclusively through Youth Training and some college-based training courses in general office skills, electronics and programming. Training or retraining occurs largely through ET and courses designed for women returners, and are carried out through both the public and the private sectors. Updating for IT takes place mainly through private companies, although colleges, ITECs and Skill Centres also offer made courses or have employer sponsorship for trainees on their existing courses – for example, through day release. Private training companies provide short courses not only in response to employers, but also as a result of demand from individuals, so there is clearly a recognition by unemployed and employed people that updating their IT skills can enhance their employability. Some private-sector manufacturing companies provide training for small firms, where they have sold them the system (Rees, G. *et al.* 1989).

While no entry qualifications are required for most of these courses for low-level IT skills, trainees tend to go straight into lower-level, routine jobs, often with small employers, with little or no prospect of opportunities for further training or advancement. The pattern seems to be that public-sector providers focus on 'general office skills' and the private sector on short courses on specific software. Large employers wanting people with low-level IT skills will recruit people from such courses. They will then add on specific software training either in-house or through the growing number of private-sector providers specialising in such training.

Within the private sector, there is specialisation between those companies focusing on Youth Training and ET programmes, and those whose business is almost exclusively for employers and individuals. A major concern about training in low-level IT skills, apart from the ghettoising effect, is that it is distinctly gendered. On ET, for example, as a private training provider in Cardiff reported to us, all the trainees on programming are men and nearly all those on word processing, women (Rees, G. *et al.* 1989).

Training for high-level skills tends to take place in the first instance through higher education, and then through in-house or external training. A small component of ET (Higher Technology National Training – HTNT) provides training from Higher National Certificate to master's degree work in technology for the registered unemployed, but only about a third are women (Wilson 1990). Some university and polytechnic computing departments have been experimenting with part-time evening master's courses in a bid to attract women returners.

Women and IT training

The polarisation of IT jobs through the 1980s has been linked to its effect on gender segregation through dual employment and recruitment structures in a series of well-documented studies (Crompton and Jones 1984; Crompton and Sanderson 1990; Knights and Sturdy 1987; Rajan 1984; Rolfe 1986; West 1982). The link with training and education systems has not been made so explicit, however. The figures clearly indicate a growing segregation, with more women coming on to training courses geared towards imparting low-level skills, and a drop in female students in IT-related subjects in higher education, from 26 per cent in 1979 to 14 per cent in 1986. Women comprised only 11.0 per cent of new graduates with first degrees in computing in 1989, a decline of 1.6 per cent women since 1986, despite an overall increase in students taking the subject (Universities Funding Council 1990; Universities Grants Council 1986). This is also, despite the proportions in other 'masculine' science subjects, increasing over the years. Given the bifurcated labour market in IT, and the lack of opportunities for progression, career mobility is limited. As a result, whereas horizontal and vertical segregation by gender in other sectors is declining or at least steady (Crompton and Sanderson 1990), it is increasing in IT occupations in the United Kingdom, in part at least because of the lack of opportunities for progression within training routes.

A major difficulty in attracting women into high-level IT jobs has been that relatively few have the essential qualifications to apply for courses in IT at degree level. This in part explains the decline in numbers of women taking relevant courses. Newton (1991:144) feels the most likely explanation is that girls have been 'systematically discouraged from applying for courses in computing given their previous experience of computers and their perceptions of computing as a career'.

She points to the exclusive nature of computer discourse, and the need to be familiar with both the technical knowledge of computers as machines *and* the social knowledge of the computer culture. Newton argues that the way in which computers are managed in schools has tended to reinforce views that they are for boys: girls are likely to have less access to computers both at home and at school. The drop in girls taking computing in schools is then manifested in a fall in the number of women studying for a degree in information technology. Wajcman (1991) develops this by discussing boys' and girls' relative levels of access to computers, and the socialisation effects of war-dominated computer games, the male territory of games arcades, and so on. Virgo and the Women into Technology Foundation argue that the careers literature for IT is highly misleading, and would only attract 'techies'; it deters both suitable women and men. He maintains that only 30 per cent of any professional IT worker's job involves technical skills; other competencies are just as important, if not more so (Virgo 1991). Hence careers literature of people sitting over a keyboard (redolent of university prospectuses for virtually all departments) gives a false impression of IT work.

The increasing credentialism of computing, argues Newton, may have the effect of conveying the image that it is a male-dominated field with set hurdles and barriers. It is certainly the case that, while graduates with degrees in any subject may enter computing, the women who do so tend to have degrees in computing itself (Virgo 1991).

The arrangements for training in IT in the United Kingdom are based upon sets of assumptions about the way in which IT jobs are organised. As Dore (1987) points out, types of jobs, skill content and associated training are changing rapidly, with the ability to learn becoming more important than formal IT qualifications. In the FRG, it was observed by AEG that those apprentices who had difficulty in learning the new pedagogics were the same ones as experienced difficulties in grasping the technological aspects of the curriculum. The new skills, such as the ability to communicate, are ones at which, on the whole, women are thought to excel. The main difficulty seems to lie then in the sets of assumptions about training meeting the needs of particular kinds of rather traditionally drawn jobs. The training infrastructure does not reflect the potential shifts in type of work; for example, decision making for clerical workers. The segmentation in IT jobs is reflected in segmentation in IT training. Because of entry requirements for high-level IT jobs, in order to progress from low-level to high-level IT work, it is currently necessary to leave the company, undertake further training (not necessarily in IT) and re-enter at another level.

Given that gender divisions are superimposed upon patterns of job and training segmentation, it is clear that there will have to be major shifts both within industry and within training in order to break down gender segregation. This becomes apparent when we look at what is available for women wanting to train in IT work through ET (for which, of course, only certain women qualify). With the exception of HTNT courses, ET on the whole prepares women for very low-level work, with few channels for progression. The experience can, if inappropriate, put women off the idea of training, in much the same way that the Youth Training Scheme was found to do for young people (Lee et al. 1990). Courses organised by women themselves for women returners have been rather more successful in creating opportunities for progression. South Glamorgan Women's Workshop, for example (see Chapter 4), although training in low-level skills, does seek to send trainees on to further training where possible: the first ex-trainee to go on to study for a degree in computer science has just graduated. It is now seeking to diversify into medium-level training in telematics and telecommunications.

Cockburn (1986b) feels that training, and in particular women-only training, is the only effective means of breaking down gender divisions in the workplace. The issue of women-only training is a recurring theme in measures designed to combat job gendering in IT, from computer clubs in schools, through to returner courses for disadvantaged women (Essex et al. 1986a, 1986b), to high-level training for returners to HTNT programmes

(Wilson 1990). Computer courses run by women for women in the FRG, too, have been found to be highly successful in training women in new technologies (Sessar-Karpp 1988).

TRAINING AND NEW TECHNOLOGIES IN THE FEDERAL REPUBLIC OF GERMANY[5]

The dual training system of the FRG has been described as the envy of the world, certainly in terms of training for intermediate qualifications. Training regulations governing the competencies which must be achieved before an individual can become a qualified worker are strictly controlled. The two sides of industry co-operate with the state, in the form of the Bundesinstitut für Berufsbildung (BIBB – the Federal Institute for Vocational Training) in identifying the required skills for any occupation. Chambers of Commerce play a crucial role at the local level in overseeing the implementation of training provision.

Some 70 per cent of school-leavers enter the training system and a further 20 per cent stay on in education, far higher figures than in other EC member states. More resources are spent on training than elsewhere. There are attempts to ensure that, as far as possible the same standards operate across regions, firms, industries and occupations. Training is part of a work culture for those people in occupations for which a graduated system of qualifications exist; that occupation becomes an important part of the package which goes to make up their personal identity. Given the significance of training in extracting the full potential of what new technologies have to offer, it is presumably no accident that the FRG has some of the most successful companies in the world, not simply in terms of using new technologies, but in their development and manufacture as well.

The very strengths of the dual training system can also be seen as weaknesses, however, in the context of training needs created by the emerging new technologies. The system provides systematic delivery of considered curricula for occupations in a range of industries, and the opportunity for both college-based teaching in theoretical aspects of work and firm-based practical learning. However, as described earlier, new technologies are having the effect of breaking down barriers both between theory and practice and between recognised occupations: workers are required to be more flexible. The nature of some jobs is changing dramatically: the new skills required are not simply technical but demand training in the new pedagogics: these are not traditionally taught in the dual training system, and trainers are not used to bringing the new skills out in their apprentices.

The dual training system is also accused of being inflexible: there is a long gestation period for introducing changes into the training regulations which govern occupations. It can take, for example, ten years between initial planning meetings between the BIBB and the two sides of industry to discuss curriculum changes, and the graduation of the first apprentices with the new qualifications. New technology is developing very rapidly; there is a danger that the training for it can lag behind by many years.

Finally, it is clear that new technologies are affecting standard patterns of division of labour in the workplace in terms of skill levels. Because jobs which are unskilled or semi-skilled are on the decrease, and others that have not involved much training after the initial period now require more, there is a rapidly growing need not simply for skill updates, but for a progressive programme of continuing education and training. Unlike initial training, this is not regulated by the state. As a consequence, access to it varies considerably, and the quality can vary too. Moreover, whereas young people are socialised to accept the importance of the initial training for their career prospects, there are cultural factors which restrict existing unskilled and semi-skilled employees' enthusiasm for continuing training. How have companies at the forefront of technological development responded?

TRAINING STRATEGIES

1 Training strategies in the FRG

Among major companies in the FRG, spending on continuing training has increased dramatically in recent years and is projected to continue doing so. Bosch, for example, a leading car component manufacturer, spent approximately DM90,000 on continuing training in 1988. In AEG, spending increased by 15 per cent in 1988 and a similar percentage again in 1989. Siemens too now spends nearly twice as much money on continuing training as on initial training.

A major reason for this is the short 'shelf-life' of techniques learnt, given the pace of technological change. The need for continuing training as a result of technological developments is brought out sharply in this account of the experience of Bosch:

> For most Bosch products there is a 'Half Value Time' of 5 to 7 years. That is, apprentices can take advantage of only 50 per cent of the knowledge gained at age 27. At that age they must relearn new knowledge. For some products Half Value Time is less than two years (car radios 15 months for example). Product life cycles are thus in rapid decline so new learning and product diversification into new areas is necessary for the company.
>
> (Quoted in Cooke and Morgan 1990:26)

While a major reason for these increases in spending has certainly been the demands of new technology, they are also due to the imperative of demographic changes. Each year there is a turnover of only 3 per cent of the entire workforce: 97 per cent is constant. This means that 80 per cent of the workforce of the year 2000 is already working. The decline in unskilled and semi-skilled jobs provides an added incentive.

What impact does the dual training system and the increase in continuing training have on women in the FRG? Gender segregation in the labour force is as entrenched as in other European countries, despite a number of measures designed to dilute it. A major difficulty facing young girls wanting apprenticeships in one of the major companies specialising in training in new technologies is that places are highly sought after and girls are less likely than boys to have taken the relevant subjects at school. Fewer girls take computing and mathematics, for example (Schiersmann 1988). Siemens confirmed a shortage of young women with the basic technical qualifications; they reported an increase in the number of girls coming on to apprenticeships, but expressed the view that it will be some generations before substantially more women are taken on.

Women are likely to benefit from the drive to increase continuing training given that they are disproportionately in unskilled and semi-skilled jobs. The Head of Technical and Professional Training in AEG reported in an interview with me in 1990:

> People who had been employed to manufacture cables had been working in one of our firms without training. The new recruits are skilled workers who know the new technologies. The unskilled workers can now have the opportunities for training as we now need more skilled workers. The machines now require people who have more knowledge about them, those who work with them need more skills. We used to have six different machines involved in the process of making cables, whereas now all that work is done by just one, highly complex machine.

Not all unskilled workers welcome the changes, of course: AEG report particular resistance from Turkish women workers. Some of these are first-generation migrants, however, and there is evidence that the descendants of migrants are likely to hold different work attitudes (see Wilpert 1988), but may experience more difficulties in securing access to initial training than indigenous Germans. The FRG has a migrant population of about 4 million, and the sons and daughters of migrant workers are less likely to be offered places in the dual training system; they figure disproportionately among the small minority of school-leaving age who neither stay on at school with a view to pursuing further or higher education nor enter the dual system. There are, of course, differences between the ethnic groups. Schweikert (1982) has shown that participation in the dual training system is much higher among the Spaniards and Yugoslavs (around 22 per cent in the early 1980s) compared with the Portuguese and Turkish populations (nearer 11 per cent). Turkish girls are the least likely of all to secure an apprenticeship. Those with the greatest impediments appear to be those who have language difficulties (particularly written skills) and/or to have arrived in the country relatively recently (Schweikert 1982). The ethnic minorities have lost their place in the queue for attention in training matters, given the urgency of harmonising training between the two old Germanies and the need to update former East German workers' skills in line with those of Western industry.

AEG have run some women-only training in the new technologies to try to break down what are seen as particular barriers facing women wanting to learn new technologies. The course is in electronics: the women do not get the full qualification, but they can enhance their pay and get better jobs within the company.

In the FRG, then, a national strategy of updating apprentice training requirements by including the new pedagogics and constructing new occupations (particularly in the metal trades – see Rees, G. 1990) is complemented in these major companies by a vastly increased expenditure on continuing training and an attempt to desegment the labour force. This is taking place within a culture that values training, and recognises qualifications as a route to progression.

2 Training strategies in the United Kingdom

Training in the United Kingdom is not part of the culture of employers or employees, and this has been recognised as a major stumbling block in companies' prospects of surviving post-1992. A survey of employers' perspectives on human resources found 'Training decisions tend to be made in the light of immediate requirements, and what is possible and do-able' (Centre for Corporate Strategy and Change 1989:20).

New technologies are on the whole introduced incrementally and do not trigger off an awareness of training needs. Christie *et al.* (1990), reviewing the findings of four surveys of 1,200 factories representative of British manufacturing industry between 1981 and 1987, discovered that only a third of their respondents had an identifiable training culture. Reasons given by British manufacturers for this included a cutback in resources for training since the 1980s recession which were never reinstated, the 'pressure of work', which being translated, meant that staff could not be spared, and a fear of expensively trained staff being poached. According to Christie *et al.* (1990), companies revealed that they were only likely to introduce a general training strategy in response to a change of ownership; a management decision to develop multi-skilling, Just in Time or integrated information systems; or to facilitate a quality awareness and improvement policy.

As a consequence, employers are increasingly likely to try to attract or poach skilled experienced staff from other companies by offering higher pay or other inducements. A training strategy in this case in effect becomes a recruitment, retention and pay strategy.

Locksley *et al.* (1989) identified four training strategies in their study of the telematics services sector. The first is to undertake no training at all, but to recruit trained people from the open market. The more skills required, the wider the net will have to be cast. This tends to characterise smaller firms. The second is to use external training providers. This is used particularly to learn specific software packages. Both large and small firms may use this approach for such training needs. The third strategy is to provide on-the-job training. In the study conducted by the Centre for Corporate Study and Change (1989) for the TA, this accounted for most of the training in the companies sampled. Basic skills are required at recruitment, and employees then learn by watching and doing. The final strategy, characteristic of larger firms, is a whole training package, which may combine in-house training and purchasing off-the-shelf courses as required.

On introducing new technology, employers have a number of options open to them. They can train existing staff, they can sub-contract specific tasks, or they can recruit or even poach people with the appropriate skills. In our case studies in South Wales, we found little evidence of training strategies at all, particularly in the smaller companies. Training on the whole amounted to induction training. In the financial services sector, training was limited to software specific courses, and there was a real fear that introducing more training would simply mean that staff would have more transferable skills: employers would not only lose their investment: they would be involved in additional replacement costs. For many, their training strategy was to recruit people with appropriate skills.

RECRUITMENT STRATEGIES

There is plenty of evidence to demonstrate the fact that in the United Kingdom, with a shortage of school-leavers from which to recruit, most employers' strategy is simply to step up their recruiting edge, by (for example) commissioning recruitment videos, developing better links with schools and the careers service, and entering into 'Compact' arrangements with school-leavers (National Economic Development Office/Training Agency 1989). This is an arrangement whereby employers contract with individual pupils to offer them a job when they leave school in return for the fulfilment of certain conditions, such as a good school record. It is widely reported, too, that employers believe that only young people can learn new technology. Certainly they are increasingly likely to be brought up with video recorders, microwaves and home computers. It is difficult to find any sound empirical evidence that older workers have more difficulty in learning new technologies, although there is research that suggests that the kind of training offered is not always appropriate and puts people off (see Sessar-Karpp 1988). Nevertheless, it is clear that the *belief* that older workers have more difficulty in adapting to new technologies itself informs employers' recruitment strategies. And indeed, older workers themselves may have those views, which would effect their confidence level and hence their ability to learn.

In South Wales, we found plenty of examples of firms preferring to recruit young people for work involving low-level IT tasks, despite the declining numbers. Indeed, a Cardiff-based accountancy firm reported to us that its secretarial and administrative staff were exclusively women aged between 24 and 30. A major investment bank employed only under 25-year-olds in its word-processing unit, despite the fact that it offered pay and conditions far better than its competitors; that is, this was not seen as a young person's job in the traditional sense.

In the experience of the head of a South Wales firm of solicitors, both solicitors and the older secretaries tended to balk when a computer was delivered to the office. Most of the secretarial work had been done by women who had returned to the firm after a period off having children, or young women recruited from the local technical college. As he put it:

> when you produce a computer on somebody's desk . . . they would have the equivalent of a heart attack. . . . So we got . . . panicky about . . . trying to do it all in the right way . . . [but] it was all rubbish . . . all you had to do was to get a sixteen year old child from the Tech and they would be much better.

In the South Wales companies we studied, the response to projected shortages of school-leavers was indeed to intensify recruitment strategies to attract those that would be available, rather than to consider introducing training for other potential recruits such as the existing workforce, the unemployed, ethnic minorities or women returners.

In the FRG, age plays a significant role in recruitment strategies, too. In Siemens, new apprentices are recruited every year. Increasingly they come with a 'rough' knowledge of new technology as they have had experience of playing with computers. Because of the shortages of school-leavers, the company is making more use of continuing education and training to update the skills of existing older workers. But difficulties have been experienced: the younger workers learn so quickly that they soon have more skills than the older workers. This can lead to resentment by the older workers, who feel that the status and pay differential between them will be eroded. As a result, old systems of production are used alongside the new machines, the latter being operated by the younger workers. The long experience of the older workers has to be recognised and rewarded as part of a 'social policy' introduced to deal with the effects of the recruitment and training policy.

The introduction of new technology in Siemens means that for the new generation of apprentices, the quality of job will be enhanced, and the prospects for advancement will be greater than those for older workers, some of whom will be encouraged to take early retirement. This means that there will be more opportunities for taking further training and advancing within the company than before.

WORK ORGANISATION

In an earlier section, I outlined how introducing new technologies can both enhance and deskill jobs at various levels. Appelbaum and Albin (1989) stress the importance of management strategies in shaping the impact of new technology, based on a study of computing in the insurance industry in the United States. They outline two major strategies. The first is a *robust* strategy, whereby the skills of clerical workers are upgraded, and they become more involved in decision making and more complex work. This clearly flies in the face of the Braverman (1974) deskilling thesis. The alternative strategy is described as *algorithmic*; this is where deskilling does occur, and clerical work becomes more routinised and fragmented. Jobs such as data-entry clerk evolve from this process.

Clearly, the major German companies described here can be seen as adopting a robust strategy, whereas in our South Wales studies, we came across far more evidence of algorithmic strategies (although there were some interesting exceptions). Essentially, the introduction of new technology appeared to lead to further polarisation between the professional and support workers in terms of their scope for job satisfaction. That polarisation was gendered.

In secretarial and clerical work, two studies have outlined the different kinds of experiences of jobs with the same name. Crompton and Jones (1984) describe the distinctions between the recognised and reasonably well-rewarded skills of secretaries at the 'personal assistant' end of the spectrum and the position of those undervalued and increasingly marginalised women in the 'typing pool'. Lane (1988) similarly distinguishes between those clerical staff who are career-graded, with promotion chances and access to training, and those who are relegated to non-career, part-time and temporary work. We found a similar pattern of polarisation. In a major Cardiff accountancy firm, the personnel officer distinguished between 'personal assistants', many of whom were graduates and spoke second and third languages, and secretaries, whose function was straight word processing. He described the likely advent of further polarisation made possible by the introduction of networking systems, which would involve some women being employed solely to 'type like billyo' all day long (presumably until they retired with repetitive strain injury), while the manipulation of the data so entered would be shifted upwards to technical specialists and the accountants themselves.

This form of organisation certainly does involve deskilling for some and upgrading of skills and job enrichment for others. Because it is the image of a typist who can 'type like billyo' that is seen as appropriate for this new job, it is women who are recruited. The pay levels are low. Hence, when we found and interviewed a sole young man in a room of fifty word processors (or WPs, as they were known in the company), he explained that he would shortly be moving on to another job as he would not be able to support himself on his WP's wages once he had left his parents' home. The women WPs continue to need financial support either from parents or partners. There is no technical necessity for this form of work organisation and infirm labour segmentation.

Some employers recognise that creating low-paid, low-valued jobs where women input data all day long is not conducive to keeping staff. A large firm of commercial solicitors had experienced considerable difficulties in recruiting and retaining secretarial employees of sufficient calibre to meet the demands rising from a major expansion of the firm's work and the adoption of more sophisticated information technology. Its response had been to improve pay and conditions; to develop a specialist internal training programme for its staff; and to abandon separation of Visual Display Unit (VDU) operators from other areas of its work: 'people just aren't happy spending all day doing that [operating a VDU], so [in future] it would be as part of another job' (interview with firm's recruitment officer).

In another firm of solicitors, but this time based in a South Wales Valleys town, information technology had been introduced in a much more haphazard way and primarily as a result of the head of chambers' own personal interest in it. He bought himself equipment, took it home and taught himself how to use it. As so much of his work involved editing text, he found it more efficient to do it himself on screen. This freed up the time of his secretary, who began to see clients on matters (such as conveyancing) that did not really require the attention of the solicitor. Gradually the pattern of work organisation evolved to such an extent that the secretary demanded, and was given, a larger office, a new title (of legal executive) and more pay. She would see the clients (and also apparently started to wear silk frocks) while the solicitor worked on the keyboard. She subsequently went on to undertake full legal training.

Local labour-market conditions and the characteristics of the available labour force both inform recruitment, training and patterns of work organisation practice and are also influenced by them. The introduction of new information technologies can both lead to further polarisation in the quality and rewards of jobs, or can free up hitherto under-used talent. Although few patterns of work organisation are technologically deterministic, some patterns are still clearly shaped by sets of expectations about what jobs are appropriate for what gender: the introduction of new technology simply brings its own version of that segmentation.

CONCLUSION

This chapter has raised some issues about the relationship between gendering in technology and gendering in training, and has sought to illustrate them through making some comparisons between companies in the FRG and the United Kingdom, particularly South Wales. It is clear that skills shortages in the future are a vital issue, and that the lack of progression within organisations and within training systems will impede employers' attempts to fill those shortages. In the FRG, there is evidence in the most advanced companies of reorganisation and desegmentation. In a culture which is 'qualification-driven' and where individuals' experience of training leads them to believe it can be transformative, enthusiasm for continuing training coupled with desegmentation may well dilute the impact of class and gender on occupational mobility. In the South Wales companies we studied, on the whole there is less evidence of both opening up channels within organisations, and individuals who have experienced training as a route to progression. Moreover, segmentation within the training infrastructure compounds the problem.

Although all women experience aspects of patriarchal relations at work and the effects of the masculinisation of technology to a greater or lesser extent, it is important to recognise that as well as commonalities there are differences between women too. Clearly, an individual's gender, race and industry are significant, but so too is the training culture of the country, region and firm. Living in Baden-Württemberg rather than Bridgend can make a significant difference to chances of securing access to training and employment in a high-tech job.

Chapter 8

Women and the enterprise culture[1]

This chapter explores the potential of self-employment and small-business proprietorship as a mechanism to challenge the restrictions of existing gender relations in the labour market. It examines the concept of 'enterprise' which underpins the policies in the United Kingdom, and the extent to which such measures have in effect excluded women. It draws upon experiences of other countries, in particular Australia, which have targeted women in local economic development initiatives to explore both the barriers to women's enterprise and the potential that an enterprise economy might have for providing opportunities for women to create their own jobs and improve their life chances.

In the spring of 1989, three-quarters of a million women of working age reported that they were self-employed; this is considerably fewer than the figure for men but more than double the number of a decade earlier (Department of Employment 1990a:620). Most of the increase took place in the latter part of the 1980s. This is despite the fact that women have not been targeted in state measures to foster enterprise. Business start-up courses that are available for both women and men to attend are usually designed to meet the needs of male proprietors, often with the support of a family behind him, rather than the circumstances that face women. As a result, they usually fail to address the needs of women and as a consequence fail to attract them. There are hardly any women-only enterprise courses. Moreover, given the projected labour shortage (see Chapter 6), it is unlikely that there will be more tailor-made courses for potential women entrepreneurs in the future.

Some of the initiatives in the New Right's package of measures to foster enterprise actually specifically exclude certain women, most notably the Enterprise Allowance Scheme, which insists upon applicants being registered unemployed and in receipt of benefit.[2] Unsurprisingly, relatively few women have taken advantage of the scheme. So far, attempts to foster the 'enterprise culture' appear to be passing women by, particularly black women. Finance houses are reluctant to invest in women, and, with the exception of some organisations in Scotland and some Co-operative

Development Agencies, advice and business support agencies do not target them. The only identifiable British initiatives that are geared specifically to women, the Women's Enterprise Development Agency (WEDA) (which started in 1987) and the networking organisation Women in Business (which dates from 1985), were both set up by women for women.

Figures from the LFS on self-employment and small-business start-ups suggest that enterprise has grown substantially in the 1980s. However, such figures need to be interpreted with some caution. It is clearly the case that much of the growth in 'entrepreneurialism', particularly that of women, is actually 'pseudo-self-employment' (Curran and Roberts 1989). Sets of flexible arrangements such as 'self-employed' home-working and sub-contracting (which do not bring the autonomy that self-employment suggests) account for some of the apparent growth. It is particularly women who are likely to feature in such arrangements: their domestic commitments can severely restrict the terms on which they can sell their labour.

Patriarchal relations in the home and the uneven division of domestic labour fashion the type of businesses that many other women set up. Phizacklea (1988), among others, has done much to deconstruct the apparent increase in entrepreneurialism among some women from Asian cultures by demonstrating that their exploitation within the family is simply being extended to their working lives. The success of some ethnic businesses is in part at least a result of the strength of patriarchal relations, which allow women to provide essential cheap labour. As this chapter seeks to illustrate, much of the hype in the growth of both men and women's increased participation in the small-business sector is illusory, and access to true self-employment is gendered.

In excluding, or at least not catering for would-be women entrepreneurs' needs, the United Kingdom's economic development policies are sharply at odds with those of other countries and rest upon a highly specific and limited notion of enterprise. In most European countries, in particular Sweden, the FRG and Portugal, there are special training schemes that target underprivileged women; indeed, in Europe as a whole there has been a substantial increase in women entrepreneurs during the 1980s. In the United States, Gould and Lyman (1987:2–3) report that 'smokestack chasing' models of economic development are meeting with increasing frustration; hence

> The idea of sponsoring a program that will draw upon previously unrecognized strengths of disadvantaged women (including some of those receiving public assistance), and will create more jobs and stimulate local economic activity is increasingly attractive to cities and states all over the country. In fact, such efforts are gaining popularity around the world – in both developed and developing countries.

Gould and Lyman document examples of such initiatives from all over the world, including some particularly imaginative projects from Third World countries. The OECD maintains that special encouragement needs to be afforded women to enable them to use their potential for initiative and creativity, and the EC has shown great interest in the contribution that women can make to local employment initiatives and enterprise through a series of research projects (see Centre for Research on European Women 1984; European Commission 1989; Halpern 1988; May 1987). It has also established a Network for Women in Local Employment Initiatives and financed a number of women's businesses, while the OECD has offered guidelines for supporting women's enterprise (OECD 1990).

In the United States, some of the schemes, incentives and training courses on offer have been directed in particular to the needs of the disadvantaged job-seeker, a category which, of course, includes the woman returner. In Australia too, particularly in the State of Western Australia, schemes have been introduced with the result that women in the late 1980s were setting up in business twice as fast as men, and their businesses were lasting longer (Rees, T. 1989b).

In both countries, there are two categories of women coming forward to such courses. One comprises disadvantaged women, often from ethnic minorities, subsisting on benefits or low wages, who see self-employment as a route out of poverty; the other consists of educated, professional, well-resourced would-be entrepreneurs, apparently fed up with the deleterious effect that their gender has on their promotion prospects (I return to these two categories later). In both cases, stepping outside the existing job market and creating their own employment reduces the disadvantage experienced because of gender, and for some, because of race as well.

To what extent could measures to foster the enterprise culture be an agent of social change to break down the reproduction of inequality in the labour market? For those traditionally denied equal access to good jobs, are there any benefits in responding to the exhortation to self-employment or setting up a small business as a means of acquiring autonomy almost certainly not available in the kinds of jobs open to them? More specifically, would it behove women returners to set their faces against employers attempting to seduce them back into low-paid, dispensable jobs and to create instead their own, alternative employment?

These questions are in essence unanswerable in the context of the United Kingdom. As this chapter seeks to demonstrate, without a structure of support mechanisms to foster women's entrepreneurialism, the extent to which women could or would flourish in the enterprise culture can only be a matter of conjecture. However, the experiences of the United States and Australia illustrate what policies aimed at women can achieve. Although it is too early to say whether such policies will survive, let alone impact upon gender relations in the business world or the home, it is clear that for many women they have provided opportunities for taking control of their working lives. The chapter concludes with a review of the merits and demerits of social targeting in enterprise.

FOSTERING AN ENTERPRISE CULTURE

Conceptualising enterprise

The word 'enterprise' seems to defy satisfactory definition: Keat (1991:2) refers to its 'elasticity' as a concept, and its proponents in the education for enterprise movement will often maintain that to define it is to shackle the spirit of invention, or to prevent a thousand flowers from blooming. Despite the centrality of the concept to Conservative education and economic development policies during the 1980s, until relatively recently it received attention almost exclusively from those commentators concerned with the education for enterprise movement. Only in the late 1980s and early 1990s were there attempts to deconstruct its meaning more broadly, through an analysis of ministerial speeches, government documents and policies, or through surveys of the self-employed (see Blanchflower and Oswald 1990; Burrows 1991; Cross and Payne 1991; Keat and Abercrombie 1991; Rees, G. and Rees, T. 1989, 1992; Rees, G. and Thomas 1991).

In school-based education for enterprise, activities that could be loosely described as action learning, interdisciplinary teaching or project-based, student-led, experiential learning came to be called 'enterprise' exercises and as such were eligible for small grants from a range of government departments, banks and private industry, even when that particular initiative had formed part of the school's programme for some years. Through re-labelling, the phenomenon was seen to be growing before our very eyes (rather reminiscent of the growth of 'mugging' effected by the re-designation of a set of crimes previously called something else – see Hall *et al.* 1978). In so far as there is an essential point to the concept of enterprise in the education for enterprise movement, it involves helping young people to move towards independence and autonomy, a notion similar to the concept of 'empowerment' that was the currency in the 1970s. Johnson (1988) contrasts the pedagogic emphases of 'conventional education' with enterprise education approaches to illustrate how the former moulds pupils into passive recipients of knowledge, and the latter produces independent young people who know 'how' rather than knowing 'that'.

Fostering the enterprise culture through education for enterprise, I have argued elsewhere (Rees, T. 1988b), represents a highly ambitious attempt by the state to retain positive attitudes to the work ethic among the unemployed and the future workforce, while changing their aspiration to secure a job as an employee to an expectation that they may have to take responsibility for creating their own. To be unemployed then becomes inexcusable. Focusing on the young is, of course, wholly appropriate as a means of resocialising the future labour force. At the same time, who would maintain that enterprise education is not pedagogically worthwhile in its own right? Who can argue that it is not a good idea to teach young people to think and be 'enterprising'? Teachers claim that enterprise education appears to be popular with schoolchildren, particularly among those who have tended to give up on, and absent themselves from, more traditional educational provision. On the other hand, there can be no doubt that the DTI and DES, which sponsor the Mini-Enterprise in Schools Project (MESP), would be disappointed that the experience of setting up small companies in schools appears to be having the effect of turning pupils off the idea of self-employment and small businesses, if indeed, they had ever entertained the idea in the first place (Jamieson *et al.* 1988; Williamson 1989).

An analysis of the school-based companies that were set up suggests that what might be regarded as essential components of 'enterprise', such as innovation and risk-taking, were distinctly lacking (see Rees, T. *et al.* 1990; Williamson 1989). Nevertheless, the concept became increasingly popular as a solution to the problems both of youth unemployment and of other groups in society suffering the effects of industrial restructuring (see MacDonald and Coffield 1991). Scarman (1981) identified enterprise as a means through which ethnic minorities could make a 'stake in the community', in the wake of the Brixton riots. The enterprise culture, as proselytised through Conservative ideology, and embodied in a series of Government initiatives has in effect, then, come to mean the advocacy and encouragement of self-employment and small businesses (see Rees, G. and Rees, T. 1991), targeted at the people most likely to suffer the effects of industrial restructuring and recession. As the White Paper, *Building Businesses . . . not Barriers* (Department of Employment 1986), put it: 'The prime aim of the Department of Employment is to encourage the development of an enterprise economy. The way to reduce unemployment is through more businesses, more self-employment and greater wealth creation, all leading to more jobs.'

Burrows (1991:1) states that 'The discourse of the enterprise culture has become one of the major articulating principles of the age'. However, the UK Government version of enterprise is arguably a very narrow one. Measures to promote it have focused on increasing self-employment and small-business creation to the exclusion of alternative models of economic development, such as co-operatives and community businesses, that might suit specific individuals, families or communities rather better. Moreover, although the concept of enterprise might imply risk-taking and innovation, it is evident that for many of the small businesses so created, there is nothing particularly innovative or risk-taking about them, nor are they job- or wealth-creating. The association of such forms of employment with the rebirth of 'enterprise' in such cases is a complete misnomer.

Indeed, MacDonald and Coffield (1991) describe young people's 'risky businesses' in the North East of England as having more to do with a 'culture of survival' than a 'culture of enterprise'. Nevertheless, successive Labour Force Surveys reveal a significant increase in the numbers of 'self-employed' between 1981 and 1988, from 2 to 3 million, and this is heralded as a sign of the success of the policies and the fostering of new attitudes.

The 'new entrepreneurs'

Where does this growth in self-employment and small business come from? Is it indeed the unemployed embracing the new philosophy? Most of the growth is in the form of one-person businesses (Hakim 1989), which rather cuts across Conservative hopes that the small-business sector will expand to create further jobs. Between a third and a fifth of new entrants are 'reluctant' entrepreneurs, who turn to self-employment in the absence of other opportunities (Bevan *et al.* 1988). Some of these are people made redundant or people whose employers wish to change the basis upon which they engage their services. Fevre (1987), for example, describes how the 'slim down' of British Steel in South Wales involved buying back on a sub-contracted basis the labour of former employees. The growth in home-working, franchising and sub-contracting all lead to an apparent increase in the small-business sector, although, in fact, much of this should be offset against concomitant losses of 'employees in employment'.

Despite the focus of government policies, the main entrants to self-employment and small businesses have come from the ranks of the employed rather than the unemployed, the young, or the economically inactive, although Blanchflower and Oswald (1990) found no evidence of an increase in *desire* for self-employment among employees during the 1980s. For some, however, redundancy acted as a trigger to fulfil a long-held ambition to become self-employed (Carter and Cannon 1988a). The types of enterprise set up vary to an extraordinary degree; there is often very little in common between enterprises that fall into the same category of employing one or a small number of people. Most of those who take advantage of the Enterprise Allowance Scheme are in low cost-of-entry, low-skilled, labour-intensive work. More successful and lucrative business starts are in the high-tech industries, and financial and professional services.

It is wholly unsurprising that relatively few unemployed people started new businesses given the social characteristics that people who set up *successful* (defined as profitable and sustained) small enterprises tend to have. Previous managerial experience, experience in the chosen market, the availability of capital, and significant levels of family support are all key factors in determining success (see Rees, G. and Rees, T. 1992; Storey 1982), and these features are more likely to figure in the cultural capital of the employed than the unemployed. They are also more likely to be available to men than to women.

HIS FAMILY, HER FAMILY: OBSCURING AND OBSTRUCTING WOMEN'S ENTERPRISE

The importance of a family background in small business for the social reproduction of the entrepreneur, and of family support to the success of a venture have been well documented in the 'small firms' literature. Hakim (1989) reports that lapsed entrepreneurs were less likely to have such a family network compared with those contemplating expansion. However, the extent to which an entrepreneur can count on support from members of the family takes on a distinctly gendered pattern. In effect, it means that men are able to count on (frequently unpaid) labour from their wives and indeed other members of the family (Finch 1983).

Family and community support networks have been particularly important for Asian entrepreneurs in making available resources such as cheap female labour and alternative sources for capital for new small-business ventures. I have already referred to Phizacklea's work, which shows that in Asian businesses in particular, the labour of women family members is essential. Phizacklea (1988:23) reports that 'In the clothing industry many wives and daughters of Asian, Turkish, and Greek Cypriot entrepreneurs supply unpaid labour as machinists and finishers, but also as supervisors, mediating between the "boss" and other machinists'. While the marginality and disadvantage experienced by Asians applying for jobs because of discrimination (Jenkins 1988; MacDonald and Coffield 1991) provide a push factor, tight social networks provide socialisation mechanisms that encourage entry into the small-business economy, as Ward and Jenkins (1984) have shown. But access to that support is highly gendered, and Asian women who experience particular sets of exclusionary devices from employers also have specific difficulties in becoming self-employed in their own right.

Moreover, not only are many women expected to contribute to the 'family business', but Goffee and Scase (1985) reveal that the women entrepreneurs they interviewed had received little or no input into their businesses from other members of their families, nor was their domestic load lightened in response to their business commitments. The likelihood of those women's businesses succeeding and prospering in those circumstances is thus inhibited. Carter and Cannon (1988a, 1988b) report that some husbands join their wives' companies after they have been set up, either because they offer better employment prospects or because the woman entrepreneur feels she can trust him with management responsibilities better than an outsider. Such experiences have not always worked out well, however; the authors report cases where the women feel that their enterprise is being 'taken over' and their own credibility diminished. Similarly, a group of Bangladeshi women wanting to set up a co-operative in Rochdale experienced difficulties when the men in their community involved themselves in their plans (Greater Manchester Economic Development Officers' Association 1990).

MEASURING WOMEN'S ENTREPRENEURIALISM

The number of women among the ranks of the new self-employed and small-business proprietors has increased at a faster rate than that of men in the late 1980s; women are thought now to comprise about a third of the new entrepreneurs (Hakim 1989; Reeves 1989). However, just as the number of women employees in employment has historically been, and still is, systematically under-recorded in official statistics (see Alexander 1976), so, too, figures on self-employment and small business do not 'count' all of women's endeavour, so this 'rise' needs to be interpreted with some caution. In the nineteenth century, for example, women's work taking in laundry, selling food from the kitchens and taking in lodgers was not recorded as 'work' in the Census, due to the enumerators' implicit theories of social processes which led to sets of assumptions about the respective roles of men and women, and the separation of home and work (see Hakim 1980, 1985; Roberts 1988; and Chapter 2).

More recently, a European Commission (1987) study of 17,000 'non-employed' women revealed that definitions of self-employment used by national governments for the compilation of statistics exclude many women who run their own businesses or who work independently. Allen and Truman (1992) explore the discrepancies between operational definitions and women's own accounts of their activities to measure the extent to which women's small-business activity is thereby rendered invisible. Comparing Eurostat statistics with the EC survey results, it was calculated that, rather than there being 3 million self-employed women in the European Community, there are nearer 4.4 million, and a further 8 million non-salaried but working in their partner's business (Allen and Truman 1992). Work by Finch (1983) has illustrated at the micro level how wives' incorporation into their husband's jobs takes place. Such contributions to the economy are obscured. A secondary analysis of Inland Revenue files on tax deductions claimed on wives' contributions to their husbands' businesses would be a fascinating and revealing, if perhaps not wholly reliable, measure.

The social construction of the statistics means that activities which are rather more visible, but which are undertaken on a less than full-time basis or on a casual basis, are likely to be ignored. Most research on the small-business sector has tended to focus on manufacturing, whereas women's contribution is more likely to be in the growing service sector (Curran and Burrows 1989). For these kinds of reasons, our understanding of women's strategies for earning an income on their own accord, or contributing unpaid labour to family businesses, is quite inadequate. Nevertheless it is clear, as studies such as that conducted by the European Commission (1987) reveal, that the extent of such activity is grossly underestimated, and that a similar construction of 'what counts' as employment governs what is recognised as self-employment. In both cases, the fact that women are frequently in a position of having to fit their economic activity around domestic commitments determines both its visibility and its status.

Women entrepreneurs

Leaving aside, then, the pseudo-self-employed (as defined by Curran and Roberts 1989), what have been the experiences of women entrepreneurs in Britain? To what extent is it the case that women who set up in business are indeed seeking an alternative form of employment where their gender is less of an impediment to their progress? What motivates women entrepreneurs, and does this differ from what motivates male entrepreneurs?

The recorded increase in women entrepreneurs in the United Kingdom has been relatively recent and there have been few systematic studies of them. Carter and Cannon (1988a, 1988b) conducted a detailed study of sixty female business-owners from London, Glasgow and Nottingham, and revealed their heterogeneity. Although they resisted constructing a typology, they did identify five ideal types of behavioural classifications: *drifters*, *young achievers*, *high achievers*, *returners* and *traditionalists*. It was possible for women to move from one type to another over time. For example, *drifters* tended to be young women who turned to business as a response to unemployment: their subsequent experiences would make them give up or move into the *young achievers* category. *Young achievers* tended to have high aspirations, be well educated and used training to make up for lack of experience. The achievement-orientated group also had strong ambitions but were older and had career-related experience. Some were mothers, others had no intention of having children. *Returners* tended to have qualitatively different experiences: their businesses were built around domestic commitments following a career break. *Traditionalists* were mostly older, and few had had to choose between prioritising family or business.

Goffee and Scase's (1985) study of fifty-four female business proprietors found four distinct categories of women entrepreneurs. The *radicals* were thought to be feminists who were engaged in collective political and economic ventures to promote women's issues; the *innovators* were reacting against experiences of restricted career prospects in conventional employment; the *conventionals* were predominantly working class and had checkered work histories in the secondary labour market, and were forced by economic necessity to engage in their own business; and the *domestics* prioritised their home duties and fitted in small-scale businesses around them. Goffee and Scase suggest that the *conventionals* and the *innovators* had high attachment to entrepreneurial roles and that the *conventionals* and *domestics* had a high attachment to conventional gender roles. The *radicals* had a low attachment to both.

In a study based on thirty-four female entrepreneurs in Northern Ireland, Cromie and Hayes (1988) identified three types. The first they too named *innovators*, as they were similar to those identified by Goffee and Scase. They were less likely to have any children than the other two groups and essentially used proprietorship to develop their work careers. Their reasons for starting up were similar to those of men. For this group alone, the authors felt there was scope for reducing their degree of dependence. The *dualists*, who wanted to fulfil two roles, had started businesses because it allowed them to spend more time with their children than conventional employment: their business ownership had not altered their conjugal roles and the business sectors they had entered were traditionally female. The *returners* tended to be older because of their career break, they had restricted prospects in the labour market and opted for entrepreneurialism as an alternative.

These studies demonstrate that women entrepreneurs are widely hetero-geneous and, as Carter and Cannon stress, their businesses can be highly dynamic. Both the experience of running a business and changes in the life cycle can facilitate women's movement from one category in these schema to another. Domestic commitments are clearly crucial for many women in determining where and how they organise their businesses. As Allen and Truman (1992) argue, whether the motivating factors are push or pull ones, they have to be understood in terms of women's position in the formal labour market and how this articulates with unpaid domestic labour.

Women's motivations for setting up in business

Creating one's own job may seem an obvious option for women. There are those who are unable, because of child-care commitments, to sell their labour on terms that local employers are prepared to reward. There are women who, because of direct or indirect discrimination, are likely to be held back in their careers. And there are women who, because of gender, race and class discrimination in recruitment, are unlikely to have access to jobs that have career tracks at all.

Autonomy has been identified as the single most important motivation for men and women wanting to set up in business in a number of studies (for example, Hakim 1989). At a European level, a recent CEDEFOP survey of women's enterprises also revealed that the most frequent reason given by women for setting up in business was 'to gain autonomy' (May 1987:2). Most entrepreneurs are attracted by the idea for its own sake, rather than because they have a specific business idea that they wanted to realise; indeed, for many, the specific nature of the business was not decided upon initially (Hakim 1989).

However, the 'attractions of being one's own boss', the 'challenge of self-employment' and 'the freedom to choose when to work' take on rather different complexions when looked at from the perspectives of men and women. Hakim (1989) reports that flexibility to choose hours was particularly important to women, outweighing financial considerations. Some 38 per cent of Cromie and Hayes's sample cited wanting to spend more time with their family as a reason for setting up. One-third of the 2,000 small firms surveyed by the National Westminster Bank had women proprietors (Reeves 1989), and the study showed that while both men and women identified economic necessity as the driving force behind setting up, again there were gender differences, women emphasising the need for 'work flexibility' in order to cope with the demands of young children. Just as Main's (1988) secondary analysis of the Women and Employment Survey showed a high workforce attachment on the part of women, but one that had to be manoeuvred around domestic commitments, so too self-employment and small-business activities are both prompted by and moulded around such demands. This is borne out by the fact that women are particularly found among the 80 per cent of the self-employed who work from home, are more likely to be one-person businesses than businesses employing others, and are more likely to be among the 25 per cent of self-employed who work part-time (Curran and Roberts 1989; Hakim 1989).

The desire for independence is a recurring theme in studies of entrepreneurs, but it can clearly imply different things to different people, and there is likely to be a gender dimension to that meaning. Carter and Cannon (1988a:10) deconstruct how women 'at different stages of their lives cited the need for independence from different circumstances'. For some this meant freedom from the restrictions of the formal labour market, either because of race or sex discrimination, or both.

Members of ethnic minorities may have traditionally had to resort to setting up their own small businesses in response to the disadvantage they experience in recruitment and promotion practices (Stanworth and Curran 1973), but this has been far more of an option for some ethnic minorities than others. Marlow (1990) found that in her study of 400 small businesses employing more than twenty people in the West Midlands, hardly any were owned by black Afro-Caribbean entrepreneurs, and she attributes this to special difficulties in obtaining start-up funding and developing marketing opportunities outside their own communities. Asian men and women, who tend to work in labour-intensive industries, are more likely to be self-employed than whites, who in turn are more likely to be self-employed than Afro-Caribbeans, according to Brown (1984).

The 'glass ceiling' (Morrison 1987) has been identified as a major motivating factor for female entrepreneurs to set up in business, particularly in the United States, although some men also report that frustrations with prospects in their previous employment led to their starting up in business. It is clear, from patterns of occupational segregation and women's highly restricted access to top jobs, that they are particularly likely to experience such frustrations as a group.

The Hansard Society Commission on Women at the Top (1990) revealed how desperately few women there are on the boards of British industry. Headhunters for top jobs estimate that 10 per cent of their clients 'would subtly or otherwise reject a woman candidate' (Hansard Society Commission on Women at the Top 1990:58), and the Ashridge Management College's survey of the few women who are on boards reveals all too starkly the narrow pool of candidates from which they tend to be drawn: 'The profile of the average woman board member is someone in her fifties with an international or Oxbridge education and with a family connection to the company or a title' (Holten and Rabbetts 1990:1–2).

Unsurprisingly, then, the National Westminster Bank survey found career blockage to be a major motivating factor (Reeves 1989). As Cromie and Hayes (1988:93) suggest:

> One key advantage of business proprietorship as a female occupation is the absence of organisational selectors. A woman contemplating entrepreneurship does not need to meet organisational selection criteria based on age, gender, experience etc. If the business product or service is well produced and marketed then the fact that a woman runs the business is unimportant.

This rather rosy picture overlooks the extent to which the selectors have the same gatekeeper effect in filtering out women applying for loans and credit or attempting to establish business contacts, however.

Another motivating factor for some women is the desire to work in less rigidly hierarchical organisations than most employers offer. For these women, the notion of 'autonomy' may be interpreted as not only retaining control over when and where to work, but a preference for the lack of hierarchy that a co-operative venture allows. This form of business organisation certainly appears to be particularly popular with women. The Industrial Common Ownership Movement (*Everywoman* 1990:11) reports that 'It has been estimated that over 50% of management positions in co-operative enterprises are held by women – surely the highest ratio for any commercial sector in Western Europe, if not the world'.

Co-operatives and community businesses can be highly appropriate forms of economic organisation for women (and indeed men) living in areas of economic decline. They can negate the need for status differentiation (especially useful in phoenix co-operatives, where workers attempt to construct a co-operative venture from the ashes of a failed business), provide employment in areas where inward investment is unlikely to occur and develop goods and services for the locality not available on the open market. Co-operatives are, however, also highly difficult to organise and can mean substituting self-exploitation for exploitation by others. A major failing has been insufficient understanding of and training in co-operative working and principles, together with the raft of problems faced by any small business. Moreover, they often start with inauspicious beginnings as phoenix co-operatives or with woefully inadequate start-up funds and a restricted market. Finance houses are suspicious of non-hierarchical management structures and prefer to deal with more traditional arrangements; the knock-on effect can be underfunding. Setting up co-operatives in the United Kingdom, given these kinds of difficulties, has tended to be extremely difficult. Wajcman (1983) gives a moving account of the attempts of one group of women to establish a shoe co-operative in Norfolk, which eventually foundered. By contrast, Castelberg-Koulma (1991) shows how women in Greece successfully formed co-operatives to respond to the growing tourist industry, and through them have gained more independence.

It is important to separate out the potential that co-operative organisation can offer, from the experiences of the co-operative movement in the United Kingdom. In Ireland, and in Italy (where co-operatives enjoy a fifth of the market share), producer and distribution co-operatives have been extremely successful and long-lived.

Barriers to women's enterprise

Women who are self-employed and small-business proprietors clearly constitute a highly differentiated group: it is hard to imagine that there is much in common between a pseudo-self-employed garment home-worker, a co-op member in a bakery and a marketing consultant. And yet they share some common barriers to their success as entrepreneurs, over and above the impediments experienced by men. These barriers have their roots in business support mechanisms and training courses that are designed for the particular needs of men. They are exacerbated in structures that have at their root the ideology of the family and assumptions about the roles of men and women within it.

As a consequence, women do not on the whole benefit from measures designed to foster enterprise, but are relied upon to assist men's entrepreneurial activities in direct and indirect ways. Women are then seen as having 'special needs'. The manifestations of the privileging of men's needs within the enterprise economy are expressed in lack of child-care facilities, women having the prime responsibility for domestic commitments within the family; lack of targeting in training and business support agencies; women's relative lack of skills and experience; women's probable lack of family support relative to men; their lack of credibility with customers and suppliers; and their lack of credibility and collateral when negotiating loans and investment capital. Women who live outside conventional nuclear families – for example, as single parents or in lesbian households – are likely to find it more difficult to acquire a mortgage because they challenge finance houses' images of a good investment.

Despite the fact that women are increasingly turning to self-employment, there has been very little targeting of women in courses aimed at people setting up in business. Given that more than one member of a family is frequently involved in starting up a business, it is surprising that the training provided for those wanting to start up has not geared itself more to the family as a unit. This, at the very least, would address the issue of women's marginalisation in their partner's business or within genuine family businesses.

The failure to target women and provide training geared towards their needs has several implications. Those women who do try to start up are at a disadvantage, certainly compared with those who have opportunities for training in other countries. Women entrepreneurs are unlikely to reach their full potential without training and support. Training is needed in business matters, but it is also often needed in substantive skills too because of the ghettoisation of women in a narrow range of low- or semi-skilled, poorly paid work. Offering similar goods and services in an independent capacity does not necessarily mean that the woman will then be earning a good income: she needs to diversify. Moreover, the emphasis on self-employment and small business in existing training and support measures means that alternative models which might appeal to some women more are not on offer.

In Scotland, there are far more support agencies for the development of co-operatives and community businesses than in England, while in Wales a substantial proportion of the ventures supported by the Wales Co-operative Centre have been phoenix co-operatives run by an all- or predominantly female workforce. Co-operative Development Agencies have a relatively small market share of the mushrooming business support services, but they have a conscious policy of targeting both women and the ethnic minorities. This contrasts with Enterprise Agencies in Britain (those which monitor their records) which report that between 25 and 30 per cent of those using their services are women (although some have been able to access ESF funds for women-only courses). The figure for local authorities is lower still, at 10 per cent (Business in the Community 1989). Business advisers are overwhelmingly men.

Finally, unless finance houses themselves learn to be more enterprising, by investing more readily in people without bricks and mortar collateral, the development of some women's businesses will always be constrained. Three of Carter and Cannon's (1988a) sample reported having to use their partners as guarantors for borrowing: one Glasgow-based engineer seeking finance for a management buy-out in 1987 explained:

> Well, we needed £10,000 each. The other two [men] took the business plan to their bank managers and raised the money no problem. I really didn't think that I would have any problem either, you see I had £8,000 of my own personal savings – which were nothing to do with my husband – plus the house in my name not his. So I went to my bank manager, told him about the buy-out, showed him the business plan and asked him for the extra £2,000 that I needed, and he said no, he just turned me down flat. I was absolutely furious, I just couldn't believe it. So I said to him, if I had wanted the money for a car loan would he give it to me and he said, well, of course I would Mrs ——, it's just that we don't lend to women for business ventures.
>
> (Respondent quoted in Carter and Cannon 1988b:15)

These barriers are not, of course, peculiar to the United Kingdom: similar impediments to women's enterprise were identified in both the United States and Australia.

The focus now turns to exploring what lessons might be learned from experiences Down Under (if that is not inexcusably Northern Hemispherist).

THE 'PRODUCTIVE ECONOMY' IN AUSTRALIA

The emphasis on self-employment and small businesses is part and parcel of an ideology that celebrates self-sufficiency. However, the notion of self-sufficiency is one that can be equally popular with the Left and the Right, albeit for different reasons. Hence it is the case that, while not necessarily couched in the same discourse, the concept of enterprise is one that can be traced in countries with social democratic and Labour governments, such as Sweden and Australia. This also explains the acceptability and prioritising of measures designed to explore and promote enterprise in international organisations such as the OECD and the EC. While macro-economic policies are deemed able to contain national unemployment levels, local employment initiatives are increasingly viewed as the means to reduce them in disadvantaged regions where capital is unlikely to invest of its own accord.

In Australia, in the late 1980s, the term 'enterprise' was not part of the daily discourse of government ministers and civil servants. Rather, the talk was of the need to foster a 'productive economy'.[3] The argument ran that, with a vulnerable overdependence on, and depletion in, natural resources, human resources must be used more effectively for the creation of wealth. In the late 1980s, when unemployment levels began to rise to unacceptable levels, the Federal Government explored the extent to which local employ-

ment initiatives could be used to create work in areas of high unemployment, and individual states introduced a range of measures.

The focus on human resources implies both a need for skills and making
use of them efficiently; some of the initiatives at state level show an attempt
to focus on workers disadvantaged in the labour market. In the more
progressive states in the late 1980s, there was a growing number of schemes
aimed at encouraging or enabling women to set up their own businesses.
One-third of the population is composed of people who are migrants or the
first-generation offspring of migrants, and schemes are particularly targeted
towards them. Kalatzis (1990) reports that between 9 and 14 per cent of
employed Australian women own their own businesses, and that women of
Third World and Mediterranean origin are more likely to be among them
than other groups. Italians and Vietnamese have particularly strong traditions of self-employment (Johns *et al.* 1983).

These schemes, it should be emphasised, need to be seen in context.
Overall, the approach to the problem of skills shortages in Australia is to
recruit from abroad. The desire to develop jobs through entrepreneurialism
informs migration policies; the wealthy and those promising to create jobs
are excluded from the clamp-down on immigration. More significantly, the
schemes described in this section were introduced by Labor administrations,
and since the research was conducted in 1988, some states have had a change
of government, some have been involved in other difficulties such as
financial problems or corruption charges, and the state of the national
economy generally has worsened considerably. The net result is that the
schemes have to be viewed as examples of what is possible by targeting
women in enterprise measures: the future of such schemes is not necessarily
assured. Finally, it should be said that they have not been subject to a
rigorous evaluation; the impact described is on start-ups rather than
prolonged, successful business activity.

The targeting of women in these initiatives is in stark contrast to the
United Kingdom but again, seen in context, is less surprising. Successive
Labor administrations at Federal Government level and in some of the
states have implemented a series of legislative measures designed to foster
equality of opportunity. The scope of the 1983 Sex Discrimination Bill was
claimed at the time to be 'more far reaching than in the US, Britain and
Canada' (reported in Sullivan 1990), and the 1986 Affirmative Action
(Equal Employment Opportunities for Women) Act required both public-
and private-sector employers to institute an eight-step affirmative action
programme. Such measures are not without their critics for leaving
structural barriers intact and doing more for the relatively small number of
women on career tracks than the majority in low-skilled, low-paid work.
Patterns of occupational segregation remain more marked than in most
European countries. Nevertheless, the legislation, combined with the opening up of an already fluid (relative to the United Kingdom) Civil Service, has

facilitated the movement of many women into senior positions in government departments. Some were feminists, initially attracted into the Civil Service through openings in offices specifically set up to advise the state premiers on women.

These 'femocrats' or 'sisters in suits' are in themselves a source of interest as a new dynamic in the workings of the state (see Eisenstein 1991; Franzway *et al.* 1989; Sawer 1990; Yeatman 1990), and they certainly amaze foreign academics with their designer suits and Italian shoes (see Rees, T. 1988d; Watson 1990). They were undoubtedly instrumental in ensuring the delivery of training schemes and support for women wanting to set up in business. It is important to stress, too, that the enterprises supported are real companies; the women concerned have not simply swapped exploitation for self-exploitation. They earn a living wage and increasingly employ other women. Many are set up as partnerships.

The inspiration for some of the measures in Western Australia came from the United States in the form of the National Coalition for Women's Enterprise (formerly known as HUB Co-Ventures, or the HUB Program for Women's Enterprise), a national programme that was launched in the United States in 1983. It supports women wanting to set up in business largely through women-only seminars and training courses. It was pioneered by Jing Lyman, who quickly identified two very different groups of women who were particularly interested in setting up in business. There were well educated, relatively well resourced women who wanted the independence and freedom from what they saw as promotion blockages because of their gender, and, by contrast, poor, disadvantaged women, often suffering the double discrimination of being female and black, who saw self-employment as a route out of subsistence living on low wages and/ or welfare. HUB has concentrated on the latter, by working with community-based women's organisations, community leaders and existing successful women entrepreneurs to build up support and information for women's small-business activities. The courses designed to help these women set up in business have been remarkably successful in leading to start-ups of genuine small companies employing others (Mercaldi 1985).

When Lisa Baker of the Employment Division of the state of Western Australia was approached by a small group of businesswomen wanting advice, she flew Jing Lyman over from the HUB Program for Women's Enterprise in New York to run a seminar. Expecting a very limited interest in the seminar, she arranged a low-profile event. Nevertheless, 400 women turned up, and further hastily arranged seminars were also packed out.

The courses and the other measures designed to support women in business specifically tackle those problems identified by local women who had made attempts to set up in business. Some of these problems were identical to those described in Chapter 4 as problems of re-entering the labour market as an employee. Some were those that a man might equally encounter in the process of starting a business. However, there were other, more specific needs that were identified as crucial, too. The two main groups of women were clearly in very different circumstances and in some respects had different needs, but these needs overlapped under three broad headings:

1 Women have poor access to start-up capital.
2 Women considering setting up in business lack confidence and skills.
3 Women have domestic commitments.

A range of measures designed to support the women entrepreneurs were set up, including specialist advice, access to guaranteed loans and training sessions. The main focus of the measures in Australia, however, has been the crucial one of finance, and this is the issue that I want to discuss here. Confidence and child care are considered more generally in the chapters on women returners and positive action, respectively.

Finance

State governments in Western Australia, New South Wales and Victoria have all made available loan funds earmarked for women. Women on the whole not only have access to fewer resources than men which can be used as collateral, but they also earn on average in Australia about two-thirds of the salaries of men. These factors clearly affect their ability to raise substantial personal funds to invest in an enterprise. Low-income women are seen as a high risk and therefore have difficulty in getting investment capital.

Women 'high fliers' who leave professional jobs to set up in business experience less difficulty than low-income women in securing start-up capital. However, while banks may give a medium-income woman A $50,000 to set up, they are less likely to follow that up with funds for expansion five years later than they would if she were a man. Part of the difficulty tends to lie in the fact that women are not immersed in male business networks; this means that they are relatively unlikely to know potential loan guarantors. Although studies have shown that, as far as banks are concerned, women are less likely than men to default, they tend not to have any capital or insurance behind them.

Some of the Australian states analysed the structural and institutional constraints that restrict women's entrepreneurialism in some detail, and are seeking to redress them. Financing emerged as the key issue, however, and loan funds earmarked for women's business projects have been an important development. Victoria was the first state to set up a trust fund (the Victorian Women's Trust Fund Ltd), the interest from which is used to provide start-up loans for women who would be unlikely to secure funding from conventional finance houses.

In Western Australia, a start-up fund was given over to a finance house which was asked to make the final decision on investing in women, after they had been screened by the Employment Division of the Department of Employment and Training. As the funds did not belong to the bank, the gatekeepers could afford to relax the normal stipulations of 'bricks and mortar' collateral, access to which women are patently less likely to have. Financial institutions were thus persuaded by the Western Australia state government to use criteria for loans that are more appropriate for women.

Finance houses were encouraged to consider other criteria, to recognise that a woman's commitment, indeed desperation, to make an enterprise work, together with the business idea itself, were more relevant than actual resources for collateral. The initiative in Western Australia met with some success in so far as the banks did invest in women who would not otherwise have received funding, and did learn to recognise the validity of alternative criteria.

Ethical investments

Women's businesses can benefit, too, from ethical investments, the growth of which has been described as the single biggest change in post-crash investment behaviour, and one that is designed to tap into 'yuppie' money (Fitzgerald and Associates 1987:43). Whereas ethical investments in the United Kingdom tend to imply a negative selection, such as not investing in countries with oppressive regimes, the tobacco industry, arms manufacturers or companies known to be polluters or despoilers of the environment, in Australia they are used far more for positive selection. Specific localities or projects may be targeted to be the recipients of ethical investments. While the return on the investment may be lower in terms of interest rates, this is willingly sacrificed because of the knowledge that the money is being used to a particular effect: for example, sustaining local jobs. It is an important development in Australia in that it releases funds for investment in the poorer regions.

One such region in Western Australia is Esperance, which suffered general rural decline and a high level of farm debt. Quotas on tuna fishing also adversely affected the regional economy. The Esperance Enterprise Committee was set up to attempt to support job creation in local employment initiatives in the region; it has achieved a degree of success in providing professional support, training and access to networks of key individuals in finance houses and government circles. About seventy businesses have been set up, and the economy has diversified. One of the most innovative projects to have been helped by the Committee is a wild-flower enterprise; there is a growing market for them in urban and suburban Perth (Western Australia is known as the 'Wild Flower State' although admittedly not until a proposal to call it the 'State of Excitement' was turned down).

As an aside, in the United Kingdom, some 'ethical companies', mostly within the co-operative sector, have managed to raise capital through the issue of non-voting shares or stock loan (non-voting shares are important if the members of the co-operative or community business wish to retain control of their organisation). However, there are difficulties such as the multitude of legal restrictions which need to be unravelled and understood. Ethical investments are, initially at any rate, unlikely to match market interest-return rates, and this severely restricts the number of potential investors. It is enormously expensive to launch targeted share issues to those investors who would be attracted by them; these are clearly more likely to be individuals than, for example, pension funds, which are obliged to seek the highest return rates.

One solution to this latter problem is for ethical investment share issue to be managed through umbrella organisations. The Industrial Common Ownership Fund (ICOF), which supports co-operatives, has created a £500,000 revolving loan fund for non-voting shares. The Ethical Investment Research and Information Service advises people wanting to make ethical investments.

As yet, the number of examples of co-operatives, community businesses receiving support from ethical investments in the United Kingdom remains meagre, and the support mechanisms, such as brokers, are not yet effectively in place.

Developing skills and providing child care

In Western Australia, in addition to access to guaranteed loans, measures were introduced to tackle the other two needs identified by women entrepreneurs: lack of skills and child-care provision. Women-only training sessions were held where crèches were provided and the hours arranged to suit women with child-care commitments. The courses tackled confidence building, but also developed women's ability to recognise that they had talents that were appropriate to running a business without necessarily realising it. Managing a household on a low budget, for example, demands cash-flow skills. Organising baby-sitting circles or fund-raising events involve personnel and managements skills that are used in business. An important task was to demystify the jargon used in the business world and to alert women to the fact that they have experience of some of the processes involved, if not access to the discourse used to describe them. This approach is similar to the notion of 'accredited learning', which is gaining ground in courses directed at women returners in the United Kingdom, where attempts are made to recognise and value skills acquired by women during periods out of the labour market.

Specialist advice was also made available and women business advisers appointed. Supporting a network of women entrepreneurs to act as 'mentors' to new entrepreneurs had the effect of supplying crucial support in the event of crises of confidence or need for advice, and providing a circle of potential guarantors and business contacts.

In New South Wales, in 1987, a series of studies and consultative meetings commissioned by the State Government concentrated on areas of high migrant and ethnic minority populations and identified the same three barriers to women's economic activity: access to finance for women wanting to set up in business, lack of child-care facilities more generally, and lack of skills. An initiative followed that was directed at migrant women in particular. The then Minister for Industry and Small Business was concerned about 'hidden unemployment' among women who had ideas about what work they would like to do but who needed flexible working arrangements to accommodate their domestic commitments. He saw them as being mostly married women who did not appear in the unemployment statistics. There was particular concern about 'home-based' women who were engaged in less than fifteen hours a week paid employment outside the home. An A $2 million Women's Employment Trust was set up to be administered by the 'NSW Women's Employment Company' to help overcome the discrimination that the studies showed women were experiencing in financing. The State Bank agreed to participate in vetting applications for funding. Training measures were also announced and A $1.5 million was set aside to fund six new child-care centres in areas of highest need in West Sydney.

There are, then, projects to assist women from ethnic minorities, and women in depressed regions, although again it should be emphasised that the numbers benefiting remain modest. But what about the original inhabitants of Australia, among whom unemployment rates are far higher than any other group, Aborigine people?

Aborigine women

Measures designed to encourage Aborigine people to set up their own businesses have, as yet, not on the whole been successful. All too often they have been predicated upon an inappropriate set of cultural and economic assumptions. However, there are examples of initiatives – for example, from the Appropriate Technology Development Group Incorporated (APACE), based in Western Australia – which have very sensitively enabled groups of Aborigines to remain where they want to live, retaining their own culture and lifestyle, and yet be assisted in creating their own employment on their own terms, and using technology which is appropriate to life in the bush. For example, while semi-automatic washing machines were given to some Aboriginal communities, they proved totally inappropriate when used to clean blankets ingrained with sand and grit, the main washing need. Lack of servicing networks and electricity, together with heavy water consumption, rendered such machines useless. APACE was involved in developing hand-powered machines that are made by unemployed Aborigines. Similarly, water flush toilets have not been successful, so APACE invented the 'Ventilated Improved Pit Latrine', which 'eliminates the problems associated with water flush systems and provides a healthy alternative to the expensive and troublesome septic and sewer systems' (Walker 1987:17). Other businesses that Aborigines themselves have developed include arts and crafts and bush-walking holidays.

There is understandable resistance among many Aborigine people to Government schemes that foster dependency, as Rose Wanganeen (1990:69), an Aborigine herself, writes: 'The authorities removed any aspect of self-determination and attempted to make Aboriginal people totally dependent on government facilities and hand-outs.' Schemes designed to empower Aborigine people to develop their own enterprises require considerable thought, understanding and flexibility; to respond adequately implies a high degree of specificity determined by local circumstances. Few as yet are directed exclusively at women. Successful examples are outnumbered by less sensitive measures, which can be extremely wasteful of resources and can cause a backlash among white Australians.

Since the late 1980s, the state of the economy has worsened, the Australian Labor Party (ALP) has lost control of the Government in New South Wales and there has been a change of ALP Premier in Victoria and Western Australia (both the new incumbents are women). These shifts have implications for the kinds of policies that will be developed and the measures that will be financed in the future. However, the idea of women's venture-capital funds is receiving continued support.

SOCIAL JUSTICE AND TARGETING

I believe the questions posed by these measures are these. Can 'enterprise', be it self-employment, partnerships, small businesses, co-operatives or even community businesses, provide an alternative set of life chances for people disadvantaged by the rigid sets of structures and processes that determine the allocation of opportunities and rewards in the traditional labour market? And is the vision offered by radical feminists, of 'opting out' into a totally separate labour market peopled by women only, an option that would indeed eradicate the impact of gender and race on promotion and pay levels? *Everywoman*, a magazine published by a women's co-operative in the United Kingdom, publishes directories that enable the reader to buy most goods and services exclusively from women; they are compiled for the purchaser wishing to discriminate positively for ideological reasons, or from fear of male tradesmen calling at the house (*Everywoman* 1987, 1990). *Everywoman* argues in its introduction that as men have more access to resources than women, and as this underpins other inequalities, then buying exclusively from women helps to restore the balance:

Green consumerism has fuelled the environmental movement with real financial power. Feminist consumer choices can make an equally powerful contribution to equality . . ..

Let's not forget, if (when?) we are accused of discrimination, that men in business gravitate naturally to each other, feel far more comfortable doing business with other men, and in many cases have a vast network of organisations to promote their mutual interests which specifically discriminate against women (such as the Freemasons; many of the City of London livery companies; elite men-only clubs; and most branches of the Rotary).

(*Everywoman* 1990:6, 11)

The measures designed to foster women's entrepreneurialism in Australia certainly do not emerge from a radical, separatist movement, rather they are rooted in good old-fashioned capitalist ideology tempered with a dose of liberalism in the spirit of giving women 'a fair go'. They are aimed at encouraging the market to operate more efficiently by making the most of human resources. But could a by-product of these attempts to produce better capitalists be social change, through the redistribution of resources? More specifically, could the productive economy actually provide an alternative for women who are otherwise destined to be economically dependent on either a man or the state. Could it offer a route to financial autonomy, and all that follows from that? Could women benefit from the surplus value extracted from their own labour?

Many (not all) employment-creating and training agencies recognise that they face a central dilemma as to whether or not to target certain categories of unemployed people. Is it most cost-effective to provide more opportunities for those who stand a good chance of being able to find or make work for themselves in a labour-market economy that privileges certain social attributes and has need of certain skills? This option ensures having a high 'success' rate in a relatively short space of time. On the other hand, should the disadvantaged be targeted? This option means less likelihood of a successful outcome, and it may take considerably longer and cost more to turn someone who has been unemployed or not employed for some time into an employee or self-employed statistic. However, such endeavours may result in a net increase in human resources that can be of benefit later on.

The hurdles facing the second option are high. The need for confidence building is the overridingly significant finding in studies of women returners and the long-term unemployed (see Chapter 4). But confidence building is time consuming, it can only be tackled in small groups, it needs special skills on the part of tutors, and trainees can find it patronising if it is not handled sensitively. Opportunities which target the disadvantaged may be the only hope for such people of ever securing employment again. But courses directed at them should not equip trainees only to get low-paid, insecure employment. They should be followed through with opportunities to change their life chances. Otherwise, they merely reproduce and perpetuate existing patterns of inequality. Unfortunately this has, in the past, been the case with so many Wider Opportunities for Women (WOW) and New Opportunities for Women (NOW) courses, and 'pre-vocational courses' for the ethnic minorities.

In a study of schemes of direct job creation that I carried out in Ireland for the EC in 1979 (Rees, T. 1980), I made the criticism of the Work Experience Scheme (based on the British model operating at the time) that it provided superfluous help to the more marketable school-leavers at the expense of the 'hard to place'. On paper, however, the scheme was a good investment. Substantial proportions of young people on placement with an employer were subsequently offered jobs by them. Indeed, so keen were employers to snap up school-leavers with certain social characteristics and ability level that the placement officers would have to go to the schools to recruit them before their last term had ended. Evaluations that rely upon an examination of placement statistics would not reveal that the scheme was most definitely subsidising the wages bill of employers who would have recruited those school-leavers anyway, leaving disadvantaged youngsters with no employer to offer them a job, and government agencies with no resources left to help them either.

The issue of targeting is one that was a central element in the debate surrounding youth unemployment and state intervention in the 1970s and early 1980s, and is one that I believe should occupy us now in training provision for the enterprise culture. Rather than reproducing inequality, state intervention designed to foster the enterprise culture could prove a force for social change, provided that women are not lured in ever-increasing numbers back into secondary labour-markets jobs in industry into the vacancies left by the short-fall of school-leavers.

CONCLUSION

In the United Kingdom, a considerable amount of effort has gone into fostering an enterprise culture. The measures have been highly restricted in their impact on women, despite the fact that women have much to gain from setting up their own businesses. The difficulty lies in the androcentricity of the policies, the ideology of family life which underpin them, and sets of assumptions about gender roles within the family. Individual entrepreneurs who live outside a nuclear family, if they are women, are at a disadvantage. But entrepreneurs within a nuclear family have a resource, if they are men, and an incumbrance, if they are women. Traditional patterns of patriarchal relations in the family inform gatekeepers' decisions which determine women's access to start-up capital and the appropriateness of training courses and business support mechanisms. The same assumptions throw into question her credibility, and the seriousness with which her enterprise is taken by suppliers, creditors, investors and customers. Because the measures are designed to assist men in setting up in business, and to resocialise the young and the unemployed to take responsibility for their own employment, other categories of would-be entrepreneur, such as women, and in particular black and Asian women, are then marginalised by being identified as having 'special needs'.

It is clear that people set up in business for different purposes and with different ideas about what a successful business means to them. Carter and Cannon (1988a) showed that, whereas men may think of success in terms of financial rewards, some women construe their business as successful if they are able to combine domestic responsibilities with income generation. But survival, as well as 'success', is linked to 'family support', business networks, access to finance, being part of a small-business culture, and relevant business and other skills, quite apart from having a good business idea. The implications for state policies that seek to foster enterprise is that crucial stumbling blocks need to be addressed, not in the sense of addressing 'women's special needs', but in the spirit of widening provision from the narrow client group for which it currently caters. TECs need to invest in skills and confidence training for women. Sponsorship of women's business networks can help to offset the exclusionary effects of male networks. Child-care facilities are needed if women are to be able to develop their businesses. And most important of all, access to capital must not be restricted by the social construction of gender and the ideology of the family.

Chapter 9

Conclusion

The chapters of this book have focused on women's experiences of the labour market in a range of sites, at different stages in the life cycle, and in a number of regions and countries. The sites explored are clearly not exhaustive – they were not intended to be; they are snapshots of a diverse range of women which reveal both their differences and their commonalities. Other studies have produced other kaleidoscopes, reflecting the cross-cutting impact of racism, heterosexism, spatial specificities and prejudice against the disabled, but they all have in common a recurring pattern, produced by those pieces of coloured glass which they share.

Women's ability to make choices, to a greater or lesser extent, is constrained by the effects of the inter-relationship between capital and patriarchy. Their activities within the labour market are bounded and circumscribed by both the forces of capital and the prescriptions of power relations between men and women. But the labour market is experiencing a number of far-reaching changes which challenge the logic of traditional patterns of work organisation and gender segregation on both economic and social justice grounds. Arguably, not since the Second World War has there been such interest in women as workers. Demographic changes, the climate of Opportunity 2000, technological changes, the new emphasis on training, the 'feminisation' of the unions and the fostering of an enterprise culture all have the potential to lead to the re-design of jobs, in content, prospects and conditions. However, as some of the studies described in this book show, gender and class relations can be reinforced or even further polarised rather than blurred during periods of change.

There are signs for both optimism and pessimism. The chapter on schoolgirls showed how the paralysis some girls feel when it comes to taking decisions about their future in effect condemns them to low-skilled, low-paid and low-regarded work, interspersed with periods of full-time child care and domestic responsibilities. 'Choices' made about options in school and early labour-market forays make that future almost unavoidable. As Cockburn (1987) has remarked, at 16 it is too late to alter that course: a set of expectations becomes a self-fulfilling prophecy. The messages the girls internalise about gender roles within the family, combined with the realities of patterns of work organisation among local employers, prescribe a lack of interest in paid work as an arena of fulfilment or reward. Like Westwood's (1984) and Pollert's (1981) factory women, the family becomes the focus in the search for an identity.

Careers officers in Valleys communities, as no doubt elsewhere, report that local employers, when addressing careers conventions, habitually address their audience in a gender-specific way, and will only accept people of the appropriate gender for work-experience placements. As the co-operation of employers is both vital and difficult to secure, teachers and careers officers collude. At a key stage in young people's 'career path', exclusionary mechanisms operated by key actors shape and determine decisions, perpetuating patterns of gender segregation. They will continue to do so throughout those girls' working lives.

It is too early to judge the effects of the TECs and LECs on women's labour-market prospects, but so far it seems unlikely that their training needs will be prioritised over other, employer-led considerations. Trade unions need to facilitate the involvement of women with domestic commitments in order not simply to represent the men and child-free, full-time, working women who tend to be the activists. Women entrepreneurs are not getting the training, advice and financial backing they need to become successful entrepreneurs and they are restricted in their business contacts through exclusion from male networks. Many employers are introducing and developing new technologies in such a way as to deskill women's work.

But there are grounds for optimism too. Some new technologies are facilitating women to get more skilled, better-paid jobs (even if those jobs become devalued as soon as they are feminised). Some women, particularly in the United States and Australia, are setting up successful businesses. More women are breaking the glass ceiling; management training courses for women and some returner courses are breeding more assertive women, clutching their action plans in their briefcases albeit also armed with cues on how to 'hide' their gender and, if necessary, their race through their clothes and their behaviour. Women's own business networks are developing. More employers are considering positive action schemes, others may become concerned that they will be conspicuous by their absence if they do not have a career break scheme, a target or a policy, irrespective of their efficacy. These activities may have the effect of moving more women into male space, providing more role-models, mentors, possibilities for an old-girls' network, and so on. For some women, this is good news.

But it is clear, as this book and many others have shown, that while women experience commonalities, there are significant differences too. Turkish women in Siemens in Berlin cannot engage with the changes on offer which would enhance their opportunities; the insecurities of being a working-class migrant may lead to resistance to change, suspicion of the unknown. Although it may become easier for middle-class white women to convince a bank manager to invest in their companies, working-class black women will rarely have the cultural capital available that a bank manager would recognise as indicating a sound investment, irrespective of the merits of the business idea. Moreover, although some well-qualified, talented, under-promoted women may have opportunities denied their predecessors, this will have little effect on the culture of the organisation, or on assumptions made about women as a category. Some women may be acceptable *despite the fact that they are women*. And they are likely to incur male backlash (Cockburn 1991).

What emerges, then, is a conflicting set of pictures. Positive action can enhance women's position; it can also lock them into jobs where there is no need for employers to pay more or alter existing segmented, gendered patterns of working. New technology can enlarge jobs and it can deskill them. Training unqualified women returners can facilitate their re-entry to the labour market; it can also channel them into dead-end jobs. Trade unions can introduce measures to enable women with children to participate; but in so doing they add a third parcel to their double load.

There are, to my mind, two main signs for optimism for the future. The first is found in the tiny number of employers who appear genuinely to be examining their organisations in order better to understand how their structures impede women. Saner patterns of work organisation could emerge, including policies for the 'family-friendly' firm, most of which currently appear to be inspired by the need to recruit and retain women in a period of labour shortage, rather than a reponse to the needs of women *and men* as members of families, with responsibilities.

The second sign of optimism is the increased activity of women themselves. It was women working through the voluntary sector and local authorities who pioneered women-centred training programmes, with such vigour that there is a European Community-wide network (IRIS) of such workshops in existence. It is women in business who are setting up clubs and networking; it has largely been women who have been the prime movers in launching and running women-only training initiatives. Now that there is more support for women as members of the workforce because of demographic, technological and cultural imperatives, it will be easier for those women to make progress.

As the chapters in this book show, tensions between patriarchy and capitalism continue to shape and structure the opportunities for women within the labour market. But the 1990s are a decade of change: the demographic imperative, the removal of trade restrictions in the European Community in 1992, and technological developments all point in the direction of better use being made of human resources, and therefore a greater investment in training. The impact of the ideology of the family, the material reality of women's lives, and the effects of male exclusionary practices will undoubtedly still be felt, but the combination of changes in the labour market in the 1990s are likely to improve prospects for some women, in the workforce, if not in the home. The danger is that women's access to training will be polarised by, for example, their class, race, region and level of qualifications: differences between women may well become even more marked.

Notes

1 WOMEN AND TRAINING IN A CHANGING LABOUR MARKET

1 I do mean ideal (not idea), despite coming from the Bristol areal.

2 THE REPRODUCTION OF GENDER SEGREGATION

1 Weekly earnings, full-time, all industries and services, excluding those whose pay was affected by absence, April 1990, UK figures. This is almost certainly an underestimate for the reasons mentioned in the earlier section on measuring women's employment.

3 SCHOOLGIRLS' OCCUPATIONAL 'CHOICES'

1 I am particularly grateful to Sara Delamont, Andrew Metcalf, Jane Pilcher and Juli Southall for their comments upon an earlier draft of this chapter.
2 This chapter focuses principally on working-class girls because they were the main focus of the studies described. It is important, however, to consider the contrasted experiences of middle-class girls: Connell *et al.* (1982) have made a useful contribution to this area drawing on Australian data.
3 I am grateful to Sara Delamont for pointing this out to me.
4 The Manpower Services Commission was renamed the Training Agency before most of its functions were taken over by the local Training and Enterprise Councils in 1990–1. I, for one, was relieved that the name was dropped, after an interpreter at a conference in Berlin rendered my account of youth unemployment and state intervention measures in the United Kingdom, based upon MSC activities, sound decidedly risqué.
   It was the part where I described the MSC as a state agency using public money to fund some projects designed to train unemployed young women to do things normally done by young men which caused the most gasps of disbelief in the German audience. It transpired that 'Manpower' had been translated into 'Manneskraft', literally, male virility! I had been heard to claim that the 'Male Virility Services Commission' was a state agency, using public money, etc., etc., etc.
5 The Evaluation of the Cardiff Women's Training Roadshow (1987–88) was funded by the Welsh Office Education Department. My co-investigators were Professor Gillian Powell, Dr Sara Delamont and Jane Pilcher, who was also the

research assistant on the project. (See Delamont 1990; Pilcher *et al.* 1988a, 1988b, 1989a, 1989b, 1990a, 1990b.)
6 The study, a comparison of a cohort of 1973 girl school-leavers' life and work experiences with 1989 leavers' aspirations from the same school was conducted by Juli Southall for her M.Sc. Econ. Women's Studies dissertation, which I supervised (see Southall 1990). I am grateful to Juli for permission to draw upon her work here.
7 This is reminiscent of how women teachers described their own lives in a study conducted by Acker (1992: 3):

> Moreover, life was full of what I came to think of as 'accidents'. Career plans on the stereotypically male professional model would have been highly unrealistic, as real life produced an unpredictable mix of health and illness, domestic stability and upheaval, childbirths and miscarriages.

4 WOMEN RETURNERS' TRAINING 'CHOICES'

1 I am most grateful to Gill Boden (a member of the construction course working group and a founder member of the South Glamorgan Women's Workshop Management Committee) and Madelon Hopkins (a tutor at the Workshop), for comments on this chapter.
2 An Evaluation of South Glamorgan Women's Workshop (1985–86), funded by the Equal Opportunities Commission. Co-investigators were Dr Claire Callender, Dr Victoria Winckler, and Sue Essex, who was also the research officer on the project. We interviewed the 1984 and 1985 cohorts of trainees, and followed the latter with a postal questionnaire six months after they had left. Interviews were also held with Management Committee members and staff. The research style was interactive (see Essex *et al.* 1986a, 1986b).
3 A study of South Glamorgan Women's Workshop trainees, five years on (1989–90), was conducted by Freda MacNamara for her M.Sc. Econ. Women's Studies dissertation, which I supervised (see MacNamara 1990). I am grateful to Freda for permission to refer to her work here.

5 THE FEMINISATION OF TRADE UNIONS?

1 An earlier version of this chapter appeared in P. Fosh and E. Heery (eds) (1990) *Trade Unions and their Members: Studies in Union Democracy and Organization*, London: Macmillan. I am indebted to the editors for comments on the earlier version, and to the British Sociological Association, the copyright holders, for permission to include this revised version here.
2 An example of a trade union colluding with management to ensure that women were the first to lose their jobs in a retrenchment occurred at the washing-machine manufacturing plant Hoover, in Merthyr Tydfil. The bitter struggle was the subject of a documentary video (*Political Annie's Off Again*), made by Richard Davies and Aileen Smith of Chapter Video Arts, Cardiff.
3 The survey of over 5,000 members and branch officers of NALGO on the theme of 'Equality' was commissioned by NALGO and conducted between 1979 and 1983 with my colleague Martin Read, and Stephen Davies (now of NUCPS), the project research officer (see Rees, T. and Read 1981). The 'Women in USDAW' Study was a survey of USDAW members and corresponding secretaries carried out in 1983–84. It was commissioned by USDAW and conducted by the same team (see Davies, Rees and Read 1983; USDAW 1987). I am grateful to the

unions concerned for the opportunity to conduct the work and disseminate the findings.

4 This table is reproduced with the kind permission of *Labour Research*.

6 DEMOGRAPHIC CHANGE AND POSITIVE ACTION MEASURES

1 Indeed, there is a demand among some men to reduce their hours, as Bell *et al.* (1983) found in their study of fathers, childbirth and work.

2 The review of positive action measures in the United Kingdom was commissioned in 1989 by CEDEFOP (the EC's Centre for the Development of Vocational Training, based in Berlin) and was carried out with Dr Anna Pollert of the Industrial Relations Research Unit, University of Warwick (see Rees, T. and Pollert 1989). Our three case studies of in-firm positive action training schemes in the United Kingdom were the Civil Service, which runs the women-only management training course (Rees, T. 1990b); Esso UK plc, which sponsors a women-only training course, places on which are given to the winners of a competition run by a women's magazine (Rees, T. and Pollert 1990); and British Telecom, which sponsored telephonists to go on a conversion course and then a degree course to become qualified engineers or IT specialists (see Pollert 1990). The studies were commissioned by CEDEFOP as part of an international comparative study.

3 Indeed, women can be excluded from eating! A Christmas lunch organised at a golf club for social-work senior management of a South Wales authority had to be hurriedly moved to an ante room when the club staff realised that the party included a woman. Women were not allowed in the room which had been booked. Similarly, a senior local authority subject adviser for physical education was unable to attend a meeting held at a South Wales rugby club because the facilities were for men only (apart from bar and cleaning staff).

4 See 7 note 2.

7 THE NEW INFORMATION TECHNOLOGIES AND DESEGREGATION

1 The study of the demand for and supply of low-level IT skills in South-east Wales was conducted in 1989 and funded by the Training Agency. Co-investigators were Gareth Rees, and Sarah Fielder and Nina Parry Langdon, who were the research officers on the project (see Rees, G. *et al.* 1989).

2 The Institutional Determinants of Adult Training: the Bridgend Case Study, 1988–90. This was awarded to Gareth Rees and me by the Economic and Social Research Council (Grant No. XC1125009); Sarah Fielder was the research officer (see Fielder *et al.* 1990; Rees, G., Fielder, S. and Rees, T. 1991). The parallel case study of Swindon was conducted by Martin Boddy, Kevin Doogan and John Lovering, School for Advanced Urban Studies, University of Bristol (see Doogan and Lovering 1991).

3 *Employment and Training Perspectives in the New Information Technologies in the European Community*, 1990. This study was funded by EC and sub-contracted to Gareth Rees and myself by the Science Policy Research Unit, University of Sussex. It was designed and co-ordinated by Gareth Rees; Paul Stokes conducted the case studies of Ireland and Greece while I did those of Germany and the United Kingdom (see Rees, G. 1990). The study was part of a much larger project funded by the EC on changing information technologies which was co-ordinated

by the Maastricht Economic Research Institute on Innovation and Technology (MERIT) at the University of Maastricht in the Netherlands (see Freeman and Soete 1991). I have since conducted a study for the EC on 'Skills Shortages, Women and Training' (Rees, T. 1992).
4 See note 2.
5 The research on which the rest of this chapter is based was conducted in the FRG shortly before reunification. As the study refers to the old West Germany, I have kept to the term FRG. Clearly the training agenda generally has shifted considerably in the new Germany; nevertheless, the developments in the technologically advanced companies remain of strategic importance.

8 WOMEN AND THE ENTERPRISE CULTURE

1 This chapter draws upon three studies of the 'enterprise culture': (1) 'Measures to Foster the Enterprise Culture in Australia' (1988), funded by the Scottish and Welsh Development Agencies and conducted while on study leave at the School of Sociology, University of New South Wales (see Rees, T. 1989b); (2) 'Evaluation of Mini-enterprise in Schools' (1988), funded by DTI and DES. Co-investigators: Dr Howard Williamson, and Professor Ian Jamieson, School of Education, University of Bath (see Jamieson *et al.* 1988; Rees, T. *et al.* 1990; Williamson 1989); and (3) 'An Analysis of the "Enterprise Culture" and its Relationship to Economic Development', 1989; commissioned by the Scottish Development Agency, co-investigator Gareth Rees (See Rees, G. and Rees, T. 1989, 1992).
2 Married women are viewed as an appendage to men in the UK social security system, with the effect that those who are only available for part-time work, or who have acquired insufficient contributions through working in low-paid or part-time work, and those who opted to pay the 'reduced married woman's stamp', are all ineligible for the Enterprise Allowance Scheme, certain training opportunities and some benefits (Whitting and Quinn 1989).
3 I am grateful to John Freeland of the University of Sydney for drawing this to my attention.

References

Abbott, P. and Wallace, C. (1990) *An Introduction to Sociology: Feminist Perspectives*, London: Routledge.

Acker, S. (1992) 'Critical introduction: travel and travail', in J. Gaskell *School, Work and Gender*, Milton Keynes: Open University Press.

—— (ed.) (1989) *Teachers, Gender and Education*, London: Falmer.

Adam, B. (1989) 'Feminist social theory needs time', *Sociological Review* 37 (3): 458–73.

Alexander, S. (1976) 'Women's work in nineteenth century London – a study of the years 1820–1850', in J. Mitchell and A. Oakley (eds) *The Rights and Wrongs of Women*, Harmondsworth: Penguin.

Allat, P., Keil, T., Bryman, A. and Bytheway, B. (eds) (1987) *Women and the Life Cycle: Transitions and Turning Points*, London: Macmillan.

Allen, I. (1988) *Any Room at the Top? A Study of Doctors and their Careers*, London: Policy Studies Institute.

Allen, S. and Truman, C. (1992) 'Women, business and self-employment: a conceptual minefield', in S. Arber and N. Gilbert (eds) *Women and Working Lives: Divisions and Change*, London: Macmillan.

Allen, S. and Wolkowitz, C. (1987) *Homeworking: Myths and Realities*, London: Macmillan.

Allin, P. and Hunt, A. (1982) 'Women in official statistics', in E. Whitelegg, M. Arnot, E. Bartels, V. Beechey, L. Birke, S. Himmelweit, D. Leonard, S. Ruehl and M. A. Speakman (eds) *The Changing Experience of Women*, Oxford: Martin Robertson.

Anthias, F. (1980) 'Women and the reserve army of labour: a critique of Veronica Beechey', *Capital and Class* 11 (10): 50–63.

Appelbaum, E. and Albin, P. (1989) 'Computer rationalisation and the transformation of work: lessons from the insurance industry', in S. Wood (ed.) *The Transformation of Work*, London: Unwin Hyman.

Arnot, M. (1986) 'State education policy and girls' educational experiences', in V. Beechey and E. Whitelegg (eds) *Women in Britain Today*, Milton Keynes: Open University Press.

Ashburner, L. (1988) 'Just inside the counting house: women in finance', in A. Coyle and J. Skinner (eds) *Women and Work: Positive Action for Change*, London: Macmillan.

Association of London Authorities (1989) *Women Returners – the Potential for the 1990s*, London: Association of London Authorities.

Atkinson, J. and Meager, N. (1986) *Changing Patterns of Work: How Companies Achieve Flexibility to Meet New Needs*, London: NEDO.

Atkinson, P. and Delamont, S. (1990) 'Professions and powerlessness: female marginality in the learned occupations', *Sociological Review* 38 (1): 90–110.

Atkinson, P., Rees, T., Skone, J. and Williamson, H. (1982) 'Social and life skills: the latest case of compensatory education', in T. Rees and P. Atkinson (eds) *Youth Unemployment and State Intervention*, London: Routledge and Kegan Paul.

Baker, C. and Davies, B. (1989) 'A lesson on sex roles', *Gender and Education* 1 (2): 59–76.

Bamford, C. and McCarthy, C. (eds) (1991) *Women Mean Business: a Practical Guide for Women Returners*, London: BBC.

Baran, B. (1988) 'Office automation and women's work: the technological transformation of the insurance industry', in R. E. Pahl (ed.) *On Work: Historical, Comparative and Theoretical Approaches*, Oxford: Blackwell.

Bargh, L. (1991) 'Women and confidence', in C. Bamford and C. McCarthy (eds) *Women Mean Business: a Practical Guide for Women Returners*, London: BBC.

Barker, J. and Downing, H. (1985) 'Word processing and the transformation of patriarchal relations of control of the office', in D. MacKenzie and J. Wajcman (eds) *The Social Shaping of Technology*, Milton Keynes: Open University Press.

Barrett, M. (1987) 'Marxist-feminism and the work of Karl Marx', in A. Phillips (ed.) *Feminism and Equality*, Oxford: Blackwell.

—— (1988) *Women's Oppression Today: the Marxist/Feminist Encounter*, London: Verso (2nd edn).

Barrett, M. and McIntosh, M. (1980) 'The family wage: some problems for socialists and feminists', *Capital and Class* 11: 51–72.

—— (1982) *The Anti-social Family*, London: Verso.

Barron, R. D. and Norris, G. M. (1976) 'Sexual divisions and the dual labour market', in D. L. Barker and S. Allen (eds) *Dependence and Exploitation in Work and Marriage*, London: Longman.

Batstone, E. and Gourlay, S. (1986) *Unions, Unemployment and Innovation*, Oxford: Blackwell.

Beccalli, B. (1984) 'Italy', in A. H. Cooke, V. R. Lorwin and A. K. Daniels (eds) *Women and Trade Unions in Eleven Industrialized Countries*, Philadelphia: Temple University Press.

Beck, J. and Steel, M. (1989) *Beyond the Great Divide: Introducing Equality into the Company*, London: Pitman.

Beechey, V. (1977) 'Some notes on female wage labour in capitalist production', *Capital and Class* 3: 45–66.

—— (1978) 'Women and production: a critical analysis of some sociological theories of women's work', in A. Kuhn and A. M. Wolpe (eds) *Feminism and Materialism: Women and Modes of Production*, London: Routledge & Kegan Paul.

—— (1983) 'The problem with official statistics', in *The Changing Experience of Women*, Course U221, Unit 10, Women and Employment, Milton Keynes: Open University Press, Section 6: 35–9.

—— (1986) 'Familial ideology', in V. Beechey and J. Donald (eds) *Subjectivity and Social Relations*, Milton Keynes: Open University Press.

—— (1987a) *Unequal Work*, London: Verso.

—— (1987b) 'Some notes on female wage labour in capitalist production', in *Unequal Work*, London: Verso.

—— (1987c) 'Conceptualising part-time work', in *Unequal Work*, London: Verso.

Beechey, V. and Perkins, T. (1987) *A Matter of Hours: Women, Part-time Work and the Labour Market*, Cambridge: Polity Press.

Bell, C., McKie, L. and Priestley, K. (1983) *Fathers, Childbirth and Work*, Manchester: Equal Opportunities Commission.

Beneria, L. (1988) 'Conceptualizing the labour force: the underestimation of women's economic activities', in R. E. Pahl (ed.) *On Work: Historical, Conceptual and Theoretical Approaches*, Oxford: Blackwell.

Bernstein, B. (1971) 'Education cannot compensate for Society', ch. 10 in *Class, Codes and Control*, Vol. 1, London: Paladin.

Berry, K., Grogan, K. and Hudson, G. (1987) *Hereford TVE Evaluation Pilot Project Final Report*, Worcester: Worcester College of Higher Education.

Berry-Lound, D. (forthcoming) *Demographic Change: an Employers' Workbook*, Aldershot: Gower.

—— (1990a) 'Towards the family-friendly firm', *Employment Gazette* 98 (2): 85–91.

—— (1990b) *Work and the Family: Carer-friendly Employment Practices*, Wimbledon: IPM National Committee for Equal Opportunities and Pay and Employment Conditions.

Bevan, J., Clark, G., Banerji, N. and Hakim, C. (1988) 'Barriers to business start-ups', *Research Paper No. 71*, London: Department of Employment.

Bird, E. and Skinner, L. (1989) 'Maximising the potential of women returning to work: aspirations, opportunities and policies', Bristol: Department of Continuing Education, University of Bristol, mimeo.

Bird, E. and West, J. (1987) 'Interrupted lives: a study of women returners', in P. Allatt, T. Keil, A. Bryman and B. Bytheway (eds) *Women and the Lifecycle: Transitions and Turning Points*, London: Macmillan.

Blackburn, R. and Mann, M. (1979) *The Working Class in the Labour Market*, London: Macmillan.

Blanchflower, D. G. and Oswald, A. J. (1989) 'International patterns of work', in R. Jowell, S. Witherspoon and L. Brook (eds) *British Social Attitudes: Special International Report*, Aldershot: Gower/ Social and Community Planning Research.

—— (1990) 'Self-employment and the enterprise culture', in R. Jowell, S. Witherspoon and L. Brook (eds) *British Social Attitudes: the 7th Report 1990/91 Edition*, Aldershot: Gower/Social and Community Planning Research.

Blue Arrow Personnel Services (1989) 'Recruitment in a changing world – employers and the skills shortage', London: Blue Arrow Personnel Services.

Bradley, H. (1989) *Men's Work, Women's Work*, Oxford: Polity Press.

Brannen, J. and Moss, P. (1991) *Managing Mothers – Dual Earner Households*, London: Unwin Hyman.

Braverman, H. (1974) *Labor and Monopoly Capital: the Degradation of Work in the Twentieth Century*, New York: Monthly Review Press.

Braybon, G. (1981) *Women Workers in the First World War: the British Experience*, London: Croom Helm.

Breakwell, G. (1985) *The Quiet Rebel: Women at Work in a Man's World*, London: Century Publishing.

Brelsford, P., Smith, G. and Rix, A. (1982) *Give us a Break: Widening Opportunities for Young Women within YOP/YTS*, Research and Development Series No. 11, London: Manpower Services Commission.

Brenton, M. and Russell, J. (1989) 'Bridging the gap between hospital and home: two models of discharge care for elderly people', in M. Jeffreys (ed.) *Growing Old in the Twentieth Century*, London: Routledge, pp. 218–29.

Breugel, I. (1979) 'Women as a reserve army of labour: a note on recent British experience', *Feminist Review* 3: 12–23.

Brimelow, E. (1981) 'Women in the Civil Service', *Public Administration* 59: 314–35.

Brittan, A. and Maynard, M. (1984) *Sexism, Racism and Oppression*, Oxford: Blackwell.

Brown, C. (1984) *Black and White Britain: the Third Policy Studies Institute Survey*, London: Heinemann.

Brown, P. (1990) 'The "Third Wave": education and the ideology of 'parentocracy', *British Journal of Education* 11 (1): 65–85.

Brown, P. and Ashton, D. (eds) (1987) *Education, Unemployment and Labour Markets*, Lewes: Falmer Press.

Brown, R. (1976) 'Women as employees: some comments on research in industrial sociology', in D. L. Barker and S. Allen (eds) *Dependence and Exploitation in Work and Marriage*, London: Longman.

Brownmiller, S. (1976) *Against our Will: Men, Women and Rape*, Harmondsworth: Penguin.

Burgess, C. (1985) 'The impact of new technology on skills in manufacturing and services', MSC *Research and Development No. 28*, Skill Series No. 1, Sheffield: Manpower Services Commission.

Burrows, R. (ed.) (1991) *Deciphering the Enterprise Culture: Entrepreneurship, Petty Capitalism and the Restructuring of Business*, London: Routledge.

Business in the Community (1989) 'Women's enterprise and training: a briefing paper on women's economic development', London: Business in the Community.

Butt, R. (1990) 'Girls won't be boys', *The Times*, Sept.: 10.

Bynner, J. and Evans, K. (1990) 'Does pre-vocational education work?' *Research Papers in Education* 5 (3): 183–201.

Cabinet Office (1984) *Equal Opportunities for Women in the Civil Service: Programme of Action*, London: Management and Personnel Office, Cabinet Office.

Cabinet Office/Office of the Minister for the Civil Service (1988) *Equal Opportunities for Women in the Civil Service: Progress Report 1984–87*, London: HMSO.

Callender, C. (1987) 'Women seeking work', in S. Fineman (ed.) *Unemployment: Personal and Social Consequences*, London: Tavistock.

Cane, A. (1990) 'UK lags behind the computer times', *Financial Times* (11 July).

Carby, H. V. (1982) 'White women listen! Black feminism and the boundaries of sisterhood', in Centre for Contemporary Cultural Studies, *The Empire Strikes Back: Race and Racism in '70s Britain*, London: Heinemann.

Carter, S. and Cannon, T. (1988a) 'Women in business', *Employment Gazette* 96 (10): 565-571.

—— (1988b) 'Female entrepreneurs: a study of female business owners, their motivations, experiences and strategies for success', *Research Paper No. 65*, London: Department of Employment.

Castelberg-Koulma, M. (1991) 'Greek women and tourism: women's co-operatives as an alternative form of organization', in N. Redclift and M. T. Sinclair (eds) *International Perspectives on Labour and Gender Ideology*, London: Routledge.

Cavendish, R. (1982) *Women on the Line*, London: Routledge & Kegan Paul.

CEDEFOP (1989) 'New information technologies and office employment – European comparison', Berlin: European Commission Centre for the Development of Vocational Training (CEDEFOP).

CEI Consultants (1989) *Women and Business Creation in Scotland and Northern Ireland 1989 Review*, CEI Consultants.

Central Statistical Office (1990) *Social Trends 20: 1990 Edition*, London: HMSO.

—— (1991) *Social Trends 21: 1991 Edition*, London: HMSO.

Centre for Corporate Strategy and Change, Warwick University in conjunction with Coopers and Lybrand Associates (1989) *Training in Britain, a Study of Funding, Activity and Attitudes: Employers' Perspectives on Human Resources*, Sheffield: Training Agency.

Centre for Research on European Women (1984) *New Types of Employment Initiatives Especially as Relating to Women*, Brussels: Commission of the European Communities.

Chambers, G. and Horton, C. (1990) *Equality: the Role of the Industrial Tribunals*, London: Policy Studies Institute.

Charles, N. (1986) 'Women and trades unions', in Feminist Review (eds) *Waged Work: a Reader*, London: Virago, pp. 160–85.

Child, J. (1986) 'New technology and the service class', in K. Purcell, S. Wood, A. Waton and S. Allen (eds) *The Changing Experience of Employment: Restructuring and Recession*, London: Macmillan.

Chisholm, J. (1987) 'Girls and occupational choice: in search of meaning', GAOC Working Paper No. 120, London University Institute of Education.

Chisholm, L. A. and Holland, J. (1986) 'Girls and occupational choice: anti sexism in action in a curriculum development project', *British Journal of Sociology of Education* 7 (4): 353–66.

Christie, I., Northcott, J. and Walling, A. (1990) *Employment Effects of New Technology in Manufacturing*, London: Policy Studies Institute.

Clarke, K. (1991) 'Women and training: a review', *EOC Research Discussion Paper No. 1*, Manchester: Equal Opportunities Commission.

Cockburn, C. (1981) 'The material of male power', *Feminist Review* 9: 41–58.

—— (1983) *Brothers: Male Dominance and Technological Change*, London: Pluto Press.

—— (1985) *Machinery of Dominance: Women, Men and Technical Know-how*, London: Pluto Press.

—— (1986a) 'The relations of technology: what implications for theories of sex and class?' in R. Crompton and M. Mann (eds) *Gender and Stratification*, Cambridge: Polity Press.

—— (1986b) 'Women and new technology: opportunity is not enough', in K. Purcell, S. Wood, A. Waton and S. Allen (eds) *The Changing Experience of Employment: Restructuring and Recession*, London: Macmillan.

—— (1987) *Two Track Training: Sex Inequalities and the Youth Training Scheme*, London: Macmillan.

—— (1991) *In the Way of Women: Men's Resistance to Sex Equality in Organisations*, London: Macmillan.

Coffield, F., Borrill, C. and Marshall, S. (1986) *Growing Up at the Margins: Young Adults in the North East*, Milton Keynes: Open University Press.

Cohen, B. (1990) *Caring for Children: the 1990 Report*, London: Family Policy Studies Centre.

Collinson, D., Knights, D. and Collinson, M. (1990) *Managing to Discriminate*, London: Routledge.

Confederation of British Industry (1989) *Workforce 2000 – an Agenda for Action*, London: CBI.

Connell, R. W., Ashenden, D. J., Kessler, S. and Dowsett, G. W. (1982) *Making the Difference: Schools, Families and Social Divisions*, Sydney: George Allen & Unwin.

Connor, H. and Pearson, R. (1986) 'Information technology manpower into the 1990s', Brighton: Institute of Manpower Studies.

Cooke, P. and Morgan, K. (1990) 'Industry, training and technology transfer: the

Baden-Württemberg system in perspective', Cardiff: Regional Industrial Research, Department of City and Regional Planning, University of Wales College of Cardiff (mimeo).

Coote, A. and Kellner, P. (1980) 'Hear this brother: women workers and union power', *New Statesman Report* No. 1.

Corby, S. (1983) 'Women in the Civil Service: holding back or held back?' *Personnel Managment* 15 (2): 28–31.

Coyle, A. (1984) *Redundant Women*, London: The Women's Press.

—— (1988) 'Behind the scenes: women in television', in A. Coyle and J. Skinner (eds) *Positive Action for Change*, London: Macmillan.

—— and Skinner, J. (eds) (1988) *Positive Action for Change*, London: Macmillan.

Cragg, A. and Dawson, T. (1984) 'Unemployed women: a study of attitudes and experiences', *Research Paper No. 47*, Department of Employment.

Cromie, S. and Hayes, J. (1988) 'Towards a typology of female entrepreneurs', *Sociological Review*, 36 (1): 87–113.

Crompton, R. and Jones, G. (1984) *White Collar Proletariat: Deskilling and Gender in Clerical Work*, London: Macmillan.

Crompton, R., Jones, G. and Reid, S. (1982) 'Contemporary clerical work: a case study of local government', in J. West (ed.) *Work, Women and the Labour Market*, London: Routledge & Kegan Paul.

Crompton, R. and Sanderson, K. (1990) *Gendered Jobs and Social Change*, London: Unwin Hyman.

Cross, M. and Edmonds, J. (1983) 'Training opportunities for ethnic minorities in the UK', Report prepared for CEDEFOP, West Berlin.

Cross, M. and Payne, G. (eds) (1991) *Work and the Enterprise Culture*, London: Falmer.

Cunnison, S. (1983) 'Participation in local union organisation: school meals staff – a case study', in E. Garmarnikow, D. Morgan, J. Purvis and D. Taylorson (eds) *Gender, Class and Work*, London: Heinemann Educational Books.

—— (1987) 'Women's three working lives and trade union participation', in P. Allat, T. Keil, A. Bryman and B. Bytheway (eds) *Women and the Life Cycle*, London: Macmillan, pp. 135–48.

Curran, J. and Burrows, R. (1989) 'Sociological research on service sector small businesses: some conceptual considerations', *Work, Employment and Society* 3 (4): 527–40.

Curran, J. and Roberts, L. (1989) 'Why single-minded operators reap rewarding benefits', *Guardian* (28 March).

Curran, M. (1985) *Stereotypes and Selection: Gender and Family in the Recruitment Process*, Equal Opportunities Commission Research Series, London: HMSO.

Dale, A. and Glover, J. (1989) 'Women at work in Europe: the potential and pitfalls of using published statistics', *Employment Gazette* 97 (6): 299–308.

Dale, R., Bowe, R., Harris, D., Loveys, M., Moore, R., Shilling, C., Sikes, P., Trevit, J. and Valsecchi, V. (1990) *The TVEI Story: Policy, Practice and Preparation for the Workforce*, Milton Keynes: Open University Press.

David, M. (1983) 'Sex, education and social policy: a new moral economy?' in S. Walker and L. Barton (eds) *Gender, Class and Education*, Lewes: Falmer Press.

Davies, S., Rees, T. and Read, M. (1983) 'Women in USDAW Working Party: Report of the survey of branches', Manchester: USDAW.

Deem, R. (ed.) (1984) *Co-education Reconsidered*, Milton Keynes: Open University Press.

—— (1986) *All Work and No Play*? London: Routledge & Kegan Paul.

Delamont, S. (1989) *Knowledgeable Women: Structuralism and the Reproduction of Elites*, London: Routledge.
—— (1990) *Sex Roles and the School*, London: Routledge (2nd edn).
Delmar, R. (1976) 'Looking again at Engels' *Origin of the Family, Private Property and the State*', in J. Mitchell and A. Oakley (eds) *The Rights and Wrongs of Women*, Harmondsworth: Penguin.
Deloitte, Haskins and Sells in conjunction with IFF Research Ltd (1989) *Training in Britain: a Study of Funding, Activity and Attitudes – Employers' Activities*, London: HMSO.
Delphy, C. (1984) *Close to Home: a Materialist Analysis of Women's Oppression*, London: Hutchinson.
Department of Education and Science (1983) *Education Statistics for the UK: 1983 Edition*, London: DES.
—— (1986) *Education Statistics for the UK: 1986 Edition*, London: DES.
—— (1989) *National Curriculum: From Policy to Practice*, London: DES.
—— (1991) *Education Statistics for the United Kingdom: 1990 Edition*, London: HMSO.
Department of Employment (1990) *Labour Market and Skill Trends 1991/2: Planning for a Changing Labour Market*, Sheffield: Employment Department Group.
Department of Employment (1986) *Building Businesses . . . not Barriers*, Cmnd 9794, London: HMSO.
—— (1988) *Employment for the 1990s*, White Paper, London: HMSO.
—— (1990a) 'Women in the labour market: results from the 1989 Labour Force Survey', *Employment Gazette* 98 (12): 619–43.
—— (1990b) *Training Statistics 1990*, London: HMSO.
—— (1991) Employment Statistics, *Employment Gazette* 99 (6).
Dex, S. (1985) *The Sexual Division of Work: Conceptual Revolutions in the Social Sciences*, Brighton: Wheatsheaf.
—— (1987) *Women's Occupational Mobility: a Lifetime Perspective*, London: Macmillan.
—— (1988) *Women's Attitudes to Work*, London: Macmillan.
—— (1989) 'Women and unemployment', *Employment Institute Economic Report*, 4 (5): 1–4.
Dex, S. and Shaw, L. (1986) *British and American Women at Work: Do Equal Opportunities Policies Matter?* London: Macmillan.
—— (1988) 'Women's working lives: a comparison of women in the United States and Great Britain', in A. Hunt (ed.) *Women and Paid Work*, London: Macmillan.
Dilnot, A. and Kell, M. (1987) 'Male unemployment and women's work', *Fiscal Studies* 8 (3): 1–16.
Dobash, R. and Dobash, R. E. (1980) *Violence Against Wives*, London: Open Books.
Dobash, R. E. and Dobash, R. (1992) *Women, Violence and Social Change*, London: Routledge.
Doogan, K. and Lovering, J. (1991) 'Training needs and provision, the Swindon case study', The Determinants of Adult Training: End of Award report to Economic and Social Research Council, Bristol: School for Advanced Urban Studies, University of Bristol.
Dore, R. (1987) 'Citizenship and employment in an age of high technology', *British Journal of Industrial Relations* 25: 201–6.
Dowling, C. (1982) *The Cinderella Complex: Women's Hidden Fear of Independence*, London: Fontana.

Ducatel, K. and Miles, I. (1990) 'New information technologies and working conditions in the European Communities', Report to the Science Policy Research Unit, University of Sussex/ European Commission, Manchester: University of Manchester.

Edwards, R. C., Reich, M. and Gordon, D. M. (eds) (1975) *Labour Market Segmentation*, Lexington, Mass.: Lexington Books.

Eisenstein, H. (1990) 'Femocrats, official feminism and the uses of power', in S. Watson (ed.) *Playing the State: Australian Feminist Interventions*, London: Verso, pp. 87–103.

—— (1991) *Gender Shock: Practising Feminism on Two Continents*, Boston: Beacon Press.

Eisenstein, Z. R. (ed.) (1979) *Capitalist Patriarchy and the Case for Socialist Feminism*, New York: Monthly Review Press.

Elger, T. (1987) 'Flexible futures? New technology and the contemporary transformation of work', *Work, Employment and Society* 1 (4): 528–40.

Elias, P. (1988) 'Family formation, occupational mobility and part-time work', in A. Hunt (ed.) *Women and Paid Work*, London: Macmillan.

Ellis, V. (1988) 'Current trade union attempts to remove occupational segregation in the employment of women', in S. Walby (ed.) *Gender Segregation at Work*, Milton Keynes: Open University Press, pp. 135–56.

Elson, D. and Pearson, R. (1981) ' "Nimble fingers make cheap workers": an analysis of women's employment in Third World export manufacturing', *Feminist Review* 7: 87–107.

Engels, F. [1884] (1972) *The Origin of the Family, Private Property and the State*, New York: International Publishers.

Epstein, C. F. (1970) *Women's Place: Options and Limits in Professional Careers*, Berkeley: University of California Press.

Equal Opportunities Commission (1987) *Women and Men in Britain*, Manchester: Equal Opportunities Commission.

—— (1990) *The Key to Real Choice: an Action Plan for Child-care*, Manchester: Equal Opportunities Commission.

Essex, S., Callender, C., Rees, T. and Winckler, V. (1986a) *New Styles of Training for Women: an Evaluation of the South Glamorgan Women's Workshop*, Manchester: Equal Opportunities Commission.

—— (1986b) *An Evaluation of South Glamorgan Women's Workshop*, Cardiff: South Glamorgan Women's Workshop.

European Commission (1987) *Non-salaried Working Women in Europe: Women Running their Own Businesses or Working Independently – Women Involved in their Husband's Professional Activity*, Brussels: Commission of the European Communities.

—— (1989) *Business Creation by Women: Motivations, Situation and Perspectives*, Brussels: Commission of the European Communities.

Eurostat (1990) *Labour Force Survey*, Luxembourg: Office for Official Publications of the European Community.

Everywoman (1987) *Everywoman Directory of Women's Co-operatives and Other Enterprises*, London: *Everywoman*/Industrial Common Ownership Movement.

—— (1990) *Women Mean Business: the Everywoman Directory of Women's Co-operatives and Other Enterprises 1990*, London: *Everywoman*.

Fevre, R. (1987) 'Subcontracting in steel', *Work, Employment and Society* 1 (4): 509–37.

Fielder, S., Rees, G. and Rees, T. (1990) 'Regional restructuring, services and women's employment: labour market change in South Wales', *Institutional*

Determinants of Employers' Training Strategies, Project Paper No. 3, Cardiff: Social Research Unit, University of Wales College of Cardiff.

—— (1991a) 'Employers' recruitment and training strategies', *Institutional Determinants of Adult Training Strategies, Project Paper No. 4*, Cardiff: Social Research Unit, University of Wales College of Cardiff.

—— (1991b) 'The new services: contract cleaning and catering', *Institutional Determinants of Adult Training Strategies, Project Paper No. 5*, Cardiff: Social Research Unit, University of Wales College of Cardiff.

Financial Times (1990) 'Income tax on childcare facilities will be removed', *Financial Times*, (21 March).

Finch, J. (1983) *Married to the Job: Wives' Incorporation in Men's Work*, London: George Allen & Unwin.

—— (1989) *Family Obligations and Social Change*, Oxford: Polity Press.

Finch, J. and Groves, D. (1980) 'Community care and the family: a case for equal opportunities?' *Journal of Social Policy* 9: 437–51.

—— (1983) *A Labour of Love: Women, Work and Caring*, London: Routledge & Kegan Paul.

Firestone, S. (1974) *The Dialectic of Sex: the Case for Feminist Revolution*, New York: Morrow.

Firth-Cozens, J. and West, M. (eds) (1991) *Women at Work: Psychological and Organizational Perspectives*, Milton Keynes: Open University Press.

Fitzgerald, F. G. and Associates (1987) 'Sources of alternative finance for the funding of local employment initiatives in Australia', *Research Paper No. 4*, Prepared for the National Advisory Group on Local Employment Initiatives, Canberra: Australian Government Publishing Service.

Fogarty, M., Allen, I. and Walters, P. (1981) *Women in Top Jobs 1968–79*, London: Heinemann/PSI.

Fosh, P. (1981) *The Active Trade Unionist*, Cambridge: Cambridge University Press.

Fosh, P. and Heery, E. (eds) (1990) *Trade Unions and their Members: Studies in Union Democracy and Organization*, London: Macmillan.

Foster-Carter, O. and Wright, C. (eds) (1989) *Gender and Education Special Issue: Race, Gender and Education* 1 (3).

Franzway, S., Court, D. and Connell, R. W. (1989) *Staking a Claim: Feminism, Bureacracy and the State*, Sydney: Allen & Unwin.

Freeman, C. and Soete, L. (1991) 'Macro-economic and sectoral analysis of future employment and training perspectives in the new information technologies in the European Community: policy conclusions and recommendations', Report to the European Commission, Maastricht, Netherlands: Maastricht Economic and Research Institute on Innovation and Technology (MERIT), University of Maastricht.

Fuller, M. (1980) 'Black girls in a London comprehensive school', in R. Deem (ed.) *Schooling for Women's Work*, London: Routledge & Kegan Paul.

Gallie, D. (1988) 'Introduction', in D. Gallie (ed.) *Employment in Britain*, Oxford: Blackwell.

—— (1991) 'Patterns of skill change: upskilling, deskilling or the polarization of skills?' *Work, Employment and Society* 5 (3): 319–51.

Game, A. and Pringle, R. (1983) *Gender at Work*, Sydney: Allen & Unwin.

Gaskell, J. (1986) 'Conceptions of skill and the work of women: some historical and political issues', in R. Hamilton and M. Barrett (eds) *The Politics of Diversity*, London: Verso.

General, Municipal, Boilermakers and Allied Trades Union (1987) 'Winning a fair deal for women – a GMB policy for equality', London: GMB.

Gershuny, J., Miles, I., Jones, S., Mullings, C., Thomas, G. and Wyatt, S. (1986) 'Time budgets: preliminary analyses of a national survey', *Quarterly Journal of Social Affairs* 2 (1) 13–39.

Gerver, E. and Hart, L. (1991) *Strategic Women: How Do They Manage – in Scotland?* Aberdeen: Aberdeen University Press.

Glendinning, C. and Millar, J. (eds) (1987) *Women and Poverty in Britain*, Brighton: Wheatsheaf.

Glucksman, M. (1990) *Women Assemble: Women Workers and the New Industries in Inter-war Britain*, London: Routledge.

Goffee, R. and Scase, R. (1985) *Women in Charge*, London: Allen & Unwin.

Gough, C. L. (1979) 'Pay, parity and policy: an appraisal of past and present sex discrimination legislation in Britain and its consequences for women workers', Unpublished M.Sc. Econ. thesis, University College, Cardiff.

Gould, S. K. and Lyman, J. (1987) *A Working Guide to Women's Self-employment*, New York: National Coalition for Women's Enterprise.

Government Statistical Service (1989) 'Key figures of Civil Service staffing, 1989–90 edition', London: HM Treasury.

Graycar, R. (1990) 'Feminism and law reform: matrimonial property law and models of equality', in S. Watson (ed.) *Playing the State: Australian Feminist Interventions*, London: Verso.

Greater Manchester Economic Development Officers' Association (1990) 'Ethnic minority business development and employment in Greater Manchester', Manchester: Greater Manchester Economic Development Officers' Association.

Green, A. G. (1989) 'Equal opportunities in the curriculum: the case of home economics', *Gender and Education* 1 (2): 139–54.

Gregory, J. (1982) 'Equal pay and sex discrimination: why women are giving up the fight', *Feminist Review* 10: 75–90.

—— (1989) 'Trial by ordeal: a study of people who lost equal pay and sex discrimination cases in the industrial tribunals during 1985 and 1986', Equal Opportunities Commission Research Series, London: HMSO.

Grieco, M. (1987) *Keeping it in the Family: Social Networks and Employment Change*, London: Tavistock.

Griffin, C. (1985) *Typical Girls*, London: Routledge & Kegan Paul.

Grint, K. (1991) *The Sociology of Work: an Introduction*, Cambridge: Polity Press.

Guttentag, M. and Bray, H. (1976) *Undoing Sex Stereotypes*, New York: McGraw-Hill.

Hakim, C. (1979) 'Occupational segregation: a comparative study of the degree and pattern of the differentiation between men and women's work in Britain, the United States and other countries', Department of Employment *Research Paper No. 9*, London: Department of Employment.

—— (1980) 'Census reports as documentary evidence: the census commentaries 1801–1951', *Sociological Review* 28 (3): 551–80.

—— (1985) 'Social monitors: population censuses as social surveys', in M. Bulmer (ed.) *Essays on the History of British Sociological Research*, Cambridge: Cambridge University Press.

—— ([1987] 1988) 'Homeworking in Britain', in R. E. Pahl (ed.) *On Work: Historical, Conceptual and Theoretical Approaches*, Oxford: Blackwell.

—— (1989) 'New recruits to self-employment in the 1980s', *Employment Gazette* 97 (6): 286–97.

Hall, S., Crichter, C., Jefferson, T., Clarke, J. and Roberts, B. (1978) *Policing the Crisis: Mugging, the State and Law and Order*, London: Macmillan.

Halpern, M. (1988) *Business Creation by Women: Motivations, Situations and Perspectives*, Brussels: Commission of the European Communities.

Halsey, A. H. (1977) 'Towards meritocracy', in J. Karabel and A. H. Halsey (eds) *Power and Ideology in Education*, New York: Oxford University Press.

Halsey, A. H., Heath, A. F. and Ridge, J. M. (1980) *Origins and Destinations*, Oxford: Clarendon Press.

Hansard Society Commission on Women at the Top (1990) *Report of the Hansard Society Commission on Women at the Top*, London: The Hansard Society.

Hardill, I. and Green, A. (1990) *An Examination of Women Returners in Benwell and South Gosforth*, Newcastle: University of Newcastle upon Tyne, Centre for Urban and Regional Development Studies.

Hartman, H. I., Kraut, R. E. and Tilly, L. A. (eds) (1986) *Computer Chips and Paper Clips: Technology and Women's Employment*, Vol. 1. Washington, DC: National Academy Press.

Hartmann, H. (1979a) 'The unhappy marriage of Marxism and feminism: towards a more progressive union', *Capital and Class* 8: 1–33.

—— (1979b) 'Capitalism, patriarchy and job segregation by sex', in Z. Eisenstein (ed.) *Capitalist Patriarchy and the Case for Socialist Feminism*, New York: Monthly Review Press.

Healy, G. and Kraithman, D. (1989) 'Women returners in the North Hertfordshire labour market', Report for the Training Agency, Hertford: Local Economy Research Unit, Hatfield Polytechnic.

Heery, E. and Kelly, J. (1988) 'Do female representatives make a difference? Women full-time officials and trade union work', *Work, Employment and Society* 2 (4) 487–505.

Heitlinger, A. (1979) *Women and State Socialism: Sex Inequality in the Soviet Union and Czechoslovakia*, London: Macmillan.

Higgs, E. (1983) 'Domestic servants and households in Victorian England', *Social History* 8 (2): 201–10.

Hindess, B. (1973) *The Use of Official Statistics in Sociology: a Critique of Positivism and Ethnomethodology*, London: Macmillan.

Hochschild, A. R. (1990) *The Second Shift: Working Parents and the Revolution at Home*, London: Piatkus.

Holland, J. (1988) 'Girls and occupational choice: in search of meanings', in A. Pollard, J. Purvis and G. Walford (eds) *Education, Training and the New Vocationalism*, Milton Keynes: Open University Press.

Holten, V. and Rabbetts, J. (1990) *Powder in the Board Room*, Berkhamsted, Herts: Ashridge Management Research Centre, Ashridge Management College.

Honess, T. (1989a) 'A longitudinal study of school leavers' employment experiences, time structuring and self attributions as a function of opportunity structure', *British Journal of Psychology* 80: 45–77.

—— (1989b) 'Personal and social enabling conditions for the 16-year-old school leaver: a transactional model for understanding the school leaving transition', *Research Papers in Education* 4 (2): 28–52.

—— (1990) *Managing Recruitment Needs in Gwent: Retention and Career Development of Key Female Staff*, Report to the Training Agency in Gwent, Cardiff: Michael & Associates.

Horrell, S. and Rubery, J. (1991) *Employers' Working-time Policies and Women's Employment*, Equal Opportunities Commission Research Series, London: HMSO.

Horrell, S., Rubery, J. and Burchell, B. (1990) 'Gender and skills', *Work, Employment and Society* 4 (2): 189–216.

Hunt, A. (1975) *Managerial Attitudes and Practices towards Women at Work*, London: HMSO.

—— (ed.) (1988) *Women and Paid Work: Issues of Equality*, London: Macmillan.

Hyman, R. (1989) *Strikes* (4th edn), London: Macmillan.

Income Data Services (1989) 'Women in the labour market', *IDS Report* 8, Labour Market Supplement, London: IDS.

Institute for Employment Research (1990) *Projecting the Labour Market for the Highly Qualified*, Coventry: University of Warwick, Institute for Employment Research.

International Labour Office (1985) *Statistical Yearbook*, Geneva: ILO.

IRS (1991) 'New bargaining agenda for unions', *Employment Trends 479*, Industrial Relations Review and Report (11 Jan.).

Jackson, B. and Marsden, D. (1962) *Education and the Working Class*, London: Routledge & Kegan Paul.

Jackson, D. (1991) 'Problems facing qualified women returners', in J. Firth-Cozens and M. A. West (eds) *Women at Work: Psychological and Organizational Perspectives*, Milton Keynes: Open University Press.

Jamieson, I., Hunt, D., Richards, B. and Williamson, H. (1988) *Evaluation of the Mini-enterprise in Schools Project*, Bath: School of Education, University of Bath, and Cardiff: Social Research Unit, School of Social and Administrative Studies, University of Wales College of Cardiff.

Jenkins, R. (1988) 'Discrimination and equal opportunity in employment: ethnicity and "race" in the United Kingdom', in D. Gallie (ed.) *Employment in Britain*, Oxford: Blackwell.

Jenkins, R., Bryman, A., Ford, J., Keil, T. and Beardsworth, A. (1983) 'Information in the labour market: the impact of recession', *Sociology* 17 (2): 260–7.

Jenson, J. (1989) 'The talents of women, the skills of men: flexible specialisation and women', in S. Wood (ed.) *The Transformation of Work*? London: Unwin Hyman.

John, A. (1984) *By the Sweat of their Brow: Women Workers at Victorian Coal Mines*, London: Routledge & Kegan Paul.

—— (ed.) (1986) *Unequal Opportunities: Women's Employment in England 1800–1918*, Oxford: Blackwell.

Johns, B. L., Dunlop, W. C. and Sheenan, W. J. (1983) *Small Business in Australia: Problems and Prospects*, Sydney: Allen & Unwin.

Johnson, C. (1988) 'Enterprise education and training', *British Journal of Education and Work* 2 (1): 61–5.

Joshi, H. and Owen, S. (1987) 'How long is a piece of elastic? The measurement of female activity rates in British Census, 1951–1981s', *Cambridge Journal of Economics* 11 (1): 55–74.

Joyce, J. (1961) 'A research note on attitudes to work and marriage of 600 adolescent girls', *British Journal of Sociology* 12: 176–83.

Kalatzis, M. (1990) 'Ethnicity meets gender meets class in Australia', in S. Watson (ed.) *Playing the State: Australian Feminist Interventions*, London: Verso, pp. 39–59.

Kanter, R. (1976) *Men and Women of the Corporation*, New York: Basic Books.

Keat, R. (1991) 'Introduction: Starship Britain or Universal Enterprise?' in R. Keat and N. Abercrombie (eds), *The Enterprise Culture*, London: Routledge.

Keat, R. and Abercrombie, N. (eds) (1991) *The Enterprise Culture*, London: Routledge.

Kelly, A. (1978) 'Sex differences in science enrolments: reasons and remedies',

Collaborative Research Newsletters 3 and 4, Edinburgh: Centre for Educational Sociology, University of Edinburgh.

—— (ed.) (1987) *Science for Girls?* Milton Keynes: Open University Press.

Kelly, A., Whyte, J. and Smail, B. (1984) 'Girls into science and technology: final report', Manchester: Department of Sociology, University of Manchester (excerpts reprinted in A. Kelly (ed.) (1987) *Science for Girls?* Milton Keynes: Open University Press).

Kelly, J. (1990) 'British trade unionism 1979–89: change, continuity and contradictions', *Work, Employment and Society Special Issue*, pp. 29–65.

Kitsuse, J. and Cicourel, A. V. (1963) 'A note on the uses of official statistics', *Social Problems* 11: 131–9.

Kleinberg, J. (1983) 'Escalating standards: women, housework and technology in the twentieth century', in F. Coppa (ed.) *Twentieth Century Technology*, Iowa: Kendall Hunt.

Knights, D. and Sturdy, A. (1987) 'Women's work in insurance: information technology and the reproduction of gendered segregation', in M. Davidson and C. Cooper (eds) (1987) *Women and Information Technology*, London: Wiley.

Knights, D. and Willmott, H. (eds) (1986) *Gender and the Labour Process*, Aldershot: Gower.

—— (eds) (1988) *New Technology and the Labour Process*, London: Macmillan.

Kuhn, A. and Wolpe, A. M. (eds) (1978) *Feminism and Materialism: Women and Modes of Production*, London: Routledge & Kegan Paul.

Labour Research Department (1986) *Labour Research* (April), London: Labour Research Department.

—— (1988) 'Working for equality in the unions', *Labour Research* (March): 9–11.

—— (1989) 'Unions and part timers – do they mix?' *Labour Research* (March): 19–22.

—— (1991a) *Women in Trade Unions: Action for Equality*, London: Labour Research Department.

—— (1991b) 'Teleworking: a splendid isolation', *Labour Research* (Feb.): 11–12.

Land, H. (1980) 'The family wage', *Feminist Review* 6: 55–77.

Lane, C. (1988) 'New technology and clerical work', in D. Gallie (ed.) *Employment in Britain*, Oxford: Blackwell.

Lawrence, B. (1987) 'The fifth dimension: gender and general practice', in A. Spencer and D. Podmore (eds) *In a Man's World*, London: Tavistock.

Ledwith, S., Colgan, F., Joyce, P. and Hayes, M. (1990) 'The making of women trade union leaders', *Industrial Relations Journal* 21 (2) (Summer): 112–25.

Lee, D., Marsden, D., Rickman, P. and Duncombe, J. (1990) *Scheming for Youth: a Study of YTS in the Enterprise Culture*, Milton Keynes: Open University Press.

Leonard, A. (1987) *Pyrrhic Victories: Winning Sex Discrimination and Equal Pay Cases in the Industrial Tribunal 1980–84*, Equal Opportunities Research Series, London: HMSO.

Lewis, J. (1984) *Women in England 1870–1950*, Brighton: Wheatsheaf.

Locksley, G., Morgan, K. and Thomas, G. (1989) *Manufacturing Growth: Employment, Skills and Training in the Telematic Services Sector*, Brunel University, PICT Conference (17–19 May).

Lorber, J. (1984) *Women in Medicine*, London: Tavistock.

Lovering, J. (1990) 'A perfunctory sort of Post-Fordism: economic restructuring and labour market segmentation in Britain', *Work, Employment and Society, The 1980s: a Decade of Change? Special Issue* (May).

Lowe, G. S. (1987) *Women in the Administrative Revolution*, Cambridge: Polity Press.

204 Women and the labour market

McCarthy, M. (1977) 'Women in trade unions today', in L. Middleton (ed.) *Women in the Labour Movement*, London: Croom Helm.

Maccoby, E. and Jacklin, C. (1974) *The Psychology of Sex Differences*, Vol. 1, Stanford, CA: Stanford University Press.

MacDonald, R. and Coffield, F. (1991) *Risky Business? Youth and the Enterprise Culture*, London: Falmer Press.

MacKenzie, D. and Wajcman, J. (eds) (1985) *The Social Shaping of Technology*, Milton Keynes: Open University Press.

MacNamara, F. (1990) *Women and Training*, Cardiff: University of Wales College of Cardiff, M.Sc. Econ. in Women's Studies, Unpublished dissertation.

Magarey, S. (1984) 'Can there be justice for women under capitalism?' in D. Broom (ed.) *Unfinished Business: Social Justice for Women in Australia*, Sydney: George Allen & Unwin.

Main, B. (1988) 'The lifetime attachment of women to the labour market', in A. Hunt (ed.) *Women and Paid Work: Issues of Equality*, London: Macmillan.

Manpower Services Commission (n.d.) 'TVEI developments 2: equal opportunities', London: Manpower Services Commission.

Marlow, S. (1990) 'The take-up of formal training by ethnic entrepreneurs', Warwick: Small and Medium Enterprise Centre, University of Warwick.

Marsh, C. (1988) 'Unemployment in Britain', in D. Gallie (ed.) *Employment in Britain*, Oxford: Blackwell.

—— (1991) *Hours of Work of Women and Men in Britain*, Equal Opportunities Research Series, London: HMSO.

Martin, J. and Roberts, C. (1984) *The Women and Employment Survey: a Lifetime Perspective*, London: HMSO.

Martin, R. (1988) 'Technological change and manual work', in D. Gallie (ed.) *Employment in Britain*, Oxford: Blackwell.

Marx, K. [1867] (1954) *Capital*, Vol. 1, London: Lawrence & Wishart.

Maternity Alliance (1989) 'Women, work and maternity: the inside story', London: Maternity Alliance.

Matthaei, J. A. (1982) *An Economic History of Women in America: Women's Work, the Sexual Division of Labour and the Development of Capitalism*, Brighton: Harvester.

Maurice, M., Sellier, F. and Silvestre, J-J. (1986) *The Social Foundations of Industrial Power* (trans. A. Goldhammer) Cambridge, Mass.: MIT Press.

May, A. (1987) 'Equal opportunities and vocational training, establishment and management of businesses by women: a synthesis of twelve national reports and four complementary reports', West Berlin: CEDEFOP.

Megarry, J. (1984) 'Introduction: sex, gender and education', in S. Acker, J. Megarry, S. Nisbet and E. Hoyle, *World Yearbook of Education: Women and Education*, London: Kogan Page.

Mercaldi, M. B. (1985) 'The HUB Program for women's enterprise', New York: HUB Program.

Metcalf, H. (1989) 'Employer response to the decline in school leavers into the 1990s', *IMS Report* No. 152, Brighton: Institute of Manpower Studies.

Metcalf, H. and Leighton, P. (1989) 'The under-utilisation of women in the labour market: a report for the Equal Opportunities Commission', *IMS Report* No. 172, Brighton: Institute of Manpower Studies.

Milkman, R. (1987) *Gender at Work: the Dynamics of Job Segregation by Sex during World War Two*, Illinois: University of Illinois Press.

Millman, V. and Weiner, G. (1987) 'Engendering equal opportunities: the case of

TVEI', in D. Gleeson (ed.) *TVEI and Secondary Education: a Critical Appraisal*, Milton Keynes: Open University Press.

Millward, N. and Stevens, M. (1986) *British Workplace Industrial Relations 1980–84*, The Department of Employment/ESRC/PSI/ACAS Surveys, Aldershot: Gower.

Mitchell, S. (1984) *Tall Poppies: Successful Australian Women Talk to Susan Mitchell*, Victoria: Penguin.

Mitter, S. (1986) *Common Fate, Common Bond: Women in the Global Economy*, London: Pluto Press.

Moen, P., Downey, G. and Bolger, N. (1990) 'Labor-force re-entry among US homemakers in midlife: a lifecourse analysis', *Gender and Society* 4 (2): 230–43.

Morris, L. (1984) 'Patterns of social activity and post redundancy labour market experience', *Sociology* 18 (3): 339–52.

—— (1990) *The Workings of the Household: a US/UK Comparison*, Oxford: Polity.

Morrison, A. (1987) *Breaking the Glass Ceiling*, Wokingham: Addison Wesley.

Moss, P. (1990) 'Childcare in the European Communities, 1985–90', *Women of Europe Supplement No. 31*, Brussels: Commission of the European Communities.

Murphy, P. and Mullan, T. (1989) 'Time for women in IT', Jordanstown: Department of Adult and Continuing Education, University of Ulster.

Murray, M. (1990) Review of S. Walby, *Theorizing Patriarchy*, in *Work, Employment and Society* 4 (3): 473–75.

National Economic Development Office (NEDO) (1988) *Young People and the Labour Market, a Challenge for the 1990s*, London: NEDO.

National Economic Development Office/Training Agency (1989) *Defusing the Demographic Time Bomb*, London: NEDO.

Nevill, G., Pennicott, A., Williams, J. and Worral, A. (1990) *Women in the Workforce: the Effect of Demographic Changes in the 1990s*, London: The Industrial Society.

Newton, P. (1991) 'Computing: an ideal occupation for women?' in J. Firth-Cozens and M. A. West (eds) *Women at Work: Psychological and Organizational Perspectives*, Milton Keynes: Open University Press.

Newton, P. and Brocklesby, J. (1982) 'Getting on in engineering: becoming a woman technician', Final report to the Equal Opportunities Commission/Social Science Research Council Joint Panel.

Nicholson, N., Ursell, G. and Blyton, P. (1981) *The Dynamics of White Collar Unionism*, London: Academic Press.

Oakley, A. and Oakley, R. (1979) 'Sexism in official statistics', in J. Irvine, I. Miles and J. Evans (eds) *Demystifying Official Statistics*, London: Pluto Press.

O'Donovan, K. and Szyszczak, E. (1988) *Equality and Sex Discrimination Law*, Oxford: Blackwell.

Office of Population Censuses and Surveys (OPCS) (1988) *General Household Survey*, London: HMSO.

Organisation for Economic Co-operation and Development (OECD) (1990) *Local Initiatives for Job Creation: Enterprising Women*, Paris: OECD.

Orr, P. (1985) 'Sex bias in schools: national perspectives', in J. Whyte, R. Deem, L. Kant and M. Cruikshank (eds) *Girl Friendly Schooling*, London: Methuen.

Owen, S. (1987) 'Household production and economic efficiency: arguments for and against specialisation', *Work, Employment and Society* 1 (2) 157–78.

Owens, D. J., Rees, T. and Parry Langdon, N. (forthcoming) ' "All those in favour": computerised trade union membership lists as sampling frames for postal surveys', *Sociological Review*.

Pahl, J. (1989) *Money and Marriage*, London: Macmillan.
Pahl, R. E. (1984) *Divisions of Labour*, Oxford: Blackwell.
Parker, G. (1988) 'Who cares? A review of empirical evidence from Britain', in R. E. Pahl (ed.) *On Work: Historical, Conceptual and Theoretical Approaches*, Oxford: Blackwell.
Parsons, T. and Bales, R. K. (1956) *Family Socialization and Interaction Process*, London: Routledge & Kegan Paul.
Payne, J. (1991) *Women, Training and the Skills Shortage: the Case for Public Investment*, London: Policy Studies Institute.
Pennington, S. and Westover, B. (1989) *A Hidden Workforce: Homeworkers in England 1850-1985*, London: Macmillan.
Phillips, A. and Taylor, B. (1980) 'Sex and skill: notes towards a feminist economics', *Feminist Review* 6: 79-88.
Phizacklea, A. (1988) 'Entrepreneurship, ethnicity and gender', in S. Westwood and P. Bachau (eds) *Enterprising Women*, London: Routledge.
Pilcher, J., Delamont, S., Powell, G. and Rees, T. (1988a) 'The Cardiff Women's Training Roadshow: the schoolgirls' experiences', Cardiff: Social Research Unit, University of Wales College of Cardiff.
—— (1988b) 'Women's Training roadshows and the "manipulation" of schoolgirls' career choices', *British Journal of Education and Work* 2 (2): 61-6.
—— (1989a) 'Challenging occupational stereotypes: women's training roadshows and guidance at school level', *British Journal of Guidance and Counselling* 17 (1): 59-67.
—— (1990a) *An Evaluative Study of the Cardiff Women's Training Roadshow*, Cardiff: Welsh Office (Welsh and English), 35 pp.
—— (1990b) *So You Want to Run a Woman's Training Roadshow?* Cardiff: Welsh Office, 18 pp.
Pilcher, J., Delamont, S., Powell, G., Rees, T. and Read, M. (1989b) 'Evaluating a women's career convention: methods, results and implications', *Research Papers in Education* 4 (1): 57-76.
Piore, M. J. (1975) 'Notes for a theory of labor market stratification', in R. C. Edwards, M. Reich and D. M. Gordon (eds) *Labour Market Segmentation*, Lexington, Mass.: Lexington Books.
Pollard, A., Purvis, J. and Walford, G. (eds) (1988) *Education, Training and the New Vocationalism*, Milton Keynes: Open University Press.
Pollert, A. (1981) *Girls, Wives, Factory Lives*, London: Macmillan.
—— (1987) 'The "Flexible Firm": a model in search of reality (or a policy in search of a practice?)', *Warwick Papers in Industrial Relations*, No. 19, Coventry: University of Warwick.
—— (1990) 'The British Telecom Women's Bridging Course', Report to CEDEFOP, Coventry: University of Warwick Industrial Relations Research Unit.
—— (ed.) (1991) *The End of Flexibility?* Oxford: Blackwell.
Power, M. (1983) 'From home production to wage labour: women as a reserve army of labour', *Review of Radical Political Economics*, XV (1): 71-91.
Prendergast, S. and Prout, A. (1980) 'What will I do . . .? Teenage girls and the construction of motherhood', *Sociological Review* 28 (3): 517-35.
Raffe, D. (ed.) (1988) *Education and the Youth Labour Market*, Lewes: Falmer.
Rainbird, H. (1990) *Training Matters: Union Perspectives on Industrial Restructuring and Training*, Oxford: Blackwell.
Rajan, A. (1984) 'New technology and missed opportunities', *New Technology, Work and Employment* 2 (1): 61-5.

Rajan, A. and van Eupen, P. (1990) 'Good practices in the employment of women returners', *IMS Report* No. 183, Brighton: Institute of Manpower Studies.

Rees, G. (1990) *Employment and Training Perspectives in the New Information Technologies in the European Community: Vocational Education and Training Systems: the Challenge of the 1990s*, Report to the Science Policy Research Unit/ European Commission, Cardiff: School of Social and Administrative Studies, University of Wales College of Cardiff.

Rees, G. and Fielder, S. (1992) 'The services economy, subcontracting and new employment relations: contract catering and cleaning', *Work, Employment and Society* (forthcoming).

Rees, G., Fielder, S. and Rees, T. (1991) 'Training needs and provision: the Bridgend case study', Institutional Determinants of Adult Training, End of Award Report to ESRC (Grant No. XC1125009), Cardiff: School of Social and Administrative Studies, University of Wales College of Cardiff.

Rees, G. and Rees, T. (1982) 'Juvenile unemployment and the state between the wars', in T. Rees and P. Atkinson (eds), *Youth Unemployment and State Intervention*, London: Routledge & Kegan Paul.

—— (1984) 'Migration, industrial restructuring and class relations: an analysis of South Wales', in G. Williams (ed.) *Crisis of Economy and Ideology: Essays on Welsh Society 1840-1980*, Bangor: SSRC/BSA Sociology of Wales Study Group.

—— (1989) *The 'Enterprise Culture' and Local Economic Development: a Review and Evaluation*, Report to the Scottish Development Agency, Cardiff: Social Research Unit, University of Wales College of Cardiff, 26 pp.

—— (1992) 'Educating for the "enterprise economy": a critical review', in P. Brown and H. Lauder (eds) *Education for Economic Survival*, London: Routledge.

Rees, G., Rees, T., Fielder, S. and Parry Langdon, N. (1989) 'The supply of and demand for low level IT skills in Mid and South Glamorgan', Report to the Training Agency, Cardiff: University of Wales College of Cardiff, Social Research Unit, 50 pp.

Rees, G. and Thomas, M. (1991) 'From coalminers to entrepreneurs? A case study in the sociology of reindustrialization', in M. Cross and G. Payne (eds) *Work and the Enterprise Culture*, Lewes: Falmer.

Rees, G., Williamson, H. and Winckler, V. (1990) *Employers' Recruitment Strategies, Vocational Education and Training: an Analysis of a 'Loose' Labour Market*, Cardiff: Social Research Unit: University of Wales College of Cardiff.

Rees, T. (1980) *Study of Schemes of Direct Job Creation in the Republic of Ireland*, Brussels: Employment and Social Affairs Directorate of the Commission of the European Communities.

—— (1988a) 'Changing patterns of women's work in Wales: some myths explored', *Contemporary Wales* 2, Cardiff: University of Wales Press, pp. 119–30.

—— (1988b) 'Education for enterprise: the state and alternative employment for young people', *Journal of Education Policy* 3 (1): 9–22.

—— (1988c) 'Fostering the enterprise culture in Australia: a study of measures to encourage alternative employment', Report to the Scottish Development Agency, Cardiff: Social Research Unit, University of Wales College of Cardiff.

—— (1988d) 'Don's diary', *Times Higher Education Supplement* (15 April).

—— (1989a) 'Women: an underutilised resource', *Labour Market Wales*, No. 2: 3–5, Cardiff: Training Agency.

—— (1989b) 'Women and the enterprise culture: the Australian experience', *British Journal of Education and Work* 3, (1): 57–69.

—— (1990a) 'Gender, power and trade union democracy', in P. Fosh and E. Heery (eds) *Trade Unions and their Members: Studies in Democracy and Organization*, London: Macmillan.

—— (1990b) 'Management training for women by the Civil Service College in the UK', Report to CEDEFOP, Cardiff: Social Research Unit, School of Social and Administrative Studies, University of Wales College of Cardiff.

—— (1992) *Women, Skills Shortages and the New Information Technologies*, Brussels: European Commission Taskforce of Human Resources, Education, Training and Youth.

Rees, T., Cowell, A. and Read, M. (1981) 'Occupational aspirations and rising unemployment in a South Wales valley', *Education for Development* 6 (3): 14–24.

Rees, T. and Gregory, D. (1979) 'The Work Experience programme: a case study evaluation from South Wales', *Monograph No. 1*, London: Manpower Services Commission, Special Programmes Division.

Rees, T. and Pollert, A. (1989) 'Vocational training and positive action in the UK', Report to CEDEFOP, Cardiff: Social Research Unit, School of Social and Administrative Studies, University of Wales College of Cardiff.

—— (1990) 'The Esso Development Course for Women', Report to CEDEFOP, Cardiff: Social Research Unit, School of Social and Administrative Studies, University of Wales College of Cardiff.

Rees, T. and Read, M. (1980) 'NALGO Equal Rights Survey: preliminary results of the 1979 Branch Survey prepared for Annual Conference 1980', London: NALGO.

—— (1981) *Equality? Report of a Survey of NALGO Members*, London: NALGO.

Rees, T., Williamson, H. and Harris, A. (eds) (1990) *Welsh Journal of Education – Special Issue on Enterprise Education* 1 (2), Faculty of Education, University of Wales College of Cardiff.

Rees, T. and Winckler, V. (1986) 'Last hired, first fired', *Planet: the Welsh Internationalist* 57: 38–41.

Reeves, N. (1989) 'Women are making it their business', *Sunday Correspondent* (26 Nov.).

Reid, I. and Stratta, E. (eds) (1989) *Sex Differences in Britain*, Aldershot: Gower.

Rich, A. (1980) 'Compulsory heterosexuality and lesbian existence', *Signs* 5 (4): 631–60.

Rigg, M. (1989) *Training in Britain: a Study of Funding, Activities and Attitudes: Individuals' Perspectives*, London: HMSO.

Roberts, B., Finnegan, R. and Gallie, D. (eds) (1985) *New Approaches to Economic Life*, Manchester: Manchester University Press.

Roberts, E. (1988) *Women's Work 1840–1940*, London: Macmillan.

Roby, P. (1987) 'Union stewards and women's employment conditions', in C. Bose and G. Spitze (eds) *Ingredients for Women's Employment Policy*, New York: Albany, State University of New York Press.

Roby, P. and Uttal, L. (1988) 'Trade union stewards: handling union, family and employment responsibilities', in B. A. Gutek, A. H. Sromberg and L. Larwood (eds) *Women and Work: an Annual Review*, Vol. 3, London: Sage.

Rolfe, H. (1986) 'Skill, deskilling and new technology in the non-manual labour process', *New Technology, Work and Employment*, 1 (1): 37–49.

Rowbotham, S. (1980) *Hidden from History*, London: Pluto Press.

Rubery, J. and Tarling, R. (1988) 'Women's employment in declining Britain', in J. Rubery (ed.) *Women and Recession*, London: Routledge & Kegan Paul.

Ryrie, A. C., Furst, A. and Lauder, M. (1979) *Choices and Chances*, Hodder & Stoughton, Scottish Council for Research on Education.

Sarah, E., Scott, M. and Spender, D. (1980) 'The education of feminists: the case for single sex schools', in D. Spender and E. Scott (eds) *Learning to Lose: Sexism and Education*, London: The Women's Press.

Sargeant, G. (1989) *Returners' Research Project: a Report for the Training Agency on Women into the Labour Market*, Hatfield Heath, Herts: Dow Stoker.

Sawer, M. (1990) *Sisters in Suits: Women and Public Policy in Australia*, Sydney: Allen & Unwin.

Sayers, J., Evans, M. and Redclift, N. (1987) (eds) *Engels Revisited: New Feminist Essays*, London: Tavistock.

Scarman, The Rt. Hon., the Lord (1981) *The Brixton Disorders, 10–12th April 1981*, London: HMSO.

Schiersmann, C. (ed.) (1988) *Mehr Risiken als Chancen? Frauen und neue Technologien*, Hannover: Institut Frau und Gesellschaft.

Schwartz Cowan, R. (1989) *More Work for Mother: the Ironies of Household Technology from the Open Hearth to the Microwave*, London: Free Association Books.

Schweikert, K. (1982) *Vocational Training of Young Migrants in the Federal Republic of Germany*, Berlin: CEDEFOP.

Seccombe, W. (1974) 'The housewife and her labour under capitalism', *New Left Review* 83: 3–24.

Segal, L. (1987) *Is the Future Female? Troubled Thoughts on Contemporary Feminism*, London: Virago.

Seidman, J. (1958) *The Worker Views his Union*, Chicago: Chicago University Press.

Senker, J. and Senker, P. (1990) *Technical Change in the 1990s: Implications for Skills, Training and Employment*, Report to the Training Agency, Brighton: Science Policy Research Unit, University of Sussex.

Sessar-Karpp, E. (1988) 'Computerkurse von Frauen für Frauen', in C. Schiersmann (ed.) *Mehr Risiken als Chancen? Frauen und neue Technologien*, Hannover: Institut Frau und Gesellschaft.

Silverstone, R. and Ward, A. (eds) (1980) *Careers of Professional Women*, London: Croom Helm.

Skeggs, B. (1989) 'Gender differences in education', in I. Reid and E. Stratta (eds) *Sex Differences in Britain*, Aldershot: Gower.

Skinner, J. (1988) 'Who's changing whom? Women, management and work organisation', in A. Coyle and J. Skinner (eds) *Women and Work: Positive Action for Change*, London: Macmillan.

Slattery, M. (1986) *Official Statistics*, London: Tavistock.

Smail, B., Whyte, J. and Kelly, A. (1982) 'Girls into science and technology: the first two years', Equal Opportunities Commission, *Research Bulletin No. 2* (Spring).

Smart, C. (1984) *The Ties that Bind: Law, Marriage and the Reproduction of Patriarchal Relations*, London: Routledge & Kegan Paul.

Smith, D. (1987) *The Everyday World as Problematic: a Feminist Sociology*, Milton Keynes: Open University Press.

South East Region TUC Women's Committee (n.d.) 'Still moving towards equality', London: SERTUC.

Southall, J. (1990) *Girls, Women and Occupational Choice*, M.Sc. Econ. in Women's Studies dissertation, Cardiff: University of Wales College of Cardiff.

Spencer, A. and Podmore, D. (1986) 'Gender in the labour process – the case of women and men lawyers', in D. Knights and H. Willmott (eds) *Gender and the Labour Process*, Aldershot: Gower.

—— (eds) (1987) *In a Man's World: Essays on Women in Male Dominated Professions*, London: Tavistock.

Spillane, M. (1991) *The Complete Style Guide from the Color Me Beautiful Organisation*, London: Piatkus.
Stanworth, J. and Curran, J. (1973) *Management Motivation in the Smaller Business*, London: Gower.
Storey, J. (1982) *Entrepreneurship and the New Firm*, Beckenham: Croom Helm.
Sullivan, B. (1990) 'Sex equality and the Australian body politic', in S. Watson (ed.) *Playing the State: Australian Feminist Interventions*, London: Verso, pp. 173–89.
Summerfield, P. (1989) *Women Workers in the Second World War: Production and Patriarchy in Conflict*, London: Routledge.
Taking Liberties Collective (1989) *Learning the Hard Way: Women's Oppression in Men's Education*, London: Macmillan.
Tannenbaum, A. S. and Kahn, R. L. (1958) *Participation in Local Unions*, Evanston, Ill.: Row Peterson.
Taylor, F. W. [1911] (1964) *Scientific Management*, New York: Harper & Row.
Thomas, M. and Rees, G. (1991) 'National systems of vocational training: a comparative perspective', Cardiff: School of Social and Administrative Studies, University of Wales College of Cardiff (mimeo).
Trade Union Research Unit (1986) 'Women and trades unions; trades unions and women', *Technical Note No. 100*, Oxford: Trade Union Research Unit, Ruskin College.
—— (1987) 'Equality – keeping the pressure on', *Discussion Paper No. 37*, Oxford: Trade Union Research Unit, Ruskin College.
Trades Union Congress (1986) *56th TUC Women's Conference Report for 1985/86*, London: TUC.
Training Agency (1989a) *Training in Britain: a Study of Funding, Activity and Attitudes, the Main Report*, London: HMSO.
—— (1989b) *Training in Britain: a Study of Funding, Activity and Attitudes: a Research Report*, London: HMSO.
—— (1990) *Labour Market and Skill Trends 1991/2*, Sheffield: Training Agency.
Treiman, D. J. and Hartmann, H. I. (eds) (1981) *Women, Work and Wages: Equal Pay for Jobs of Equal Value*, Committee on Occupational Classification and Analysis, Assembly of Behavioural Sciences, National Research Council, Washington, DC: National Academy Press.
Truman, C. (1986) 'Overcoming the career break: a positive approach', Sheffield: Manpower Services Commission.
Universities Funding Council (1990) *Universities Statistics 1988–89*, Vol. 1, *Students and Staff*, Cheltenham: Universities Statistical Record.
Universities Grants Council (1986) *Universities Statistics 1985–86*, Vol. 1, *Students and Staff*, Cheltenham: Universities Statistical Record.
USDAW (1987) 'Getting involved: members' views and priorities', Manchester: USDAW.
Valli, L. (1986) *Becoming Clerical Workers*, London: Routledge & Kegan Paul.
Venning, P. (1983) 'From MSC dream to curriculum reality', *Times Educational Supplement* (14 Oct.).
Vickery, K. (1990) 'Impact of the current economic climate on IT', London: PA Consulting Group.
Virgo, P. (1991) 'The key to overcoming your IT skills problems: the case for joining the Women into IT Foundation', Farnborough: Women into IT Foundation Ltd (mimeo).
Vogel, L. (1983) *Marxism and the Oppression of Women: Toward a Unitary Theory*, London: Pluto Press.

Wajcman, J. (1983) *Women in Control: Dilemmas of a Workers' Co-operative*, Milton Keynes: Open University Press.
—— (1991) *Feminists Confront Technology*, Cambridge: Polity Press.
Walby, S. (1986) *Patriarchy at Work: Patriarchal and Capitalist Relations in Employment*, London: Polity Press.
—— (ed.) (1988) *Gender Segregation at Work*, Milton Keynes: Open University Press.
—— (1989) 'Flexibility and the sexual division of labour', in S. Wood (ed.) *The Transformation of Work*? London: Unwin Hyman.
—— (1990) *Theorising Patriarchy*, Oxford: Blackwell.
Walford, G. (1983) 'Girls in boys' public schools – a prelude to further research', *British Journal of Sociology of Education* 4 (1): 39–54.
Walker, B. (1987) 'Practical porcelain outback', *Work Matters: a Magazine on Local Employment Initiatives*, Canberra: Work Resources Centre.
Wallace, C. (1988) *For Richer for Poorer*, London: Routledge.
Walters, P. (1987) 'Servants of the Crown', in A. Spencer and D. Podmore (eds) *In a Man's World: Essays on Women in Male-Dominated Professions*, London: Tavistock.
Wanganeen, R. (1990) 'The Aboriginal struggle in the face of terrorism', in S. Watson (ed.) *Playing the State: Australian Feminist Interventions*, London: Verso, pp. 67–70.
Ward, R. and Jenkins, R. (eds) (1984) *Ethnic Communities in Business*, Cambridge: Cambridge University Press.
Watson, S. (1989) *Winning Women: the Price of Success in a Man's World*, London: Weidenfeld and Nicolson.
—— (ed.) (1990) *Playing the State: Australian Feminist Interventions*, London: Verso.
Webster, J. (1986) 'Word processing and the secretarial labour process', in K. Purcell, S. Wood, A. Waton and S. Allen (eds) *The Changing Experience of Employment: Restructuring and Recession*, London: Macmillan.
—— (1990) *Office Automation: the Labour Process and Women's Work in Britain*, Hemel Hempstead, Herts: Harvester Wheatsheaf.
Weedon, C. (1987) *Feminist Practice and Post Structuralist Theory*, Oxford: Blackwell.
Weitzman, L. (1985) *The Divorce Revolution: the Unexpected Social and Economic Consequences for Women and Children in America*, New York: Free Press.
Wellington, J. J. (1989) *Education for Employment: the Place of Information Technology*, Windsor: NFER.
West, J. (1982) 'New technology and women's office work', in J. West (ed.) *Work, Women and the Labour Market*, London: Routledge & Kegan Paul.
Westwood, S. (1984) *All Day Every Day: Factory and Family in the Making of Women's Lives*, London: Pluto Press.
Whitting, G. and Quinn, J. (1989) 'Women and work: preparing for an independent future', *Policy and Politics* 17 (4): 337–45.
Whyte, J. (1985) 'Girl friendly science and the girl friendly school', in J. Whyte, R. Deem, L. Kant and M. Cruickshank (eds) *Girl Friendly Schooling*, London: Methuen.
—— (1986) *Girls into Science and Technology*, London: Routledge.
Whyte, J., Deem, R., Kant, L. and Cruickshank, M. (eds) (1985) *Girl Friendly Schooling*, London: Methuen.
Wickham, A. (1986) *Women and Training*, Milton Keynes: Open University Press.

Wilce, H. (1983) 'Continuing fall in the number of women who become heads', *Times Educational Supplement* (29 July).

Williams, R. (1983) 'Developing skills for women in middle management: final report on course evaluation', London: Personnel Management Research Branch, Management and Personnel Office, Cabinet Office.

Williamson, H. (1989) 'Mini enterprise in schools: the pupils' experience', *British Journal of Education and Work* 3 (1): 71–82.

Willis, P. (1977) *Learning to Labour: How Working Class Kids Get Working Class Jobs*, Farnborough: Saxon House.

Wilpert, C. (1988) 'Work and the second generation: the descendants of migrant workers in the Federal Republic of Germany', in C. Wilbert (ed.) *Entering the Working World: Following the Descendants of Europe's Immigrant Labour Force*, Aldershot: Gower.

Wilson, E. (1977) *Women and the Welfare State*, London: Tavistock.

Wilson, J. (1990) 'High technology national training', *Employment Gazette* 98 (7): 347–52.

Winckler, V. (1987) 'Women and work in contemporary Wales', *Contemporary Wales* Vol. 1, University of Wales Press, pp. 53–71.

Windsor, K. (1990) 'Making industry work for women', in S. Watson (ed.) *Playing the State: Australian Feminist Interventions*, London: Verso.

Witherspoon, S. (1986) 'The 1984 Social Attitudes Survey, a report for the Department of Employment' (unpublished), cited in N. Millward and M. Stevens, *British Workplace Industrial Relations 1980–84, the Department of Employment/ESRC/PSI/ACAS Surveys*, Aldershot: Gower.

—— (1988) 'Interim report: a woman's work', in R. Jowell, S. Witherspoon and L. Brook (eds) *British Social Attitudes: the 5th report, 1988/89 Edition*, Aldershot: Gower/Social and Community Planning Research.

Wollstonecraft, M. [1792] (1967) *The Vindication of the Rights of Woman*, New York: W. W. Norton & Co.

Women's Returners' Network (1987) *Returning to Work: Education and Training for Women*, London: Kogan Page.

Wood, S. and Kelly, S. (1982) 'Taylorism, responsible autonomy and management strategy', in S. Wood (ed.) *The Degradation of Work*? London: Hutchinson.

Yaron, G. (n.d.) 'Trade unions and women's relative pay: a theoretical and empirical analysis using UK data', Oxford: University of Oxford, Institute of Economics and Statistics.

Yeatman, A. (1990) *Bureaucrats, Technocrats, Femocrats: Essays on the Contemporary Australian State*, Sydney: Allen & Unwin.

Zaretsky, E. (1976) *Capitalism, the Family and Personal Life*, London: Pluto Press.

Name index

Subject index